SECRET
SOCIETIES
OF
AMERICA'S ELITE

Also by Steven Sora

The Lost Treasure of the Knights Templar:
Solving the Oak Island Mystery

SECRET
SOCIETIES
OF
AMERICA'S ELITE

From the Knights Templar
to
Skull and Bones

STEVEN SORA

Destiny Books
Rochester, Vermont

Destiny Books
One Park Street
Rochester, Vermont 05767
www.InnerTraditions.com

Destiny Books is a division of Inner Traditions International

LIBRARY OF CONGRESS CATALOGING-IN-PUBLICATION DATA

Sora, Steven
Secret societies of America's elite : from the Knights Templar to
Skull and Bones / Steven Sora.
p. cm.
Includes bibliographical references and index.
ISBN 978-0-89281-959-1
1. Secret societies—United States. I. Title.
HS61 .S67 2002
366'.00973—dc21
2002153563

Printed and bound in the United States at Lake Book Manufacturing, Inc.

10   9   8   7   6

This book was typeset in Bembo with Felix Titling, Delphin, and
Avenir Light as the display typefaces

*To my wife and best friend, Terry,
and our sons, Christian and Mike.*

CONTENTS

ACKNOWLEDGMENTS

T hanks first to Terry, my wife, and our sons, Christian and Mike, who make it all the more worthwhile. Thanks to family and friends whose enthusiasm, criticism, and support are always appreciated.

Special thanks to readers of *Lost Treasure of the Knights Templar* who have taken the time to contact me and in many instances provided both inspiration and background for this book. Thanks to fellow travelers, authors and readers who share an interest in the hidden side of history. One in particular, purposely unamed, shared much insight and information on the subject matter.

Thanks to the staff of numerous libraries, bookstores, and maritime museums that serve to keep history alive. Of note are the staff of the Bethlehem Area Public Library, Bethlehem, Pennsylvania; Mystic Seaport, Mystic, Connecticut; the Maritime Museum, Salem, Massachusetts; The Cushing House, Newburyport, Massachusetts; the Museum of Fisheries, Lunenburg, Nova Scotia; and the Custom House, Saint George, Bermuda.

Deepest gratitude to everyone at Inner Traditions, especially Ehud Sperling, Jon Graham, Cynthia Fowles, Kelly Bowen, Susan Davidson, and Jeanie Levitan, for everything from encouragement and hospitality to meticulous editing and creative design.

Introduction
BORN IN BLOOD

E lite and secret societies have shaped history since the beginning of civilization. From the time of the Crusades to the twenty-first century, a handful of families have controlled the course of world events and have built their own status and wealth through collective efforts and intermarriage.

The greatest elite society was that of the Knights Templar. Admission to the organization often required breeding and wealth that were the privilege of a select few. Outside the core a larger force was needed both to fight wars and to maintain the organization's far-flung assets. These forces would grow to include an army, a navy, various real estate (including agricultural properties), and a banking empire. Admission standards changed over time to the degree necessary to maintain the needed personnel, but the elite core was always in control.

When the massive Templar organization was suddenly outlawed by the avarice of the French king, it did not die; it simply moved underground. The survival of the underground Templars has been touched upon by several authors, but only recently has more in-depth research brought the Templars' survival to light.

The Templars survived militarily. By pledging themselves to various powers, the military orders survived their open attack by both state and church and the mass executions and imprisonments of the fourteenth century. The Knights of Christ, the Teutonic Knights, the Swiss Guard, and the Scots Guard, as well as several small but powerful military orders, outlived those who persecuted them. Hydralike, the orders survived, prospered, and multiplied. Several are alive and well in the new millennium.

The Templar organization survived and regrouped financially. The massive Templar, Incorporated that would bring banking to its modern form survived by moving to Switzerland, where a handful of bankers maintained and often controlled the massive wealth of the European elite. The Swiss cantons, often flying flags only slightly different from the Templar flags, protected by the Alpine passes and the Swiss Guard, took the role of the Templar preceptory. The neutral status and the preservation of secrecy would attract the funds of Europe from the fourteenth century to the twenty-first.

The Templar ideal of commitment to learning, discovery, and brotherhood greatly affected the world over the subsequent centuries. For example, neo-Templar organizations were responsible for advances in various sciences. Prince Henry, the grand master of the Knights of Christ, made advancements in the art of navigation and funded the voyages of discovery. And various members of the Royal Society progressed in astronomy, in medical arts, and even in the transmutation of metals, and their accomplishments frequently became the foundation of modern sciences. Until the early 1300s, learning and experimentation were considered heretical and could easily place a scientist under the control of the Inquisition. Later post-Templar organizations understood the value of secrecy to avoid religious persecution for philosophical and scientific discussion.

The Masonic brotherhood created in post-Templar Scotland was largely responsible for influencing the American concepts of liberty, freedom, due process, and democracy. The concept of the "military lodge"—in which a non-permanent lodge traveled with soldiers—brought to America by the fighting units of Europe would further the ideals and fight the war for independence. Secretive groups such as those meeting at Saint Andrews Lodge in Boston would instigate the Boston Tea Party, and they spread like wildfire throughout the colonies. The Caucus Club, the Loyall Nine, and the Sons of Liberty would grow into the Committees of Correspondence, the Continental Congress, and finally fighting militia units. Many were necessarily organized in secret. Many would preserve their secrecy by oaths taken in Masonic fraternal lodges. The climax was when French forces, enlisted through Masonic channels, arrived under the command of high-ranking Masons and Knights of Saint John and defeated the British at Yorktown.

The result was an elected American president who was a Mason, sworn in on the Bible of a Masonic lodge by the grand master of New York's Masons and a new form of government. Another was the nation's capitol, which was built by employing Masonic geometric principles and was dedicated in a strictly Masonic ceremony complete with high-ranking government members in Masonic aprons.

But there was a downside.

Secret societies and the elite of mainstream society would strive to perpetuate themselves through any means possible. The higher ideals of liberty and equality were compromised by the elite, who remained in control.

The breakup of the Templars was directly responsible for the dramatic rise in piracy that plagued Europe, America, and even the Indian Ocean. The pirates themselves were organized in fraternal brotherhoods, they pledged themselves to the good of the group, they promised to share equally in the proceeds, and they even fought under the same battle flag that was flown by the Templar fighting fleet. Stranger still, the pirate bases—ports in Scotland, Ireland, and America where pirates could openly dock and sell their booty—were protected by Masonic cells that extended to the courthouses and capitol buildings.

Smuggling, too, grew as a worldwide enterprise despite its illegality. Ports from Salem and Newport to the Caribbean and Bermuda, which harbored and facilitated the trade of pirates, had no qualms about aiding and abetting smugglers. For the same reasons that Masonic organizations grew into labor and artisan guilds that protected the livelihood of their members, individuals in the smuggling business needed to be considered trustworthy. In Bermuda, where possibly two thirds of the eighteenth-century trade was illegal, trading partners had to maintain secrecy. The island was and is a bastion of Masonry; the

Customs House itself more closely resembles a Masonic temple than a government office.

Unfortunately, the slave-trading industry was also furthered by Masonic groups. The Knights of Christ were actually responsible for organizing the importation of human cargo to Europe and later for licensing the trade in the Americas. The chivalric orders that controlled the governments of Portugal and Spain sold licenses to other governments, which in turn organized companies to propagate the trade. The royals of Europe were the ultimate beneficiaries of the business; for a share of the profits, they granted licenses to elite merchants and businessmen who were part of the court. Licenses to trade in slaves were sold by the merchants and businessmen to the highest bidders, allowing newcomers to join the merchant class—yet connections would supersede wealth. In America, democracy and free enterprise theoretically allowed anyone to play a role in the buying and selling of humans, but it was a handful of elite families, connected to counterparts in England and France, that took over the business.

When the American Revolution broke out, Benjamin Franklin turned to the Masonic elite of France, who controlled the slave trade, to get arms, supplies, and military support. In the first fourscore years of American history, the slave-trading ports from Charleston to Newport were controlled by a handful of families bound by Masonic and family ties. They were not like the Jeffersons and Madisons, who saw the eventual end to the institution as befitting the new democracy; it was a mercantilist capitalism that the slave traders put above freedom and democracy.

These merchants would not relinquish the lucrative trade and seemed to stop at nothing in fighting abolition. The presidency was something members of the mercantile elite felt they could buy, and when money couldn't decide an election they used other means to seize control. In an effort to derail abolition, Presidents Harrison and Taylor suffered sudden and suspicious deaths that put pro-slave vice presidents in power. When even death failed to halt abolition, the country wound up in the most destructive war it ever fought. The Civil War ended at Appomattox, where the armies of Jefferson Davis surrendered—but not for the elite. A conspiracy organized by members of the quasi-Masonic Knights of the Golden Circle to kill President Lincoln sought to nullify the Emancipation Proclamation and its effects on the trade with England. The postwar efforts at reconstruction would also be stained by another Masonic group of "knights," the Ku Klux Klan.

Although piracy and smuggling were no longer as profitable in the newly independent America, institutions such as the slave trade and illegal drug trafficking would take their place. The latter provided riches for the elite that would become the bedrock of the American industrial age. The illegal drug trade that the Americans and British united to create in the first half of the nineteenth century would be a never-ending plague. Again, a select core of families controlled the trade, and in both Britain and America they were organized in Masonic cells. Family and lodge connections were the only tickets to admittance.

While it is not surprising that America's Founding Fathers were mostly slave owners, a legal activity, it may be surprising to discover that they were often smugglers as well. Profits from drug running, smuggling, slave trading, and even piracy are directly responsible for the founding of several of the country's most important banks, which are still in operation today. New England's staunch insurance business was born and prospered through profits earned from insuring opium and slave ships. The large railroad system that was built throughout the continental United States in the nineteenth century was funded with profits from illegal drug smuggling. And one of the greatest opium fortunes would provide seed money for the telephone and communications industry.

The European Knights Templar was a massive organization, but at the center was a hereditary elite that controlled and reaped the rewards of the group. Even after the reported demise of the group, it retained remarkable clout and power, always behind the scenes.

In America the influence of a core elite was as strong. This elite class positioned itself to control the masses no longer for holy crusade, but rather to enrich itself. Rooted in the Masonic lodge system, a new class formed through connections made at the most famous lodges, such as the Holland No. 8 Lodge in New York and the Solomon's Lodge of Charleston, where members could control politics and legitimate business while also enjoying the profits of corrupt and even criminal underworld dealings.

The family wealth of Franklin and Theodore Roosevelt had been built on drug running. As in all opium-smuggling families, inbreeding was important. The Delano side of Franklin Delano Roosevelt was an opium smuggler who made a fortune, lost it, and returned to drug running to recoup it. Ulysses S. Grant married into an opium-dealing family with connections in Europe and America. The first families of New York and New England who graciously provided funds for Harvard, Yale, Columbia, Brown, and Princeton Universities donated money earned in the illegal drug trade. The same men would build railroads and textile mills, found banks and insurance companies, and keep the family wealth intact for generations to come. Besides the Roosevelts and Grant, other presidents—including Taft and both Bushes—were connected by a bizarre cult at Yale that was founded by and funded with money from the China trade. That organization is as secretive, elite, and powerful today as it was two centuries ago.

Other presidents have been connected to piracy by their relations. John Tyler married into a family whose status was achieved on pirate booty. Millard Fillmore's great-grandfather was tried for piracy. Like opium trading, piracy was an enterprise that depended on a widespread system of recognition and trust. From Cape Cod and eastern Long Island to New York City, North Carolina, and New Orleans pirates trusted each other and knew those in power who provided shelter, legal protection, and a market for their goods. When on land, the pirate captains reported to the powerful few who protected their trade. These connections were made and preserved through the Masonic halls. Governors, mayors, and judges licensed and invested in pirate voyages, the proceeds of which helped build family fortunes.

Pirate ships were floating lodges where ritual, secrecy, and blood oaths were the glue bonding the pirates. But the rank-and-file pirate brothers were not welcome at the lodge meetings of the Holland

No. 8 in New York, where the Livingston family toasted their success in backing pirates like Captain Kidd and were still protecting pirates like Laffite a hundred years later.

Piracy was not the only crime on the high seas; the American colonies also prospered through smuggling. John Hancock was a wealthy Mason whose ship *Liberty* would put Boston on the path to the Tea Party and Revolution. With one foot in the elite Masonic lodges where shipowners and captains were welcome and another in the lodges where the workingman was accepted, Hancock provided work for one third of Boston. It was Britain's insistence on enforcing its laws against smuggling that precipitated the Revolution. The colonies relied on their smugglers to provide food, arms, and supplies to fight Britain.

The role of America's smuggling partners in the Caribbean and Bermuda has hardly been examined by historians, but it was vital. At the same time, smuggling and privateering provided a foundation for many of America's political dynasties that remain in power today.

The Revolution put an end to the large profits of the smuggling business. Piracy and privateering also ceased to be an easy road to profits. The slave trade would provide the next avenue to wealth on the seas, thriving in ports that were strongholds of Masonry. From Newport to Charleston, belonging to a lodge meant access to funding, insurance, and finding a crew for slave trading. It also meant access to the marketplace.

But Masonic membership did not merely present opportunity in the underworld. Benjamin Franklin acknowledged that success in the printing business hinged on just which Masonic lodge one belonged to in the city of Philadelphia. John Jacob Astor, who once held one fifteenth of all American personal wealth, joined the prestigious Holland No. 8 Lodge in New York to advance his businesses. Success in the legal profession, almost a prerequisite for government office, was ensured to the sons of the wealthy who could study at the Temple in London. *Passing the bar* is a term that originated in the Templar stronghold in London, and it is a rite of passage that must be achieved today in order to join the legal profession. Promotion in the military was denied to many who would not be part of the military lodge, a portable home to brothers that included George Washington, the Marquis de Lafayette, and John Paul Jones.

The secret and elite structures that have built America's business empires and family fortunes have concealed their history well. In an age when the slightest indiscretions sometimes have the potential to disqualify a candidate from public office, the tainted backgrounds and family histories of the Founding Fathers of the country and its institutions are remarkable. We have inherited colleges and universities named for slave traders and opium dealers. We honor presidents and other politicians whose families built their fortunes through crime. We patronize businesses founded by men whose fortunes are rooted in illegal activity.

Many of the families regarded as America's blue bloods, our equivalent of aristocracy, have hidden in their ancestral closets men who would make today's organized criminals look cherubic. They were not mere horse thieves and snake-oil salesmen, nor were they con men who were ridden out of town on the rail. These Founding Fathers rose to great wealth. Their legacy was passed on to heirs who still enjoy that wealth—and their power too, which is protected by the institutions they put in place and ensures their participation in the future. The system, thanks to ill-gotten gains and power, perpetuates itself.

In a country where everyone was given a new start, a fresh chance, and an equal opportunity, it is curious that the gap between rich and poor widened so dramatically after the American Revolution. But it was not by chance or hard work; institutions from Europe, often underground, established a network that would ensure the success and power of their own. The same secret societies that had been established in Europe for hundreds of years were imported into Europe's colonies from the earliest days.

To understand how pervasive secret and elite societies are today and how they played such a significant role in recent centuries, we must begin at one critical day in 1307, when the greatest organization the world had ever known saw its downfall.

PART ONE

Piracy: A Merry and a Short Life

◈

MEDIEVAL EUROPE HAD a class structure that divided the rich from the poor in more intrusive ways than does the gap that divides the classes today. From the lord of the manor to the king, life-and-death power was wielded over the common man. Society and the Church also played a great role in determining just what an individual could or could not do. Strict conventions permeated society to the point that even the clothes an individual wore were subject to law. In colonial New York, when pirates paraded from one tavern to another in silk shirts and pistol-concealing waistcoats, they defied not only a societal convention, but also the law. Wearing silk or fur was a privilege of the landed few.

From medieval times in Europe to the colonial period in America, society underwent a challenge that would change the way man perceived and indeed lived his life. In medieval times the choices for most young men (and women) were few and unappealing. Inheritance law once gave the family estate to the eldest son and allowed the younger brothers and sisters to stay only if they remained unmarried. Daughters were married off and sons apprenticed out or sent to study for the priesthood, as their fathers saw fit.

War brought opportunity. Enlisting for the Crusades gave men the chance to leave behind a predestined life. The Crusades meant adventures and the possibility of bettering one's circumstances. Going to sea offered the same escape. Life at sea was adventurous, and enabled some to return home with enough money to live out their lives. However, most men who joined the Crusades to escape the mundane fate of becoming priests or apprentices could not even step back into those vocations. When Jerusalem was lost and the Knights Templar disbanded, many had little chance of returning to society. Fearing prosecution or simply poverty, many decided to keep on enjoying the daredevil life.

For the fighting soldier, one choice was to become a mercenary in the newly emerging fighting orders from Scotland to the Mediterranean Sea. For the sailor, the life of a privateer, a smuggler, or a pirate held even more promise of reward. Both mercenary and pirate became members of a society within the society.

Pirates have been portrayed as bands of swashbuckling, peg-legged lunatics with homicidal tendencies since the days of the eighteenth-century writer Daniel Defoe. The real story is less colorful—and more interesting. Although many would live "the merry life and the short life," as Defoe's fact-bending tales called it, others enjoyed a life expectancy longer than that of sailors on British navy ships. They ate better, were treated less harshly, and shared in a greater portion of their gains.

Pirates were banded together by covenants that provided more protection than English naval law, and were regularly voted on by every sailor aboard. The pirate ship and pirate ports like Saint Mary's in Madagascar were the first instances of democratic rule. The one-man, one-vote system aboard the pirate ship was not duplicated until the

American Constitution. Even then, voting was not as democratic as was pirate rule.

Care for the injured and for the widowed, too, was usually more reliable for the pirate than for the sailor in the English navy. The navy embodied the most rigid of class structures and offered little in the way of security.

Pirates bought supplies and arms, sold ill-gotten gains from wool to jewels, and often retired to estates, or at least farms, bought with the proceeds of their life's work. To deal with conventional society, they had to have connections. To create such connections meant that they had to belong to a brotherhood. The brotherhood went much deeper than a small group banding together. As remnant Templars became organized in lodges, old ties were restored. Masonry, more or less underground until the early eighteenth century, provided lodging, employment, food, and even clothes to brothers. Masonry also provided connections to a network, underground and often above the law. When Freemasonry was finally acknowledged, a secret oath for a Master Mason acknowledged that masons were "brothers to pirates and corsairs."

Those who sailed under the skull and crossbones could rely on protection in the ports and in the courts, where a secret handshake or coded phrase required fellow Masons to come to the aid of a their brethren.

Fortunes built by pirates and by those who outfitted them with supplies and bought their goods survived the "golden age of piracy." Dynasties created through underworld activity and membership in secret societies would pave the way to power that survives into modern times.

Chapter 1
THE NEW WORLD ORDER

October 13, 1307, would go down in history as the first unlucky Friday the thirteenth. On that day the Knights Templar, who had fought so valiantly for the cause of Christianity during the Crusades, were ordered arrested by the French king. Operating on orders that were sealed until the night before the arrest, the representatives of the French crown launched an early-dawn raid on all the Templar properties in the realm of the king. Special focus was given to the center of the Templar organization, the Paris treasury. Within hours both knights and servants of the order were under arrest and in custody. Within days, interrogation under extreme torture began, and it soon elicited confessions of many of the depraved acts and practices of the order of warrior-monks. The greatest order Europe had ever seen soon ceased to exist.

When it was formed almost two hundred years before, the Templars were a military force organized like a religious order. The creation of the Templars coincided with Saint Bernard taking control of the Cistercian order of monks in France. Bernard was instrumental in molding both organizations to carry out the mission he envisioned. The rules for his order of monks were adopted by the fighting monks that would be called the Order of the Poor Knights of Christ and the Temple of Solomon. They would become known as the Knights Templar. Bernard's vision became reality. But he was not acting alone.

Saint Bernard was a member of an elite class at a time in European history when the feudal system ruled every facet of life. This handful of wealthy families, mostly centered around the town of Champagne and its count, would be responsible for the Crusades, for the rapid growth of the Cistercian order, and for the power of the Knights Templar. There were nine members of the original Knights Templar; three were pledged to the Count of Champagne. One of these was André de Montbard, the uncle of Saint Bernard. The count donated the land on which Bernard built the abbey of Clairvaux, which would be the center of Bernard's power.

Fixing on the need to take back the Holy Lands from Islam, Bernard preached a military crusade. It was said that when he reached a village, women would attempt to hide their husbands, as few could resist his call to arms. The act of seeing the world may have appealed to a peasant class that was often regarded as the property of the feudal estates that dominated the countryside. The Crusades offered adventure—and salvation. After thousands marched against Islam and recaptured the holy city of Jerusalem, thousands more desired to travel to the sacred city. The nine original Templar knights went to the Holy Lands to protect the roads for those making the pilgrimage. After several years, they returned to a hero's welcome.

With Bernard's seal of approval, the Knights Templar grew and flourished, becoming the vanguard of Europe's military. Their military exploits against Islam are legendary; their financial exploits are misunderstood and downplayed.

TEMPLAR, INC. BANKING

Although the full name of the organization was the Order of the Poor Knights of the Temple of Solomon, the order was anything but poor. It was, in fact, the richest organization that Europe had even seen and the first ever multinational corporation. The business of the Knights Templar was business, and it was conducted in a way that Europe had never seen before. The loyalty of the order was directed to itself. The Templars nominally owed their allegiance to the Roman pope, but this loyalty was more in word than in deed. They actually fought against other Christian armies and against their rival order, the Knights of Saint John, and during the Albigensian Crusade some Templars even fought against the pope and his genocidal purge of the Cathari in southern France. The Templars' true allegiance was to themselves, as together they could become masters of any industry they desired.

Banking as we know it today was an institution founded by the Knights Templar. Before the Templars there were certain individuals who would attend trade fairs for facilitating currency exchange, buying and selling shares in commercial enterprises, and lending money. Many of the early banking groups were Italian families from Florence, Venice, and Lombardy. The activities of these bankers were restricted by numerous laws.

In a world where the pope and the Catholic Church made the rules, usury, the charging of interest, was banned. For the Templars there were several ways to skirt the laws forbidding the charging of interest. One way was simply to charge a commission to procure the loan, but such a thinly disguised fee would still attract the condemnation of religious members. Another way was to call usury by a different name. The order was allowed to charge a "crusading interest" for loans. Its clients were often the same nobility that donated lands to the Temple, for which they received an income from the properties. Nobles, often the kings of England and France, needed to borrow money to fight wars and the Temple was willing to lend—for a fee. Where usury was a practice not allowed even for the Temple, the Temple would earn a profit by currency changing. For instance, wool from France that was carried on Temple ships and sold to a buyer in England was subject to a currency change that often placed less value on the payment currency.

Deposit banking was not banned by the Church, nor was the function of acting as a safe deposit. Who was better prepared than the Templars, with their numerous fortresses and strongholds stretched over Europe, to protect the wealth of the Continent's elite? The Templar bank secured the worldly possessions of merchants, knights, and royalty alike and held them in one country while allowing withdrawal in another. Fees were charged for each step of the transaction, and if the fees were not enough, wise Templar bankers would charge more if one needed to make a withdrawal of money in another currency. There was always a profit to be earned.

The few records found in the Paris Temple show the various transactions that took place on a typical day. Entries signed by the Templar cashier of the day listed the amount of a deposit, the name of the depositor, the origin of the deposit, and occasionally to whose account it would be credited if not the depositor's. A network of fortified houses throughout Europe and the Holy Lands served as the predecessor of the modern branch system of any large financial institution. Five categories of clients were served: Knights Templar (they often received payment in cities outside of their homeland and were not willing to carry money), ecclesiastical dignitaries, the king, other nobles, and the bourgeois. The records were kept in the *Journal of Treasure*.[1] This "treasure" would ultimately attract the interest of the French king, who was on the accounts receivable list.

TEMPLAR, INC. PROPERTY MANAGEMENT

Property and estate management played a large role in Templar affairs. Before the fall of Jerusalem, the Templars controlled nine thousand manors that had been donated to the order by Europe's landowners. An English property census noted, "The number of manors, farms, churches, advowsons, demesne lands, villages, hamlets, windmills and watermills, rents of assize, rights of common and free warren, and the amounts of all types of property, possessed by the Templars in England . . . are astonishing." In Yorkshire the Templars owned several large manors and sixty smaller parcels of property.[2] In Sicily they possessed valuable estates, large tracts of land, and rights of fishery, pasturage, and cutting wood. In Spain the Templars were "endowed with cities, villages, lordships and splendid domains."[3] In Aragon they had castles in several cities, were the lords of Borgia and Tortosa, and received the revenue of one tenth of the kingdom.[4]

The list of Templar property filled an entire census book; they had

lands in Germany, Hungary, and France and in the territories bordering France and Germany. In 1180 hundreds of acres were required to
support one knight in battle; a century later thousands of acres were
necessary. Templar property was exempt from local tithes yet could
receive them. While the common man would understand that the fruits
of his labors provided support to those fighting the Crusades, a neighboring noble was not as gracious. A common man was generally
required to contribute time, and for most this was easy. A noble
(landowner) paid a higher price. He experienced higher costs and more
challenge in finding workers, as he competed with the Templars for
available able-bodied men. And a landowner, unlike his Templar neighbor, paid taxes. Because the Temple employees were liable only to the
order that employed them, fugitives and felons could find refuge from
the law by working for a Templar estate.

The amalgamation of an international military force and a religious
order in the form of a business never again appears in the history of the
world. In addition to reaping profits, the Templar order was the beneficiary of gifts that were meant as penance for sins. The greatest gift to
the Templar order was required of King Henry II of England as a result
of the murder of the Archbishop of Canterbury, Thomas à Becket.
Henry donated funds to equip two hundred knights a year, as well as
more money in his will. The Templars had every advantage and no one
to report to.

TEMPLAR, INC. SHIPPING

The Templar fleet was another source of profits that aroused the envy
of the shipowners and merchants of France's port cities. In the early
years of the Crusades, the Templars required massive movement of men,
arms, and horses. They would contract with merchants of Italian city-
states like Venice and Genoa. These merchants, especially those from
Genoa and Pisa, had merchant colonies in Barcelona, Marseilles,
Mahdia, Ceuta, Tunis, and Tripoli. Their ships brought in wares from
China, India, and Ceylon. Because minor kingdoms would coin their

own money, the Italian traders were also money changers and lenders. The bankers from Venice, Genoa, Lucca, and Florence were called Lombards, and they replaced the Jews as Europe's merchant bankers. Loan rates could range from 15 percent for a business loan to 100 percent for a personal loan. Templar, Inc. would move to take business from the Italian merchants.[5]

In 1207 the Templars became shipowners. When they weren't using ships for the transport of men, they would use the vessels for trade. The profits and the fleet itself began to grow in size. By 1233 the city of Marseilles was complaining that Templar ships were taking business away from their own.[6] The Templars soon had many preceptories in port cities including Brindisi, Bari, Barletta, and Trani and on Sicily at Messina. The trans-Mediterranean trade often involved transporting goods and animals to the eastern Mediterranean Sea and returning with slaves, who would work for the Templars in the West.

The Turkish port of Ayas in Cilicia was a center for the slave trade, and the Templars established a wharf there. The Knights Templar and the rival Christian order the Knights of Malta became the largest European slave traders in the Mediterranean, and they established themselves in Venice. Perhaps the most important slave port of the Templars was the city of Acre in the Holy Lands. There all the slaves were called Muslims, regardless of their religion; this was the result of the pope in Rome declaring a ban on Christian slaves in the kingdom of Jerusalem. Muslims who sought to convert were denied. Pope Gregory was told of this and complained to the grand masters of both orders, but the trade in all its avarice continued.

The Templar fleet served both to generate profits for the order and as part of the Templar war machine. Flying the skull and crossbones as its battle flag, the Templar fleet was used in military operations against Egypt, the coast of Asia Minor, and throughout the Mediterranean Sea.

In addition to transporting troops and carrying weapons and supplies for their military operations, as well as slaves and goods for trade, the Templars engaged in piracy. *Piracy* was defined as the act of capturing another ship on the seas. But a Templar ship taking on an Islamic warship was not considered piracy, as the two were at war. There were few ships designed strictly for battle, as all shipping boats needed to be armed. Thus the act of capturing an Islamic merchant ship would be considered privateering. There was a fine line between piracy and, later, privateering, which meant that a ship's captain had the permission of a ruler, and later a letter of marque, to engage in piracy.

An English ship engaged in plundering English ships would be defined as a pirate ship, even if it shared the spoils with the English king. If an English ship took a French ship without the English king's permission, it was still a pirate ship. If, however, an English ship sailed with the permission of the English king to plunder the ships of other nations, it was a privateer ship.

The Templars answered to no one except the pope, who did not, according to record, issue letters of marque. When the Templars captured enemy ships, they claimed they were acting on behalf of their nominal ruler, the pope. But the ships of the Templar order did not stop there, and often the ships of other Christian kings were fair game.

Most of the Templar fleet was originally the low-lying galleys, which were similar to those used by the Muslim pirates of the Barbary Coast. They were ideally suited for the coastal trade and equally suited for piracy, as they could maneuver into shallow waters and were not forced to depend on the winds. The Atlantic fleet of the Templars used the sail, which allowed it to navigate the oceans as well.

Christian Europe and Muslim Africa and Asia were at war for hundreds of years, but on a cultural basis many connections were made. Simon Dansker, a Flemish adventurer, showed the North African pirates the use of the long-range sailing ship in piracy. Dansker started his career in the French port of Marseilles but soon changed sides and names. As Dali Rais, which means Captain Devil, Dansker switched to the side of the Barbary pirates and captured Christian ships. Under his tutelage the Muslim pirates extended their range into the Atlantic. A Muslim fleet even sailed to Iceland, where the pirates took slaves and plundered. But Dansker changed sides one too many times and was hanged in Tunis.

The Templar fleet was made up of whatever ships could be built or bought or captured from its enemies. The range of the Templars' sailing ships extended from the North Atlantic to the eastern Mediterranean. The ships carried goods and pilgrims from Italy to the Holy Lands. With no fear of reprisals, the Templars engaged in piracy when profit could not be made in legitimate ways. For those who manned the Templar fleet, the career jump from privateer for the order to pirate for one's own gain was small.

One early Templar-turned-pirate was Roger de Flor. The son of the falconer of Emperor Frederick II, the eight-year-old Roger was taken on as a cabin boy in the Templar port of Brindisi. Working his way up through the ranks of the Templar navy, he soon assumed command of a ship bought from the Genoese. He named his ship the *Falcon*. When the final stronghold of Acre was being besieged, de Flor learned a new skill: extortion. He used his ship to raise money for his future career as a pirate by charging to rescue "ladies and damsels and great treasure."[7] De Flor eventually fell out of favor with the order and his ship remained in Temple hands, but he had earned enough money to buy a new ship. Through piracy and later mercenary work, he built a fortune and an army. The renegade Templar even earned the hand of the niece of the Byzantine emperor.

It was not only renegade knights who would resort to piracy; both orders, the Templars and the Order of Saint John, profited from their ability to loot Mediterranean ports and merchant ships, just as the Muslim fleets profited from their capture of Christian ships.

For hundreds of years different ports around the world played host to pirates and resisted or ignored the authority of any governments. Ports such as the pirate kingdom of Saint Mary's in Madagascar, where the only government was that of pirates in exile or hiding, served the European pirates who preyed on the silver ships of the Moghuls of India. In the Americas, Tortuga and the Bahamas would enjoy shorter periods as pirate refuges. Even where ports had an official government, they were often ruled by those who supported piracy, such as those in Port Royal, Jamaica.

One of the greatest pirate ports of the medieval period was Mahdia, on the North African coast. In the three hundred years that the Knights Templar fought the Islamic conquerors of the Mediterranean Sea, there were numerous periods of truce during which Arabs and Christians exchanged ideas. The Europeans learned about history, religion (including their own), science, mathematics, and medicine from their enemies. The greatness of such interchange of culture cannot be measured, but the Crusades had an enormous effect on Europe. Academic knowledge was not all the Templars learned; they also picked up new military and naval skills and a tolerance for their Islamic counterparts. The result was that many ex-Templars simply switched sides and joined the Barbary pirates. Author John J. Robinson suspects the Scottish "Mason's word" *mahabone* is a corruption of *Mahdia the good,* just as the French *Marie le Bon* (Marie the Good) survives in English as *marylebone.*[8]

Templar sea power is often downplayed in comparison to their military land maneuvers. The Templar navy and merchant fleets were well acquainted with the Baltic Sea, the British Isles, large portions of the African coast, the Mediterranean Sea, and even the Black Sea. They sailed as far as their Norman predecessors, and their purpose was not only trade and plunder; supplying food and munitions, carrying troops and pilgrims, and playing host to kings and their goods were important in the long conflict against the Islamic nations.

When the war with these countries abated, the war between the Christians filled the gap. In 1256 two Christian factions formed over who should possess Acre. The Hospitallers came to the aid of the Genoese and Catalan merchants to fight the navy of Venice, which was joined by the Templar fleet.[9] Despite the fact that one of the Templar rules forbade killing a Christian, turf wars existed and the act of killing fellow Christians was "absolved" by the necessity of preserving the wealth and power.

THE TEMPLAR WORLD TURNED UPSIDE DOWN

In 1291 Acre fell to the armies of Islam. The Templar order would have just sixteen years before it too would fall. The knights had already lost

Jerusalem, and now their last fortress was captured by their rivals. Public opinion quickly turned against the order. In the eyes of the world the Templars had lost their mission and were now simply a fat organization of creditors, landlords, and competitors with an attitude to boot. "Haughty as a Templar" was a phrase coined by Sir Walter Scott. His novels describe an order that turned its back on its founders. Once dedicated to poverty and obedience, the Templars became guilty of pride, arrogance, and, by the beginning of the fourteenth century, possessing more wealth than European kings. Pope Nicholas IV, the theoretical commander in chief of the order, publicly directed his anger against the Templars, blaming their squabbling with the rival Hospitaller order as the reason that the last Christian bastion in the Holy Lands was now in Islamic hands. The Templars allowed themselves to be viewed as uninterested in protecting the most sacred possessions of the Christian world.

A Church council had decided that the only way to fight an effective war against Islam was to have a unified force of its own. The council proposed merging the fighting orders, but the orders refused. The Teutonic Knights of Germany and Prussia returned to Marienburg. The Knights of Saint John moved to Malta. The Templars moved to Cyprus.[10]

Although the Templar order had abandoned Acre, it would not abandon its own possessions. To an outsider, the Templars seemed to be on a crusade only to protect their enormous wealth.

In a watershed event that would become known as the Eperstoun Affair, a knight who pledged half his wife's estate to enter the order died. When the order came to claim the murdered member's property, his widow refused to leave. Templars were sent to evict the widow, and they had to literally drag the woman from her home. As she clung to the doorpost of her house, the knights chopped off her fingers. Even before public media, this was a "media" event so compelling that it reached the ears of King Edward I. When he heard about the treatment of the widow, he interceded to restore her property. Not yet comprehending the concept of public relations, the Templars would go so far as to kill the widow's son for revenge[11] and seize the property after his death.

Set against a backdrop of military losses, the transgressions of the order were becoming too much to defend. In 1306 a new pope, Clement V, was elected. Before becoming the pope he was Bertrand de Got, the Archbishop of Bordeaux. His elevation to the highest rank in the Church was engineered by his brother Beraud, who was the Archbishop of Lyon. In June 1305, when the kings of France, England, and Naples had representatives bickering over who should be the next pope, the choice came down to the least objectionable person[12]; Bertrand de Got had achieved that distinction. The French king certainly did not object to de Got, and to the dismay of the Italians, he never left France. He was considered weak and ineffective, and the Italians believed that in establishing his papacy at Avignon he gave proof that he was simply a puppet of the king of France.

The new pope was in an awkward position. On the one hand, he was related on his mother's side to Bertrand de Blanchefort, a Templar grand master. On the other hand, the power of the French king appeared more threatening. He would stall as long as he could in making decisions. It is possible that Clement V already saw the writing on the wall that told him that unless he took action he would lose both of his orders. His first act was to ask the new grand master of the Templars and the grand master of the Knights of Saint John for a written summary enumerating the reasons for and against a merger of the orders. Jacques de Molay, the leader of the Templars, answered the pope, and may have been aware that the ultimate goal of the French king was to head a united order as the *rex ballator,* the warrior king. At the very least, Molay knew he would be out of the number one position.

Despite the less-than-satisfactory answer, the pope hesitated to take action. He was not unaware that agents of the king of France had been responsible for the death of Boniface VIII and possibly the death by poison of Benedict XI, according to rumor.

King Philip of France decided the time was ripe to remedy the impasse. Because France was the home base of the Crusades and had borne the heavy cost of war, Philip was impatient to repair his finances. Earlier preachers such as Saint Bernard had often cleaned out a town of its men, inspiring them to take up the crusade. The orders had been the beneficiaries of thousands of donated estates. The Church had declared that the state should not tax the fighting men or the estates of the order. The net result to the French king was a depleted treasury. He took back from the Templars the management of his own finances in 1295, creating the Royal Treasury at the Louvre. He then debased the currency and turned on the Italian banking families.

How close the Italian banking families were connected to the Knights Templar may never be known. They initially played a role in financing the Crusades and in transporting the crusaders. In Florence, where the city minted its own coins, they would pay respect to the patron saint of the order, Saint John the Baptist, on one side of the coins. The other side depicted the lily, hinting at a royal bloodline. Florence is one of the very few places where an octagonal baptistery stands. This unusual style of baptistery was borrowed from Jerusalem and taken to many Templar strongholds. From Tomar in Portugal to Drogheda in Ireland, these structures represented the original baptism of Jesus Christ by Saint John. The baptistery in Florence was dedicated to Saint John the Baptist.

After maneuvers against the Lombards, Philip the Fair would prove himself to be anything but fair when it came to replenishing his treasury. He forced the Jews out of France in an attempt to seize their property and restore his wealth. But the Jews hadn't been as prosperous as he thought, and the move accomplished little. Philip was deeply in debt—and mostly to the Templar bank.

What better way to fix the situation than to seize that bank?

On October 13, 1307, Philip's forces descended on all the Templar preceptories in France. The pope was dismayed; technically, only he had jurisdiction over the Templars. But Philip's forces threatened the pope, so he quickly went along with the king. Philip would soon be dismayed as well. Templar spies had gotten wind of the impending arrests. Having commanded a large fighting force, a large navy, and a large merchant fleet, and having possessed the world's largest bank, through which they were close to aristocrats and clerics around Europe, the Templars had intelligence operations that were certainly superior to those of the French king. Jacques de Molay called in the order's books and had them burned. Many knights went underground. And perhaps most significantly, the treasure held in Paris, the second most desired possession of King Philip, vanished.

The combination of the missing treasure, the burned books, and the meek surrender of the Templars is intriguing. If the Templars understood that arrest was imminent, why didn't they all flee or prepare to fight back? The only explanation is that the order believed that Philip's target was strictly monetary, and that once deprived of the Templar bank, his suppression of the order would be short-lived.

If this conclusion is correct, then the members of the order who stayed behind were simply unprepared for the incredible horrors to which the arrested knights would be subjected. Under torture that included the rack, the strappado, and the burning of fat-smeared feet, the Templars confessed to anything. Because the charge was heresy, the arrested had no right to counsel. Normally torture would be allowed to the extent that it would accomplish its goal but not cause mutilation or permanent injury. For the Templars, however, an exception was made. The torture was "carried out with a barbarity which even medieval men found shocking."[13] Confined to dungeons, sustained with bread and water, accused of the most heinous perversions, and tortured beyond endurance, many knights lost their ability to reason, several committed suicide, and most confessed to anything.

Those who survived the two years of imprisonment had little to look forward to other than their death. In May 1310 the soldiers of Philip bound fifty-four Knights Templar to carts and brought them to fields near the convent of Saint-Antoine outside Paris, where they were stripped, tied to stakes, and burned to death.

The king of France broke the order but failed to confiscate their treasure. He was further disappointed by the reaction of his fellow kings; instead of the other nations suppressing the Templars within their borders, they had to be goaded into taking any steps against the knights.

In England, Edward II was very slow in reacting to the demands of the Roman pope. The new king was simply uninterested, as his focus was on the continuing war with Scotland and on his lover. After persistent pressure from the pope, Edward made a handful of arrests and later succumbed to the Church's demand for torture, which was forbidden by English law. Edward did not shield the Templar organization and allowed its property to be seized. To the disappointment of the Church, however, the property seized did not revert to the Church but instead was distributed by Edward in his own fashion, most likely to his creditors and allies.

Scotland finally agreed in principle to an inquisition of the Templars. The country had continually fought the pope, who would eventually excommunicate both the king and the nation. The degree of compliance in Scotland was minimal, with a total of two knights questioned.

In Spain and Portugal the Templar fighting force was important to the kings. After a few arrests and seizures, the Portuguese quickly reincorporated the order into the Knights of Christ, which now reported only to the Portuguese king. In the parts of Spain controlled by the Inquisition there were arrests and torture, but the order and its men were soon incorporated into several other orders of the Spanish military.

In Germany the Teutonic Knights, which had been formed separately, marched into the court at Metz armed to the teeth and challenged the court to bring charges. They were not Templars but presented their case to head off similar charges. The court assured the order its existence was not in danger.

Although all this frustrated Philip, his greatest frustration was the disappearance of the treasure from the Paris Temple Bank. It had reportedly been loaded on a wagon train that raced for the port of La Rochelle. There the treasure was placed aboard the Templar fleet, again flying the skull and crossbones, from which it disappeared once more. While many of the French Templars who were captured suffered long imprisonments and gruesome tortures, many others, who were now regarded as outlaws, used the Templar fleet as their home base. It was difficult for a large, armed group of men to escape detection on land, but the ships provided a mobile hideout as well as a place to live. With their immense treasure supplemented with piracy, the Templars who had escaped France survived.

The final act against the order was committed on March 18, 1314. The four surviving officials of the order—the grand master, the visitor, and the preceptors of Aquitaine and Normandy—were burned on an island in the Seine River in view of the Royal Gardens.

THE RESURRECTION OF THE TEMPLARS

While the arrested French Templars suffered imprisonment, torture, and often execution, the remnant Templar organization became like the mythical Hydra; one head was cut off at the neck and others sprouted. The new organizations in Germany, Portugal, and Spain were all various Templar reincarnations.

In Germany the Teutonic Knights needed their own raison d'être, and they quickly found one. They turned their attention from the armies of Islam, which were apparently too strong for Europe, to the more easily conquered pagan Lithuanians. A new northern "crusade" found the well-equipped Teutonic Knights doing battle with the Lithuanian peasant farmers and converting or killing them in short order. This new crusade was less an instrument of the Catholic Church for converting the world than a weapon in the German war of expansion.

In the Iberian Peninsula the war against Islam was still an active conflict. The kings of Portugal and Spain needed all the help they could muster. Spain's most sacred pilgrimage spot was Saint James of Compostela. The order of the Knights of Santiago (whose name was derived from the Spanish *Santo Iago,* or Saint James) performed activities that were similar to the original efforts of the Templars: It protected pilgrims along the world's second most important route. In neighboring Portugal the "new" Knights of Christ were allowed to keep the properties and preceptories of the former Templar order and even the Templar banner, a red cross on a white background. The order has survived in that form to the present.

In England the Templars' survival would not be as simple. The English version of suppression united the Templars with their rival order, the Knights Hospitaller of Saint John. This order pleased the demands of the Church, but according to some sources it was a charade. Templar property was administered separately for years.

East of France, the Alpine regions that would later become Switzerland provided refuge to the Templar knights. When their trading routes were not by sea, the Templars used the same Alpine passes to reach Italy and Germany that other merchants had used for more than a thousand years. The order had fortified preceptories in various cantons, and the power of the order soon grew. Three months after the fall of Acre, three of the cantons formed a military alliance. They were quickly joined by others, and the unified state of Switzerland would take on many of the characteristics of the order. They were respected for having a fierce army that defended itself against the expansionist German states to the north and the avaricious France to the west. The knights' reputation grew rapidly, and soon the Swiss Guard, as it became known, was contracted to defend the Vatican, just as the Templars had defended the Catholic religion.

The Swiss, of course, soon earned another reputation: that of banker to the world. In *The Warriors and the Bankers* authors Alan Butler and Stephen Dafoe point out that, although the treasury in Paris might have been the Templars' greatest central bank, the order would certainly not have kept all its valuables in one location. Switzerland grew in importance because of its political neutrality and its position as the central bank of the world. While the bank would no longer have the advantage of state and religious backing, it possessed a very advantageous geographical location. Few would underestimate the ability of a country with a well-trained military and the access of the Alpine passes. Anyone who has had to deal with an Alpine banker might be reminded of the "haughty" description of the Templars given by Sir Walter Scott, as more than one trait was passed from the Templars to the Swiss. The discipline and secrecy maintained by Swiss bankers, however, allowed them to achieve dominance both for their bank and for their currency.

The Swiss franc took on a mantle of stability that was possibly second only to gold.

Butler and Dafoe refer to the survival of the Templars as well as Switzerland's inheritance of the world banking industry. The authors observe the stunning resemblance of the Templar red-cross motif to the emblems of Switzerland—the country as well as its cantons. The Templar cross has been simply reversed in color to become the flag of a united Switzerland, and other variations would become the canton flags.

THE TEMPLAR UNDERGROUND

Most dramatically, the post-1307 Templar order took the form of a huge underground organization. This form developed in the north where the resurrected French Templars who sailed with the Templar treasure fleet to Scotland reunited under the Anglo-Norman cousins of the French Normans.

In France, the St. Clair family had been one of the handful of elite families that were instrumental in founding the new Templar order. The Scottish branch of the St. Clair family, which had Anglicized the spelling of its surname to Sinclair, would preserve the order. They allied themselves with Robert the Bruce, of the French Norman de Brus family, whose name had also been Anglicized. At Bannockburn, Robert defeated the English in the most decisive battle the Scots had ever experienced against their oppressors. The victory came shortly after a fresh force of Templar cavalry charged onto the battlefield.

But the Templars remained underground in Scotland, even after the end of the War of Scottish Independence. Some of the more noble knights continued their careers as mercenaries. Evidence shows that twelve years after the Battle of Bannockburn the Scottish mercenaries returned to France under the employ of the D'Anjous, another Norman family that helped found the Templars. There they fought under Joan of Arc in a war that history has done little to explain.

Others, more often the rank and file, put their skills of construction and engineering to work in the trades. As a military force, the Templars spent more time building than fighting. Thus the knights learned the building trades by constructing houses, bridges, and castles. After 1307 they put these skills to work in building many of Europe's finest monuments, including cathedrals.

French Templars had little trouble fitting in, as the French language was spoken in the British Isles and was for years to come the language of the court. French Templar words were corrupted into their British counterparts. Remnant Templars, while fighting as paid mercenaries, building bridges, or working in the trades, remained organized in underground lodges. They often employed secret words and handshakes to recognize each other and came to one another's aid. Their sons, too, would keep up the tradition.

The term *Freemason* entered the English language in the same century that the Knights Templar, as an order, was officially dissolved. The term was another corruption of the French language; the Templar knights originally referred to each other as brother, or *frère* in French. What was *frère maçon* in France became *Freemason* in English. When the Templars traveled they erected quarters, and these became lodges, so named after the French *loges.* The guard posted at the door of the lodge during meetings was the *tyler,* in English, derived from *tailleur,* meaning "one who cuts." But the term *Freemason* soon took on a new meaning. Unlike most of the populace, which was shackled to the land by the feudal system that prevailed in England and France, the former Templars became working craftsmen who were free to travel to find employment.

At a construction site, which could be a cathedral, a castle, or a public building, the masons would band together and erect a lodge. Most lodges were not permanent, but would be built to protect the property of the traveling men. Masons promised that if a brother mason came to them, they would find him work, give him money, and, when he was ready to leave, direct him to another lodge. Why would this be such an important charge for Freemasonry? Because in a feudal system, finding a home was nearly impossible for the remnant members of an outlaw order. All their old ties were broken and there was no home to return to—certainly not back in France. Freemasonry was created to protect those whose lives were threatened because of their association with the Knights Templar.

A Masonic initiation specifically states that the brothers are there to feed you, to clothe you, and to protect you from your enemies. The initiation also enigmatically states, "We will keep your secrets."[14] Why a simple stonemason would attract enemies and have secrets that needed protecting is questionable. But it is not so hard to understand the need for secrets and protection from enemies for an outlaw Templar.

The building trades and crafts were an opportunity for ex-Templars and later for their sons. The name *Lewis* came from a term meaning "son of a mason," a status that was usually the only requirement needed for entrance into a lodge. It was also helpful in gaining employment. In *The Hiram Key,* Christopher Knight and Robert Lomas write, "Now we are certain, without any shadow of a doubt, that the starting place of Freemasonry was the construction of Rosslyn Chapel."[15] This chapel was built on Sinclair property under the direction of the Sinclair family, members of whom would become the hereditary grand masters of the crafts and guilds and orders of Scotland. For many former knights, Scotland was now home and building was their trade.

Some ex-Templars did not fit into the new way of life. Not all the former Templars were masons and craftsmen; some took to the highways as brigands and some to the seas as pirates. The skull and crossbones, the same battle flag that had been used for piracy by the Templars, remained the flag of choice for pirates after the Crusades. The skull and bones announced the ship was a pirate ship. While it had a religious significance, to the elite order it also had a more practical use: to instill fear in the hearts of those under attack. It warned that there was not to be any other action except surrender. If that was not heeded, an all-red flag declared no quarter to be given. Like many of the Scot Templar words that have been derived from French, the battle flag was called the Jolly Roger, from the French *joli rouge* (pretty red). Later, the name Jolly Roger was given to both flags.

The black skull and crossbones flag would come to be recognized as an indicator of a pirate ship. The skull and two bones, however, had a much deeper meaning to the original Templars who sailed under the flag. Their insignia represented resurrection. The Catholic Church taught that the resurrection of man was a bodily resurrection. But the Templars believed, contrary to the Church, that only a skull and two bones needed to be buried in order for a person to be admitted into heaven. The skull and crossed bones became a popular motif on Templar graves. To those who had dedicated their wealth and committed their lives to the Templar order, the skull and bones suggested that the Templar organization itself had been resurrected. The Templar fleet, in particular, was alive and well. It had survived the army of the French king and the Roman pope and would conquer again.

Just as the Templars had used military organization during the long war against Islam, they now used military organization against their new enemies. Upon coming into contact with a ship, the skull and cross-bones would be raised. If this was not enough to make the pursued ship surrender, the Templars raised the red flag, the Jolly Roger, meaning that "no quarter," or no mercy, would be granted. The message was quickly learned by the captains who plied the seas with the wares of merchants. Few would wait for the red flag.

The skull and crossbones continued to rule Europe's seas long after the Templar order was officially in the grave. The New World too would be threatened by the skull and crossbones, and well after America's independence the remnant Templars would still exert their influence and power.

Chapter 2

BROTHERS TO PIRATES AND CORSAIRS

Under the skull and crossbones, the fleet of the ex-Templars roamed the seas. The menacing flag that to the Catholics had represented resurrection now represented the resurrection of the outlawed order. Lacking the same allegiance to the pope in Rome, the order now served mostly to preserve and enrich itself. The ships that were once manned by knights and sworn to protect religious pilgrims now threatened anyone who traveled, transported goods, or traded on the high seas. Rarely was retaliation considered. Even more rare was the capture of a pirate ship; it was said that in that event, a flash of a secret signal might allow a pirate ship a pass from its captors. Templar power was not to be underestimated.

The fragmented Templars had succeeded in the goal of resurrecting the order. At the same time, the pirates who ravaged the seas would keep alive the Templar ideals of liberty, equality, and the protection of their own. Ironically, the ideals of a corrupt organization would become the basis of American democracy.

Pirates aboard a former Templar ship ran the ship in the same fashion as a Templar preceptory, a model that was based on life in a Cistercian chapter house. What did monks, pirates, and Templar knights have in common? Democracy. While there was no example of a democratic nation at that time and writers such as Voltaire, Jefferson, and Rousseau would not be born for another four hundred years, Templar pirates and Cistercian monks practiced democracy. Within the confines of the monastery, the preceptory, and the pirate ship, leaders were elected by their peers and could be removed by them. It was a concept foreign to a feudal system, where birth and property determined title and position. No one person was absolute; leaders were expected to act in the interest of the group.

The Cistercian monks, ex-Templar pirates, and Templar knights had other interesting similarities. In a world dominated by a feudal order that used taxes and duties to force all wealth to the top, the Templars, the Cistercian monks, and the pirates held wealth in common for hundreds of years. This is not to be confused with a vow of poverty or even with socialism. Rewards such as greater amenities were given to those who exercised more responsibility. A pirate captain was often entitled to a double share of booty, and the quartermaster might get a share and a half for his role. It was strictly a result of merit. The failure to lead or a propensity for greed could bring down a knight, an abbot, or a pirate captain.

The ultimate irony is that democracy arose within orders created by feudal powers. In this new social experiment, title, family name, and appointed power were all secondary to the ability to lead and bring benefit to all. The ideals of liberty and fraternity surfaced despite the intentions of the feudal rulers.

Of course, not all pirates were Templars, and the order did not invent the art of robbery on the high seas. The ex-Templar pirates, however, were very distinct from other organized pirates. The pirates who served aboard the ships of Islam, or even on the ships of the rival order of Saint John, had more in common with the later English navy. The captain of the ship, who was most often appointed as a result of high birth or favor, would get the majority of the spoils; the common seamen were often treated only a little better than the galley slaves who served the fleets of Rome.

Life aboard the pirate ship was democratic, but it was still a feudal world on the shores of the civilized world. Pirates were still forced to deal with this reality. For example, ships were enormously expensive, and therefore piracy was an institution that was generally not open to the average man. In a world that knew no form of capitalism, there were few ways to accumulate the funds to buy a ship. If a ship was captured, it still had to be allowed to land in a safe port and to sell its captured wares. This meant having the right connections. In the world of the former Templars, connections often came in the form of elite families that served to assist the remnant Templars and benefited from the role played behind the scenes. Both the Templar version of piracy and the non-Templar version of piracy depended on hidden guardians. The institution of piracy was allowed to exist by the various states and kingdoms as long as it could be officially denied and it provided a benefit to the monarch who had domain over the pirate's home port.

MEDIEVAL PIRACY

Pirates often enjoyed the lackadaisical approach of the various monarchs. Well before becoming the ruler of the high seas, England had one of the poorest defense forces. Dutch, Flemish, and Breton pirates raided the English Channel from the twelfth through the sixteenth centuries, simply because it was frequently easy to do. The king would benefit little by wasting resources to protect the goods of merchants.

Prior to the arrest and prosecution of the Templar order, Henry III ignored the piracy the various French states inflicted upon English merchants.[1] English pirates were given carte blanche to plunder if they would offer a share in the spoils to their corrupt monarch. This pattern repeated itself in the American colonies centuries later when governors turned not a blind eye but a greedy eye on the profits made by pirates. A share in the spoils was usually enough to buy clemency.

Edward I, the successor to Henry III, attempted to attack pirate bases by land, as England had no real navy at the time. He was alternately at war against the Welsh and the Scots, who considered English merchants easy targets. Failing in his attempt to fight a war against the pirates by land, Edward I instituted the practice of issuing marques, or letters of reprisal. Such letters granted a merchant or shipmaster the right to attack the pirates or their home port if the merchant or shipper could claim to have suffered a loss at the pirates' hands.[2] Other ports would then have their monarchs issue the same type of documents, which allowed them to plunder an English port should they be the victims of an English pirate.

Edward's lack of ability to rule the seas was matched by his ineptitude at ruling on land. His interference in the morass of bloody politics that was Scotland led to many wars. The wars against Scotland and the lack of centralized order in England would allow Scotland to flourish as a pirate haven.

THE TEMPLARS AND SCOTLAND

A simple act would serve as the catalyst for new hostility between England and Scotland. Alexander III, the Scottish king, had preserved neutrality, but in 1284 he was killed—not in battle, but from falling off his horse after a night of partying. Six guardians were appointed to ease the successorship, and for a brief time these guardians ruled Scotland. But Edward I of England exercised his right to choose who would succeed Alexander. Of the handful of claimants to the Scottish throne, the leading candidate was John Baliol, who was supported by the powerful Comyn family. The other main candidate was Robert the Bruce, who had the support of his country.[3] Edward's court picked Baliol.

When Baliol and the Comyns would not back Edward in internal conflicts, Robert would support Edward, which gave Robert the opportunity to reclaim his lands from Baliol and the Comyns. After the Wallace Revolt, Scotland was controlled by the triumvirate of Bishop William Lamberton of St. Andrew's, Robert the Bruce, and John Comyn. On February 10, 1306, Robert somehow managed to get Comyn to meet him at the Church of the Greyfriars in Dumfries. While neither side trusted the other, the hallowed sanctuary made Comyn assume he was safe from violence. He was wrong.

Robert the Bruce eliminated Comyn in the church by stabbing him and leaving him to die on the stone floor. There are several versions of what transpired, but it is very likely that the attack was spontaneous. When Robert ran from the church and told his confederate what he had done, the man ran into the church. Seeing Comyn already in the care of the friars, the confederate rushed to the wounded man and stabbed him again until he was sure Comyn was dead. Robert then had himself sworn in as king by Bishop Lamberton in the Abbey Church at Scone.

Despite the official coronation, both England and the Catholic Church made sure that Robert the Bruce would not take a throne. For several years he was an outlaw king, pursued first by Edward, who died in the campaign against Robert, and then by Edward's son, Edward II. Robert spent the early years of his reign living in caves and traveling in disguise. He was not only outlawed by the king of England, he was also excommunicated by the pope.

Robert's exile did not last forever. His salvation was realized at the Battle of Bannockburn, but events that took place hundreds of miles away from the battlefield helped tip the scales in his favor. The same papacy that made Robert an outlaw of the only official religion in Europe had also declared the Knights Templar to be outlaws. The Templar fleet and the remnant organization that managed to escape from La Rochelle in the nick of time found refuge in Scotland. The St. Clair family of France, a powerful force behind the Templars, had most likely negotiated an alliance with Robert through its Scottish side of the family, the Sinclairs.

The French had probably been arming Robert since 1310 by smuggling arms into Ireland and then into Scotland. At this point they smuggled an entire army to aid Robert. While the history of Scotland both before and after Robert the Bruce is riddled with one defeat after another at the hands of much more organized and better-equipped armies, the Battle of Bannockburn was the exception. In this historic battle, which was contested on June 24, 1314, a sacred day to the Templar knights, the battle at first seemed to go well for Edward's army. He had at his disposal twenty thousand soldiers and three thousand knights on horseback, who fought against a force less than half their size. But just when victory seemed at hand, a fresh contingent of knights came charging from the rear of the Scottish force to soundly and spectacularly beat Edward's troops. The remnant Knights Templar led Scotland to victory over the English army, which made Scotland independent of its overlord.

An elite group that was at the core of the Knights Templar existed in France and Scotland prior to the arrests, and they remained united afterward. At the heart of this group was the family of St. Clair. In Europe they started as part of the Norse wave of conquerors that changed the face of the continent. The St. Clairs and their Norse countrymen were called Normans, and they settled in northern France, where the king handed over great amounts of land in exchange for being allowed to keep the rest. Under William the Conqueror, the Normans successfully invaded England. This resulted in members of the St. Clair family being granted tracts of land in England and Scotland. The St. Clair branch eventually changed its name to the more Anglicized Sinclair, but the family connections in France, Scotland, and even to a degree in their Norse homeland remained intact.

The St. Clair/Sinclair family became a very strong presence in the politics of both France and Scotland. Although they preferred a secondary role in the public eye, they often controlled the politics from behind the scenes. The loyalty of a strong military was one component of their power.

After Bannockburn, Henry Sinclair, a descendant of the French noble St. Clair family, organized the remnant Templars into military units and guilds. They would become the integral force of his power base, and he in turn would become their guardian. In 1320 Sir Henry signed a letter to Pope John XXII asserting the independence of Scotland. This was a unique document in the history of the world, predating the American Declaration of Independence by more than four centuries. While Sinclair never played the leading role, he ruled quietly from behind the scenes, and the remnant Templars were his "big stick." They would remain united, and cemented their loyalty to their benefactor.

THE GUILD AND THE LODGE

In times of peace the ex-Templars used their skills as masons, carpenters, bridge builders, and merchants. The guild brought together members of a single trade. As the guilds became specialized, the Templars who had been seamen under the Templar flag now organized into a group that manned the Sinclair fleet, which was among the largest in Europe. The sea remained a gateway to riches, often more so in turbulent times. A fleet needed merchants, and the merchants themselves were also organized in guilds, which were the models for later companies.

The concept of guilds was originated by merchants and craftsmen. Their work often included secretive operations, as they had to deal with the prying eyes of the tax man, the competition of other guilds in the same craft, and even the Catholic Church. The Church had declared that a person who bought something with the intention of selling it at a higher price was cast out of "God's Temple."[4] Towns were actually created by the guilds to employ workers in the manufacturing process and for the purpose of meeting to buy and sell their wares. In modern Italy, the guild system and its secrecy prevail. Some towns are still dominated by one industry, and workers in that industry will reveal absolutely no information to an outsider.

Guilds grew into larger merchant "companies" licensed to sell goods abroad. Because Scotland and Europe exported wool, shipowners would transport the merchants who wanted to carry the products to continental Europe. In this less-than-golden age of freebooting, pirates attacked ships even for such mundane cargoes. Therefore, merchants needed a strong ship or fleet of ships to navigate the pirate-infested waters. The Templars, inheritors of a military organization, provided the strength.

Post-Bannockburn, the seas of commerce were anything but conducive to trade. The Dutch pirates would attack the English wool fleet—and often under letters of marque issued in their own country. The English king Edward II had temporarily stopped issuing such privateering papers, instead opting not to patrol the Scottish shores.

Unrestricted piracy against Scotland grew, but it had the effect of making the illegal business more lucrative. Privateers and pirates from the Low Countries, from the Hanseatic League, from France, and from the Channel Islands now regularly attacked English ships. Because the relations between Scotland and England were at best tense, the Low Countries could also be counted on to provide military equipment and food to Scotland, an act that the Scots regarded as necessary trade and the English considered smuggling.

The history of Scotland is murky at this time, and naval history even more so, as it was in no one's interest to record piracy. The fleet of Sinclair in the post-Bannockburn years is known to have been one of Europe's greatest; Sinclair had at his command more ships than Edward II of England. The same irregular coast and innumerable island hideouts had protected and hidden ships for hundreds of years before the reign of Edward II, and it continued to do so for hundreds of years after. In 1919 the German fleet was scuttled at Scapa Flow in the northern islands rather than surrender from its hiding place.

The Sinclair fleet underwent a major change in the years after Bannockburn. Sinclair ships had been built like those of their Norse relations, in the thin, overlapping oak-planked style that made them light and flexible. But Sinclair now had to react to the heavier style of ship being built in England. He built a castle in Kirkwall, in the northern islands, imported the necessary lumber, and built thicker-planked warships to accompany his Orkney galley ships.[5]

The fleet of the Sinclairs was now so strong that it was used to defend possessions of the king of Norway, who had a much smaller fleet that was "too weak to defend her own coasts against pirates."[6] At this time Stockholm had been seized by a pirate navy called the Victual Brothers, or the Victualleurs. They soon raided the Norwegian coast and sacked the city of Bergen.

The Templars who had come to Scotland to the protection of Robert the Bruce and Henry Sinclair found employment aboard Sinclair's neo-Templar fleet. They also served in their military tradition in newly formed land fighting units—and for the same elite masters.

THE RELIGIOUS WARS

The backlash against the wealth and power of the Catholic Church had started long before Martin Luther. In France the Cathar movement was a desire to return to a "pure" Christianity not obstructed by indolent priests and avaricious bishops. The Church quickly moved to stamp out the heresy and sent Saint Bernard, the Templar proponent, to investigate the Cathar sect. He discovered the movement to be larger than the Church thought, and he also believed it to be a most Christian example of living. The Church disregarded his report and sent Simon de Montfort of Leicester, England, to lead an army against them.

The viciousness of the war may be evidence of just how severe Rome regarded the threat. At Béziers the papal legate was asked how to recognize the Cathari. He responded, "Kill them all, God will know his own."[7] Simon de Montfort was brutality personified, burning many at the stake and blinding or cutting off the noses of those he allowed to live.

The order of the Knights Templar, sworn to obey only the pope, was not only visibly absent in the war against the Cathari; in some cases members fought on the side of the heretics against Rome. At Montsegur sixty knights served against the papal army. The Cathari, like the ex-Templars in the next century and the Freemasons thereafter, had secret signs and words to recognize their members. When the knights arrived in Cathar territory the password was "Have you brought the hatchets?" The answer was "We have eleven, freshly honed." Montsegur would end in defeat for the Cathari, but the anti-Rome sentiment simply went underground.

The Templar organization had less than a century to survive until Rome would turn against it. The Templars may have had more than ample reason to harbor anti-Church sentiments, but these would remain underground from the time of the battle at Montsegur until the Templar persecutions.

The Reformation that would thrive in Germany and Switzerland as a reaction to the all-powerful Catholic Church was based on religion, but the bitterness of the hundreds of years of the Inquisition, merciless taxation, and numerous wars against any non-Catholic people played a role. The Reformation also divided the former Templar knights on both political and religious grounds.

As the Reformation took hold in Scotland, the original core Templar group remained Catholic, including the Sinclair family, which was described as ardently Catholic and suffered as a result. In France, where the church and state had persecuted the Templars the most, former seaport stronghold La Rochelle would become, like many French ports, Huguenot—that is, Protestant. The religious wars pitted brother against brother, as did any civil war.

The Freemasons, the surviving ex-Templars, would remain underground, the lodge system not yet in its official (post-1717) period. The symbols of the anti-Rome movement among the Cathari and the symbol of the French Protestants in the north of France were often shared. The dove (the symbol of personal enlightenment), the eight-pointed cross, and the hatchet would grace the apparel and equipment of Huguenots and Freemasons. The wars also divided the ex-Templars and Masons along political lines, placing members of the descendant orders on both sides. The English king Edward III managed to pit his country against Catholic France in what would become known as the Hundred Years War. Some of the original founding Templar families acted for the Catholic side. The Scottish-French alliance created by the family connections behind the Templars set the ex-Templars and their heirs alongside the French in fighting England. But not all ex-Templars were seagoing warriors. On land the Scots Guard became the inheritors of the Templar tradition.

In 1445, one hundred years after the Templars were abolished and the French Templars fled to Scotland, the neo-Templar Scots Guard, or the Compagnie des Gendarmes Écossis, returned to France to intervene in French military adventures. The "auld alliance" renewed by the Robert the Bruce–Sinclair power base brought Scotland to war on the Continent. The Templar descendants often took the names of the men to whom they pledged themselves in feudal Scotland, but generations later they often kept their language and their patriotic leanings to their homeland. In France they were organized under French names. They were paid in *livres tournois*. And their officers and commanders were often invited into a new knighthood, the Order of Saint Michael.

When the French dauphin was ready to flee Catholic France and allow the victory of newly Protestant England, it was Joan of Arc who intervened. A vanguard of Scottish soldiers helped Joan's armies reverse the tide in one spectacular victory after another. The Scots Guard, a neo-Templar organization, would become the King's Guard and the King's Bodyguard, and play important roles in both military and state affairs for almost another two hundred years.

The Hundred Years War was a particularly difficult time in Europe, and England may have never seen a century of such lawlessness. On land petty thefts were innumerable; on the seas piracy reigned. Bribery secured judges and juries alike, and the ever-present tax collectors' palms could be greased. Greed was the most significant force, and even poets like Chaucer, who once denounced greed, now practiced it.[8]

The effect of the avarice was widespread poverty and economic disruption. In England the fourteenth century ended with a massive rebellion that would go down in history as Wat Tyler's Revolt.

Wat Tyler was actually Walter the Tyler, a Masonic name derived from the French word *tailleur,* meaning "one who cuts." Each lodge of Freemasons had an appointed tyler, and unlike the tailor who cuts clothes, the tyler was designated to guard the door with a sword. While it is often claimed that mob violence is spontaneous, Winston Churchill in his *Birth of Britain* and author Barbara Tuchman agree that beneath the mob violence was organization. By whom? The answer is obvious according to some, as "no single group suffered losses comparable to those inflicted over the next few days on the Knights Hospitallers, who seemed to be on an especially aggressive hit list of the rebel leaders."[9] Three generations after the Templars had been officially dissolved, they was still taking revenge on their rival order.

The Crusades were over, yet the Templars remained a force both in the public eye and underground. History records the achievements of the military units such as the Scots Guard, but history leaves uncovered the role of the ex-Templars in various forms, from merchants and craftsmen to pirates. And the Templars were not the only order to engage in piracy, although they were the only order to use the skull and crossbones as their battle flag.

RIVAL ORDERS AS PIRATES

The main rivals of the former Templars, the Knights of Malta and the Teutonic Knights, also turned to piracy to finance their orders. In the period just after the Battle of Bannockburn, when Scottish and English pirates ravaged the wool trade, the Hanseatic League turned to the Teutonic Knights to protect its shipping. The envoys of Henry VI of England who were sent to meet with the order's grand master to discuss a truce were actually captured by Hanseatic pirates. England then turned to the Knights of Rhodes, later the Knights of Malta, as they were known to provide assistance with negotiations. Oddly, two orders that had faced a common enemy during the Crusades were now enemies with each other.

The Knights of Rhodes had been organized by merchants from Amalfi. The order was created before the Knights Templar with the goal of providing medical assistance to the crusading knights and the pilgrims in the Holy Lands. The Knights of Rhodes first dedicated its order to Saint John and was called the Order of the Hospital of Saint John, or the Hospitallers. After the fall of Jerusalem, they went to Cyprus. In 1306 the master of the order, Foulques de Villaret, who had been the knights' first admiral, joined forces with a Genoese adventurer. With their combined fleet they captured the island of Rhodes. The tiny island that had served as a nest for Greek, Italian, and Saracen pirates became the order's privateer base. But the order had little to do now that Jerusalem was lost. It protected Christian shipping and attacked Muslim shipping.[10]

The Knights of Rhodes developed a distinctive style of warfare at sea, using grappling hooks and powerful soldiers to lock together ships and immediately board them, pirate-style. Little better than pirates, they launched an attack on Cairo. The first stop was in Alexandria, where twenty thousand men, women, and children were killed before the conquest erupted into an orgy of pillage and rape.[11] Many of the military contingents refused to go any farther because they enjoyed the spoils of war and "some Brethren turned pirate." [12]

From Rhodes the Hospitallers continued to harass Muslim shippers until three successive sieges by the Turks dislodged the knights. They then moved from port to port operating as pirates—even to the point of allowing the "brethren" to share in the booty. In the sixteenth century the Hospitallers resumed their naval operations from Malta. They harassed Islamic shippers. They were at war, so in their eyes the piracy was just privateering.

The Knights of Malta was very close to the various nation-states of Italy, and was often allied with other states to carry out raids. Members became known as *corso,* a word that later was Anglicized to *corsair,* or pirate. Their sea caravans enriched the order through *spoglio* (prize money) obtained in the sale of the goods they captured, including slaves, and through ransoming captives.

Both the underground Knights Templar and the legitimate Knights of Malta continued their piracy on the high seas and even in the Americas. It is surprising that the role of these religious military orders in the French settlements of the Americas largely remains secret.

THE KNIGHTS IN AMERICA

The Knights of Malta, which is active today, was influential in the settlement of Canada, in early colonization of the New World, and even in the American Revolution. In 1632 a knight of Malta, Commander Isaac de Razilly, organized the expedition to Acadia and Quebec. History records Samuel de Champlain as one of the earliest explorers but pays little attention to his top lieutenants, Marc-Antoine Brasdefer de Chateaufort and Charles-Jacques Huault de Montmagny. After Champlain's death, Chateaufort and then Montmagny served as governor of New France. Other French-Canadian knights would also play significant roles in the early history of Canada.

The counterpart of the Knights of Malta in France was the Order of Saint-Sulpice. Founded by the Abbé Jacques Olier, the order invited wealthy patrons to form another group, the Society of Notre Dame, which would in turn become the founding Seigneurs of Montreal in Canada. Serving the same role as the Cistercians in relation to the Knights Templar, the Order of Saint-Sulpice at times played a very powerful behind-the-scenes role in international affairs. Unhampered by the vow of poverty, the order grew in wealth and power. Many of Montreal's streets, named for luminaries of the Sulpicians, remind citizens of the order's key position. In the 1660s, when the overlords of Montreal, the so-called One Hundred Associates, proved themselves to be absentee landlords inclined to tax the city, the Sulpicians had them expelled and took over the governance of Montreal. To their credit, their wealth has been committed to good works, and the order remains as wealthy today as it was three centuries ago. In France the order also remains wealthy, powerful, and able to play a political role from backstage.

The Knights of Malta also colonized the Caribbean, including Tortuga, Saint Croix, and Saint Barthélemy—islands that later passed into the ownership of the French West India Company.

Another knight, Admiral François-Joseph-Paul de Grasse, delivered the coup de grâce to the British at Yorktown. His fleet arrived from the Caribbean just in time to trap Cornwallis and the British army, who were in full retreat. The British, waiting for reinforcements and supplies that would never arrive, surrendered to George Washington and ended the war. The admiral was a Knight of Malta, and he learned his seamanship skills under the tutelage of the order. Of the French ships that battled the British, several were commanded by members of the Knights of Malta, including Admiral de Grasse's *chef d'escadron* at Chesapeake Bay, Jean-Louis-Charles de Coriolis d'Espinousse.

After the war fourteen of the twenty elite Knights of Malta who fought for the American cause became members of the Society of the

Cincinnati, a closed group formed by George Washington for his officers.[13] Despite criticism that the order was a version of European aristocracy, membership was limited to a handful and future membership required that an individual be a descendant of a member of the founding group.

The French Revolution and the subsequent Napoleonic Wars saw the Knights of Malta defeated in battle. Napoleon seized the home base of Malta in 1789 because the French knights had provided Louis XVI, his rival, with funding. The Russian czar Paul I offered the knights refuge and asked them to create a new order that would answer to him. Napoleon immediately ended the order's income from its French property and evicted the knights, forcing them into a brief sojourn in Russia. In 1834 the order moved again to Rome and came under papal protection. The pope restored the office of grand master in 1879.

The order slowly rebuilt itself in the twentieth century. The Knights of Malta order survived and grew to the point that it became a very powerful, albeit secretive, force in modern world politics. In 1921 it had two hundred knights and 1,800 members of all grades.[14] Today the group is headquartered at Palazzo Malta on the via Condotti in Rome, and it has a worldwide network of nine thousand knights and thousands more lower-grade members.[15] It is the most elite of the Catholic orders, and although it remains behind the scenes, it has great power. While the Knights of Malta does not own any property outside Rome, the order is recognized as a sovereign state, complete with its own passports and stamps.

The European press often regards the order as an old boys' club for aristocrats, but it is actually active on several continents in both charitable works and political action. In the United States, a branch of the Sovereign Military Order of Malta (SMOM) was started in 1927, under the leadership of New York's Cardinal Spellman. Since its founding, the group has included the likes of Joseph Kennedy, Joseph Grace of W. R. Grace, and presidents of companies such as General Motors and U.S. Steel. The SMOM has an influence in politics and has taken activist roles from its earliest days, starting with opposition to the New Deal of

Roosevelt. In post–World War II politics the group has always leaned to the right, sometimes to the extreme. In supporting the right wing the SMOM has not shied away even from assisting Nazi war criminals. After World War II the order granted its highest honor to German army general Reinhard Gehlen, which might sound shocking but is nonetheless in line with supporting a monarchist agenda. Although the Sovereign Military Order of Malta does nothing to hide its existence or membership and does little to disguise its right-wing political agenda, it receives almost no recognition in post-Crusades history texts.

The rival order of the Knights Templar, however, is a much more secretive entity. Because it is forced to stay underground, the order goes to great lengths to conceal its existence and membership and to disguise its activities. Nevertheless, it has survived.

The Americas presented great opportunity to the remnant Templar factions. For many of the rank and file, the new lands represented a place to survive the religious wars and start a new life. Jacobin Catholics from Scotland, Huguenots and Catholics from France, and various dissenters from England found peace and brotherhood in the Americas. And the wealthy who had found power in the changing feudal hierarchy of the old order also found new types of power in the Americas. A handful of these people pulled the strings and enjoyed the fruits of criminal activity from their secret positions.

Chapter 3
UNDER A BLACK FLAG

Execution by hanging was a gruesome affair in the days of Captain Kidd, and for the convicted pirate there was no reprieve. In the city in which Kidd had lived while attempting to secure his privateering commission, he undoubtedly passed the execution dock at Wapping numerous times. Had he ever thought his own neck might end up in a noose?

Public executions were fascinating to the people of seventeenth- and eighteenth-century England. In order to have the opportunity to see the law exercise its ultimate power over man, the power to take life, people would flock in from all over London. The poor arrived on foot and the wealthy by carriage to see the wretched plead for their lives. No pains were taken to spare the public the crudeness of the death penalty. A particularly barbaric highlight was having the executioner, most likely a large specimen of a man, actually carry the condemned up a ladder to the noose. There the hooded figure would place the neck of the condemned in the noose. The victim might be given an opportunity to speak his last words, to plead for his life, or to ask forgiveness. Or he might simply have the rope tightened around his neck and be dropped to his death.[1]

If he was lucky, the convicted felon's neck would break immediately and he would be spared the horror of suffering a slow choking demise. If the convicted was able to manage it, he might tip his executioner beforehand, ensuring that the executioner would use a longer rope and thus hasten the death. If the condemned didn't have any money, he might have family or friends present who could rush in to pull on his hanging legs so that his suffering would end faster.

In all, hanging was wonderful entertainment. At Tyburn the weekly hangings drew two hundred thousand spectators. They would gather the night before outside Newgate Prison to drink, dance, and fornicate in the streets. In the morning the crowd followed the condemned in a parade through the streets of London, all the while cheering or jeering at the unfortunate criminals. The wealthy would pay as much as ten pounds sterling to sit ringside and eat and drink during the execution. This event, which might be the ancestor of the modern tailgate party, was so popular it became known as the Tyburn Fair, and the rulers made a very unpopular decision in finally ending such spectacles in the mid-nineteenth century.

A pirate could expect treatment worse than that of the common criminal. On occasion the executioner quickly cut down the hanging pirate and disemboweled him while he was still alive. His entrails would be burned before his eyes, and if he survived any longer, he could be drawn and quartered. Women were spared from this indecency because they were considered the "fair" sex. Instead they were burned to death.

On Friday, May 23, 1701, it was William Kidd's turn to provide the entertainment; the stairs at Wapping would be his place of justice. The body could be displayed for all those who traveled the Thames to see. Kidd had no plans to repent and no plans to ask for mercy. To the end he told all who would listen that he was a pawn of wealthy men. Members of the elite ruling class on both sides of the Atlantic had out-fitted his ship and helped him get a commission, and they were due a share in his gains. But none of his wealthy backers was called before the judge. None of his elite partners stood before the executioner. All were at home in landed estates, breathing a sigh of relief that they would not be tarnished by their role in Kidd's crimes.[2]

Kidd himself was once a man of property, an owner of real estate on what would become the financial capital of the world, Wall Street. He was not a career criminal, although he was certainly not without blame. He simply thought his ties to the men who pulled the strings of colonial

New York government allowed him to get away with murder. But the political tide had turned. Piracy against the Muslim trading partners of the East India Company caused trouble for many who had been shareholders. While Kidd plied the seas for booty, a power play in London put the interests of the East India Company above those of other would-be adventurers. Pressure was applied to those who interfered. Kidd was the scapegoat. The ties he relied on to protect him instead cut him loose. To his surprise, Kidd was separated from those who commissioned him. Now a convicted pirate, Kidd was at the dock in Wapping.

Those who came for a show were not disappointed. Kidd arrived drunk and unrepentant. His last words were a speech against the liars who testified against him. He was carried to the hangman's noose and dropped. The rope broke. Dazed by the fall but still alive, Kidd was quickly carried up the ladder again by his executioner. This time the fall killed him.

◈

The legend of Captain Kidd has grown out of proportion with its reality. Kidd was no swashbuckler; he was a businessman pursuing wealth in the fashion of the day.

New York City in the 1690s could be equated with the Wild West. The governor, Benjamin Fletcher, was appointed to office by the military. He arrived in New York in August 1692. As befitting a fat, greedy, minor tyrant, Fletcher attained his wealth by being corrupt. He controlled the exchange of real estate, and real estate was the first source of wealth in the colony. In a short period of time citizens understood that to favor the governor with a bribe earned them his favor. Fletcher allied himself with Stephen van Cortlandt, William Nicoll, and Frederick Philipse by giving them large pieces of land.

Fletcher soon turned his attention to another opportunity. In 1696 England passed the first of a series of ill-conceived laws limiting the colonies' ability to engage in commerce. Defying such laws built some of America's greatest fortunes and started a tradition of giving the wealthy the right to be above the law. Smuggling quickly became an accepted way to earning a living. With the European countries at war and all shipping in danger of encountering an enemy, smuggling was scarcely more dangerous than honest shipping.

Pirates and smugglers were always at risk when landing in a foreign port. Their cargoes were subject to seizure and the pirates and smugglers were subject to arrest. Governor Fletcher provided a safe haven for all who were willing to pay his personal tax. This bribery greased the wheel of commerce, and New Yorkers were able to get imported goods from anywhere in the world. Local shops in the small port city offered goods from exotic places around the world. Items such as teak furniture, Oriental carpets, and Madeira wine could be found beside the simple homespun goods of colonial New York. Currencies of European and Asian countries were exchanged by the English, Dutch, French, Jewish, Irish, and Scottish settlers in the city, which was already a melting pot. Elsewhere the British, French, and Dutch men-of-war preyed on the smuggler and legitimate shipper alike; in New York City, all who paid Fletcher's fees were safe.

Fletcher, who "undertook to mine all the known veins of gubernatorial graft, and to stake claims on some new ones,"[3] backed all forms of crime at sea. Fletcher found a way to profit from all aspects of pirate commerce. The pirate captains dined at his table while their crews swaggered around town spending their ill-gotten money. The pirate Edward Taylor is on record as having paid Fletcher £1,700 to be allowed to land in New York City and sell his wares. (In modern purchasing power, £1,700 would be about $250,000.) The privateer who applied to Fletcher for a commission to attack enemy shipping would then attack anything he could defeat. Such a commission could be procured for five hundred pounds; the pirate John Hoar is on record as having bought one of these commissions. The merchants who supplied New York's shops with exotic goods bought from pirates and often had a stake in their voyages as well.

An example of Fletcher's liberal interpretation of his powers is in his relationship with Thomas Tew. The legendary pirate was from an English Quaker family that had settled in Rhode Island. His history has not been recorded before his arrival in Bermuda, a smuggling capital, in 1692. According to sources, Tew was already enriched by piracy. There he bought a share of a ship called the *Amity* with gold he carried in his pockets. Other shareholders were Thomas Hall, Richard Gilbert, John Dickinson, and William Outerbridge, who was a member of the governor's council. Tew received a privateering commission from Governor Ritchier and headed for French West Africa to attack slave ships. On the way, Tew "turned pirate," with the backing of his crew. They headed for the Red Sea and attacked Arab shippers before settling in the kingdom of pirates, Madagascar. After several adventures, Tew returned home. He sold his Indian textiles in New York City and then headed to Newport, sent for his partners, and divided the spoils—some of which was buried near Newport and the rest in Boston.

Tew's Bermuda backers reportedly received fourteen times their investment.[4] Tew's share amounted to eight thousand pounds, enough to provide a high-style retirement. For a while Tew took part in the good life in Rhode Island, untainted by the same crimes that would see Kidd hanged. But the governor of Massachusetts denied Tew another privateering commission, so he applied to the governor of Rhode Island and for five hundred pounds received his papers.

The first order of business was sailing to New York to meet with the Philipse family. Frederick Philipse was the seventeenth-century equivalent of a venture capitalist. He provided the equipment needed for a pirate voyage, and in turn was entitled to a share of the gains. His only risk was monetary and he hedged his bets by making numerous investments. Those who came to him risked life and liberty. With Frederick Philipse's backing, Tew outfitted his second pirate expedition, one that would immensely benefit his patron.

Tew's second adventure found him capturing ships of the Great Moghul and keeping one hundred unmarried girls as well as treasure. After a sojourn in Madagascar, Tew and his crew headed home again for the quiet life. This time his treasure was said to be more than a hundred thousand pounds. Philipse, who risked only money, in comparison to the pirates who risked their lives, would earn more than a hundred thousand pounds backing numerous voyages.

Tew's weakness was that he could not retire. He sought another privateering commission, this time from the new governor of Rhode Island, John Easton, who refused. Tew then applied to Governor Fletcher of New York. Fletcher knew that Tew was a well-known sea rover, but felt justified in commissioning him to sail against the French. When later defending his actions, Fletcher claimed he did not know of Tew's reputation, but that the "stranger" had planned to attack the French at the mouth of the Canada River. Such commissions against the French were nothing unusual. But Tew saw the situation differently.

Tew outfitted his ship and then sailed between New York and Boston recruiting fellow pirates and adventurers for his fleet. Fletcher claimed the commission was for attacking the French in Canada, but Tew openly acknowledged there was more money to be gained in the Indian Ocean and that this area was his destination.

Thomas Tew made his final voyage to the Indian Ocean, where he reportedly had some early success against Indian trading ships. But he may have pushed his luck. He was never again seen in New England.

On occasion, Fletcher had to make a token charge against a pirate or smuggler to confuse his enemies. In 1694 he seized a ship that had returned from a Caribbean voyage. The ship was owned in part by one of New York's wealthiest men, Robert Livingston. Livingston not only beat the charges, but also sought a way to get rid of Fletcher at the same time. It would take four years and the efforts of two partners. It was into this early version of the "world trade center" that Captain Kidd sailed.

THE WORLD OF CAPTAIN KIDD

Born in Greenock, Scotland, in 1645, William Kidd climbed up the career ranks as a seaman and finally a captain. Scotland was pirate central after the Templar fleet had sought shelter there centuries before, and the country, along with Ireland, would be regarded as a pirate haven for another two centuries. Before the so-called Golden Age of Piracy, pirates were more likely to be found capturing ships loaded with wool or fish—but certainly not capturing the Spanish treasure fleet, plundering the ports of the Golden Main, or chasing the fleet of the Moghul of India. But piracy, like smuggling, was a living.

As Templar soldiers and their descendants remained in the military service as mercenaries, Templar sailors and their descendants spawned a culture of both legal privateering and illegal piracy. In the seventeenth century, many Scottish seamen were commissioned to battle Dutch attackers who preyed on English and Scottish shipping and fishing. Later, after one more attempt to attain independence, Scottish Jacobites swelled the ranks of the pirates in Europe and the Caribbean. It is little wonder that the best pirate literature was also spawned in Scotland; Robert Louis Stevenson wrote the classic *Treasure Island* and fellow Scot J. M. Barrie wrote *Peter Pan*.

Participation in piracy and smuggling was a frequent occurrence in Scotland, despite laws that called for the highest penalties against these offenses. The laws were only sporadically enforced and convictions were nearly impossible to achieve. An underground society prevailed; it was not necessarily hereditary, but it was so prevalent that it was not threatened by a justice system. From the days of the Templar demise until the eighteenth century, the lodges of men dedicated to a specific craft or occupation enforced their own codes and often exercised power that reached to the highest levels of government. These guilds of lawyers, sea captains, craftsmen, and soldiers were individual cells, or lodges in Masonic parlance, that operated independently yet assisted one another in ways that those outside the brotherhood would never suspect.

Freemasonry was not yet public. Before 1717 it was truly a secret society in which it was a violation of oath to admit membership or discuss anything that went on in a Masonic meeting. A major event took place less than twenty years later, when four of England's lodges met at the Apple Tree Tavern in Covent Garden in London to form the Grand Lodge. Shortly afterward the Irish, French, and Scottish lodges emerged as public societies. There is no satisfactory reason why Masonry came out of the closet, but the most plausible explanation is that the distrust those in power had for the secret organizations encouraged the orders to reveal themselves. Scotland's Masons hid a vast underground of smugglers, pirates, and revolutionaries. Rather than risk being accused of plotting against the king of England, the English lodges welcomed royalty and toasted the health of their kings and queens. Scottish Masonry was the preserve of such people as Andrew Ramsay, the tutor of Bonnie Prince Charlie. Ramsay publicly spoke of the former Crusaders setting up Masonic lodges upon returning from the wars. The lodges survived the persecution of the Templars by remaining underground. And the Bonnie Prince led a revolt by the Scottish against their English overlords.

The Scottish version of the Masons had strong political overtones, while the English version, which had distanced itself from politics, did not present such a threat. Because of this threat, the Scottish secret organization needed to remain underground.

◈

Kidd was a Scotsman and was partnered with fellow Scotsman Livingston, and both men became Masons as well. After a few short years, Livingston was very public with his membership in the guild. His family is still known as active proponents of the Masons. Kidd, of course, did not have even a few short years.

The massive immigration of Scots to America and Canada was resented by the earlier colonists. This Scottish "invasion" of America was a direct result of constant war with England, and it increased dramatically after the failure of the Jacobite Rebellion. A prejudice against Scots existed from Massachusetts to Virginia, although these immigrants still had a significant role in the formation of the new country. In 1776 a play produced in Philadelphia was dedicated to "Lord Kidnaper . . . Pirates and Buccaneers, and the innumerable clans of Macs and Donalds upon Donalds in America." [5] The dedication was in jest but the sentiment was real, and the Scots-as-pirates stereotype was not helped by the prominence of Captain Kidd in pirate lore.

In August 1689 Kidd had been on the island of Nevis in command of a sixteen-gun privateer he had taken from the French. Two years later, in another English expedition, his men—mostly former pirates—

had left him ashore, and he lost command of a ship. Later that year he received another command to take on the French.

By the time Kidd arrived in New York, his reputation had preceded him. He helped build the first Trinity Church and bought a lot on Wall Street. William Kidd, man-about-town, then married a well-to-do Dutch widow, Sarah Bradley Cox Oort.[6] It was his wife's third marriage; in fact, the marriage license was received just days after John Oort, her second husband, died. Sarah Oort brought a nice dowry to the new marriage, including a house on Wall Street and another on Pearl Street. Kidd must have felt that he was a worthy catch, and titled himself "Gentleman" on their application. Oort and Kidd lived in the fashionable part of town, their home complete with furniture and carpets that were imported from Asia. Kidd could have remained simply a gentleman, but he didn't.

As luck would have it, the acts of piracy committed around the emerging British empire were bringing complaints to the ears of King William III. Especially irritating to the court was the role that Governor Fletcher was playing in North America. King William met with his Privy Council and Richard Coote, the Earl of Bellomont. They decided that Lord Bellomont would be sent to New York to replace Fletcher as governor and stamp out the pirate haven he had created.

Piracy was a worldwide problem for empire-building Britain. In Asia the same countries that England was trying to trade with were complaining about American pirates attacking their shipping, and they held the British responsible. All the legitimate trade was carried on through a royal-sponsored monopoly called the British East India Company.

At the end of the seventeenth century, the British East India Company was trying to further establish itself in Asia. The company had been doing well and had the favor of James II until his death. With a royal monopoly, the average dividend was 25 percent in the last ten years of the century. But this monopoly inspired jealousy. Other European traders, American merchants, and even pirates were hindrances to business. In the new market the British East India Company was trying to develop, it also did not help that the company had little the customer wanted. It introduced cheap opium, and tried to hold its own against invaders and pirates.

Ironically, in this newly declared war against piracy Kidd was enlisted to fight for the cause of the British. While visiting England with New York's most respected merchant, Robert Livingston, Kidd was introduced to Lord Bellomont, who desired the job of New York's governor. Livingston, Kidd, and Bellomont plotted to get rid of Fletcher. For his part in the deal, Kidd was commissioned to fight against the pirates.

Pirates sailing out of New York, commissioned by Fletcher, frequently attacked the Moghuls' ships. John Hoar actually attacked the British East India fleet and captured and burned two company ships. Tew's attacks on the Indian fleet caused rioting in the streets. The account of Henry Every's pirate crew kidnapping and raping Indian women, some of whom committed suicide rather than submit, caused the offices of the East India Company in Surat to be attacked by mobs. Several key employees were imprisoned, where they received harsh treatment during the six months of negotiation between the Moghuls and the British East India Company. Several did not survive.

Whatever the real intentions of Kidd, Livingston, and Bellomont, the plan was first to capture the pirate Tew. Kidd, Bellomont, and Livingston would be entitled to whatever goods were taken in the process.

THE BIRTH OF AN AMERICAN DYNASTY

Robert Livingston built a dynasty as fast as he could and in any way he could. He was a Scot who had lived in Rotterdam for a time and learned the Dutch language. He sailed to America in 1674. At that time the Dutch still controlled New York, and the largest patroonship was owned by Nicholas Van Rensselaer, who had joined another very wealthy Dutch family through an arranged marriage to Alida Schuyler. Van Rensselaer was the son and namesake of the man who had actually received the grants of land and built the family wealth. Like many sons of ambitious men, Van Rensselaer had no interest in the business or his upstate lands; instead he fancied himself a mystic. He hired Livingston, an obvious go-getter, to run his empire.

A trader by profession, Livingston caught on quickly and acquired the ability to speak the Iroquois language—an ability many traders didn't have. He also helped build the Van Rensselaer fortune.

In 1678 Nicholas was only in his early forties, but he began aging rapidly. He took to his sickbed with an illness that could not be diagnosed. One day he decided the end was near and called for a servant to bring a pen and paper for his will. Instead Livingston appeared. "No, no, send him away; he's going to marry my widow," cried Van Rensselaer, just before he died.[7] If ever a will was composed, it was never found. But some have suggested that "if you believe a Van Rensselaer rumor, still circulated to this day, Nicholas was poisoned."[8]

Nicholas the mystic had been right: Within eight months Alida and Robert Livingston were married. Livingston acquired his boss's widow and became the wealthy man he had designed to become. When he met Kidd, Livingston was the wealthiest man in New York. As a Scot, Livingston was embroiled in the religious wars that raged back home and that spilled over into the colonies. His relatives in Scotland, the Earls of Callendar and Linlithgow, had fought on the wrong side of what became the Glorious Revolution. It was a precarious time because of the religious upheaval, and many Scots and French Huguenots were forced to leave the country. The hostilities did not end once the immigrants reached America.

In New York the war was between Jacob Leisler and the Catholics.[9] In his frantic effort to keep the pope from controlling New York, Leisler seized the city. When Britain later sent a new governor, Leisler attempted to defend New York against him. His rabid anti-Catholic sentiment ended with his trial and that of five confederates. The same evidence admitted in trial freed four and sentenced two to hanging. Jacob Leisler was hanged on the land where the Manhattan side of the Brooklyn Bridge would be built.

A bit of jury tampering may have helped the four who were acquitted. One of these possible beneficiaries was Peterse Delanoy. His family subsequently dropped the last letter of their name and become the Delanos. A later alliance through marriage would result in the Delano-Roosevelt family.

With Leisler out of the way, the power vacuum allowed Huguenot families such as the Delanoys and their allies among the Dutch power base, including Livingston, to prosper. Livingston was now in prime position to expand his empire. He traded with whomever he could and owned outright or owned shares in several merchant ships. One of these returned 500 percent in one 1694 voyage alone. But success had its downside: Through a customs agent of the mayor of New York City, Livingston was charged with the crime of trading with the French. It is possible that the charge was correct, as not all legitimate voyages yielded such high returns. But the mayor simply wanted a share in the profits. The case was brought before the grand jury, whose chairman was William Kidd. It is not known if this case also involved jury tampering, but Livingston was spared. Jury chairman Kidd refused to indict.

Kidd and his new friend Livingston went to England to increase their fortunes. The deal that was struck with Richard Coote, Lord Bellomont, involved several other figures who moved in commercial and government circles. The list included John Somers, the Lord Chancellor; Edward Russell, the Earl of Orford, who was the First Lord of the Admiralty; Henry Sidney, the Earl of Romney; Charles Talbot, the Duke of Shrewsbury; Edward Harrison, a director of the East India Company; and Richard Blackham, who would later be imprisoned for bribery and currency manipulation. King William III was destined to claim 10 percent of the return in exchange for his blessing of Kidd's pirate-hunting enterprise.[10]

Livingston and Kidd were the core partners of the agreement, and together they were required to put up six thousand pounds to purchase and refit a ship named *Adventure Galley*. This was approximately one fifth of the funds needed for the voyage, and in turn the partners would receive one fifth of the prizes captured and get to keep the ship. The men who signed on as crew members were on a no-purchase, no-pay contract. This type of contract was used by whalers and pirate ships, and it stated that if no prizes were obtained, no pay would be given. Therefore, the inducement to capture something was great.

Kidd and crew were commissioned to capture pirate ships. Their papers specifically targeted Thomas Tew of Rhode Island and two New York–based pirates, Thomas Wake and William Maze. For good measure the commission added any and all pirates, freebooters, and sea rovers. Commission in hand, Kidd sailed out of London to New York. Along the way he captured a French fishing ship—not much of a catch, but perhaps practice for his new crew.

In New York, Kidd recruited more men for his adventure and finally started his planned voyage on September 5, 1696. The destination was the Indian Ocean, where the large island of Madagascar was actually a pirate nation.[11] The onetime French station Fort Dauphin had become the home base of the pirate Abraham Samuel, who was called King Samuel. The pirate king welcomed other pirates who presented him with gifts. His kingdom and other pirate strongholds, as well as slave ports run by merchants with no national affiliation, made Madagascar a truly wild locale.

LIBERTALIA

Saint Mary's was a small island off the coast of Madagascar where the pirates formed a democratic nation called Libertalia. It may have been the world's first true democracy, in which each man had an equal vote. It just happened to be a pirate nation.

Upon reaching the mature age of about thirty, many of the pirates retired to Libertalia. Land was free, exotic Polynesian-African women were plentiful, and the locals were not hostile. Plantations were started and trading posts were established. Even though each man might be able to return to his home port with a small fortune, many chose to live on the island.

It is a mystery just why Kidd sailed into Saint Mary's if by this time he did not intend to "go pirate." As a pirate hunter, he apparently had no intention to attack the pirate port; instead he landed, to repair his ship and recruit new men. But once he landed, his situation grew worse. A greater enemy than the English would attack Kidd's crew: disease. On the small island in the Indian Ocean, one fifth of the crew succumbed. Kidd needed to replace even more men than he originally intended. He took on new members, all of whom were most likely experienced pirates.

The major distinction separating the privateer from the pirate was a piece of paper. The commission that gave the privateer captain the right to take certain prizes made his actions legal, whereas seizing bounty without such a commission was an offense punishable by hanging. Commissions would occasionally be honored, and sometimes would expire because of the end of a war. Unfortunately, the privateer at sea had little way of knowing that hostilities had ended and that a truce voided his commission. Another difference between privateers and pirates was the conditions in which they lived and worked. On a privateer ship the captain was chosen by the owner. He had to be tough and able to make difficult decisions, but he also had to be intelligent. The men on both merchant ships and privateer ships received very little pay, were treated as inferior by the owners and officers, and were subject to physical abuse at the whim of their masters. Such abuse was legal, and more men died of being flogged than died in battle. Alexander Falconbridge, a surgeon who served aboard the ships of the Royal African Company, reported that one captain flogged a man to death for losing an oar. Another captain forced men to eat live cockroaches for his entertainment. Falconbridge is quoted extensively for such cruelties to both seamen and slaves in Hugh Thomas's *The Slave Trade* and Patrick Pringle's *Jolly Roger, the Golden Age of Piracy*. The slaves aboard such ships often were of more value to the captain than his own crew. The average mortality rate for slaves in the seventeenth century was 25 percent; it was often as high as 40 percent for the crew.

The officers of the British navy treated their own crews just as harshly.

It was no wonder that when a pirate ship attacked a merchant ship, the crew was eager to surrender. The pirates treated them better. Those who came aboard were treated as equals. Many were invited to join, some were simply impressed by their lifestyle, but all were treated better. Four hundred years after the Templar fleet left France, the lodge system spawned in Templar preceptories and Cistercian monasteries was alive aboard the pirate ships. The ship's rules were determined by articles that each man signed. The men voted on such rules in a democratic fashion: one man, one vote. Rules included not taking women aboard, as they could cause friction; not discussing religion, as it too could cause conflict; and spelling out tasks and duties.

On a pirate ship the captain was elected by the entire crew. Like a privateer captain, he had to be tough and intelligent. He had to be well liked, too, as his crew could simply unelect him. Shares were determined, and the job of the captain and the quartermaster was to ensure equal shares to all members of the crew.

The crew on both pirate and privateer ships would sail for a share in the voyage. On the privateer ship the captain's share and that of the high-ranking officers were greater than the crew's. On many pirate ships all bounty was shared in a fairer way. The captain and the quartermaster might get a double share; a highly proficient crew member could get a share and a half. An injured pirate who was unable to return to sea might be given a greater share to aid his retirement. The average sailor on a pirate ship had a better chance of making a windfall profit for the risks and hardships he endured. Some took their shares and went back to the farm. Sometimes an agreement was struck so that all sailors remained together until every man had a certain amount of money.

Life was potentially dangerous for the pirate, but the dangers were not in attacking enemy shipping. Very rarely was a merchant ship willing to mount a defense, and few pirate ships were ever captured outside of ports. One pirate historian reports that brothel casualties were higher than battle casualties. The greatest risk a pirate might endure was expulsion by his fellow sailors. Marooning, or expelling a pirate from a crew, took place on a desert island or sometimes on a sandbar that would disappear at high tide. Pirates were usually marooned only for the worst of offenses, which included abandoning their posts during battle. The term *maroon* was coined from what the Spanish called Cimarrons, the group of people created from the marriage of escaped black slaves to native Amerindian women.

Life at sea was equally dangerous for the criminal pirate and the legitimate privateer, as the common threats—injury, imprisonment, and death—did not favor one type of sailor. For example, a privateer sailing against Spain was a criminal in the eyes of the Spanish crown, as was a pirate operating anywhere. Both could suffer equally for their offenses, and death was the most common punishment. The difference was that the pirate stood a better chance of making a profit. As a result, pirate ships often had little problem defeating better-armed naval ships, merchant ships, and privateer ships. Many times the crew of the captured ship was happy to join the pirates—and they were often delighted to see a cruel captain subject to his own medicine.

CAPTAIN KIDD AND THE PIRATES

Kidd knew the risks and the rewards of piracy. What happened aboard the *Adventure Galley* to induce the captain and crew to "go pirate" will probably never be known. But Kidd was low on supplies, had little to trade, and had a crew that was most likely unhappy with the long months at sea and his harsh leadership and lack of profit. With his leadership and judgment in question and his reward system poor, it is surprising that he was able to recruit veteran pirates. However he did it, he set out from Saint Mary's as a pirate.

Twice Kidd brought his ship to within threatening distance of British-protected shipping, and twice he was turned away. Finally he captured a lone trading ship from Bombay flying the English colors. Upon meeting the ship's captain, Kidd found out that he was already considered a pirate. Word traveled quickly.

Kidd soon took three more ships, including the valuable *Quedah Merchant* in January 1698. With his new fleet, he now broke all the rules and attacked an East India Company ship. He left the coast of India with his prizes and headed for Madagascar, where he spent six months before heading back to North America.

It is hard to believe that an experienced captain such as Kidd would think that he could return to New York and escape punishment because of his connections, but that appears to have been the case. The Earl of Bellomont, now the governor of New York, actually came to Kidd's defense. The governor said he received reports that Kidd was forced by his men to act as a pirate. But Bellomont was in an awkward position. Having replaced Fletcher, who had given a commission to the pirate Thomas Tew, Bellomont had to be careful not to cast himself in the same light. He also was entitled to a large commission should he issue a pardon. Kidd, however, had gone too far.

The capture of the *Quedah Merchant* had caused rioting in the streets of Surat, where the British East India Company maintained its offices. The company was already blamed for any acts of European piracy, but this time the ship belonged to a member of the Indian emperor's court. This news eventually reached New York—well before Kidd.

Bellomont had to distance himself from the situation and cut his losses. The governor of what is now New York and Massachusetts had never seen Boston, and he traveled there on May 26, 1699, for the first time. It appeared to his critics that he was on his way to meet his pirate-partner Kidd, who had just reached Delaware Bay and was heading north. Bellomont later explained that he wrote Kidd a letter that purposely did not threaten his arrest, as he didn't want to scare Kidd away.

Joseph Emmot, a New York lawyer whose specialty was admiralty cases, advised Bellomont that Kidd had treasure aboard and had left treasure behind in the Caribbean. Emmot also delivered two passes granted by the French that Kidd had taken from the Moorish ships he captured. These documents were evidence that the act of capturing those ships, at least, was not piracy. Had these passes made it to Kidd's trial, he might have been acquitted. But somehow Bellomont or another backer of the voyage allowed the passes to disappear.[12]

While he was conspiring to have Kidd convicted, Bellomont sent two men to get a statement from the pirate. They met with Kidd off Block Island. Afterward Kidd seemed confident he could still trust Bellomont. He set sail for a tiny island off the coast of eastern Long Island called Gardiner's Island. He unloaded three or four small boats of booty and then sent for John Gardiner, in whose care Kidd placed a chest for Bellomont.

Gardiner's area of eastern Long Island was one of the two favorite pirate places to anchor in summer; the other was across the mouth of Long Island Sound, on the islands between Cape Cod and Martha's Vineyard. Both were locales where ships, both pirate and merchant, could rendezvous to trade and exchange cargo and supplies. It was an illegal floating market at times. The mouth of Buzzards Bay was also passed by ships cruising between New York and Boston, but docking a ship there would mean drawing the attention of the navy.

As Kidd sailed around the eastern end of Long Island, he dropped treasure in various places. One stash was delivered to an old pirate by the name of Thomas Paine, who lived on Canonicut Island off Rhode Island. When the governor of Rhode Island got wind of the story, he searched Paine's house, but the gold was not there. It may have already been moved back to Gardiner's Island, but proof against the Gardiner family was not to be found.

Kidd's plan was to hedge his bets. If he hid enough treasure before meeting the authorities, it would be something to use in striking a bargain. As Kidd's real history grew into legend, people would tell tales of him dropping his treasure as far north as Nova Scotia and as far east as the South China Sea. But it's more likely that what he did not leave in the Caribbean he hid around Long Island Sound.

Kidd was also attempting to deftly play the cards he was dealt. He knew after meeting with Emmot that the situation was vastly different since he had left New York. The British were cracking down on piracy, the ships returning to New York were being seized, and the ships' captains and crews were being hunted and arrested. Kidd had put his partners Bellomont and Livingston in a very complicated position. Bellomont, in fact, had much to gain either as Kidd's friend or as the arresting officer of the court. Both scenarios allowed him to be rewarded either financially or in reputation.

Not having all the treasure available for confiscation was one of the strategies Kidd employed; the temptation to have more would serve as an inducement for Kidd's apprehensive partner. Kidd's second play was delivering to Lord Bellomont's wife an enameled box with four jewels; he hoped it might tip the scale and make Bellomont back his partner. But Bellomont did the math. Allowing that Kidd's charges might be false and pardoning him—and thereby keeping his legitimate share—could equal a thousand pounds. But seizing Kidd and claiming his legitimate share as arresting governor gave him thirteen thousand pounds.

Bellomont's advisers warned him not to go against the British East India company and the powers the company represented. Thus Bellomont decided against his onetime partner; Kidd was to be arrested. The other partner, Robert Livingston, was dismayed by Bellomont's decision. He stood to gain all if Kidd was pardoned and nothing if Kidd was arrested. In fact, Livingston had posted a bond guaranteeing Kidd's behavior. Bellomont alleged that Livingston threatened him, saying that Livingston would take reimbursement from Kidd's treasure if Bellomont didn't return the bond. Did Bellomont make up this accusation to distance himself from the crime? Or as Bellomont might have feared, were Kidd and Livingston, brother Scots, involved in a conspiracy against him?

Both Bellomont and Livingston had to bear the weight of public opinion. In America the arrest was an exciting event; in England it was a political event as well. The Tory party, closely tied to the British East India Company, wanted Kidd convicted. The Whigs, several of whom were backers of Kidd's voyage, were in a corner. In the end, all but Kidd got their way. At the trial the book listing the owners of Kidd's ship, his partners, and his instructions was missing. So were the vital passes obtained from the Moorish ships, which might have acquitted him. (The passes were discovered two hundred years later in a London records office.) The letter from Bellomont to Kidd was also missing.

There were only two eyewitnesses against Kidd: Robert Bradinham and Joseph Palmer. Both were military deserters who turned pirate. Today an American lawyer might point out that such criminals may not be credible witnesses, as they are not men of reputation, and they were very obviously testifying against Kidd for their own reprieve. Their pardons came days after Kidd's conviction.

It appears that a deal had been struck, one that convenienced all except William Kidd. Kidd was the scapegoat and, as such, was hanged. Livingston was cleared of all charges. Bellomont was enriched for his role in arresting Kidd. The other Whig partners were unsullied by what might have been a scandal, although they lost their stake in the ship and any proceeds they might have expected. For England and the ruling class, the bottom line was that Tory shipping was safe from Whig upstarts.

Livingston made out better than he thought. He received his bond back, although remarkably he was forced to pay off fellow partner Robert Blackham for his stake in the venture. The members of Captain Kidd's crew were mostly pardoned, and some died in jail. Kidd's wife, Sarah Bradley Cox Oort Kidd, was jailed and her house seized on Bellomont's order. Oort was known to have some of Kidd's loot, but it was never found. She was eventually released and married a fourth time.

Those who had received the treasure were targeted by Bellomont, who stood to gain a share of the recovered valuables. The greatest amount of treasure was on Gardiner's part of Long Island. Threatened with an enemy landing on his tiny kingdom, John Gardiner presented Bellomont with bags of gold and silver. Thus, Kidd was killed, and all those associated with him prospered.

Chapter 4

SKELETONS
IN THE CLOSET

The lifeless body of Captain William Kidd would join the bodies of other captured and convicted pirates left to greet those who sailed into London's port. The hanging criminals served as a warning for prospective sea rovers that crime did not pay. The real message, however, was that crime did pay, and it rewarded those who could pay others to do their bidding.

The feudal system that gave birth to the Knights Templar gave rise to noble ideals such as liberty, equality, and fraternity. Among those in power, however, corruption ruled. Freemasonry developed from the noble ideals of the Knights Templar, and the lodge system was created—underground—to protect its members. Some lodges became more celebrated than others, and membership in the more prestigious lodges offered greater rewards. While Livingston would survive into days of public Freemasonry, Bellomont would not. Almost twenty years passed after Kidd's body hung over the Thames before Freemasonry went public. From London to Boston, New York, and Philadelphia, the lodge system separated those who pulled the strings from those who were left hanging. Through the right connections family dynasties could survive and build on fortunes made from nefarious crimes. Profits from piracy became investments in more acceptable enterprises, and fortunes made in seventeenth-century crime were the bedrock for wealth in the twenty-first century.

THE GARDINER DYNASTY

Among those who benefited from the criminal activities of the "expendable" was the Gardiner family. It is hard not to suspect the Gardiners of running a sort of pirate bank on their tiny kingdom. They owned Gardiner's Island itself and larger tracts of land stretching from East Hampton to Smithtown on Long Island.

The progenitor of the family was an Englishman, Lion Gardiner, who was born in 1599. He came to America in 1635 as a soldier, a builder of fortifications, a trader, and a fighter against the Indians. Gardiner's son David was the first white child born in what would become the state of Connecticut. In what is now known as the Pequot War, Gardiner was instrumental in enlisting opposing tribes to join a small English force that sought to exterminate the Pequots. Gardiner's principal ally was Wyandanch, a sachem from Long Island. Gardiner agreed to trade with Wyandanch's group if he would "kill all the Pequots" that came to him and "send . . . their heads." [1] From his new friends the Montaukett tribe, Gardiner bought the self-named Gardiner's Island, a 3,500-acre island kingdom (part of modern-day East Hampton), for cloth, a gun, some gunpowder, and a dog. He added to his Long Island holdings by rescuing Wyandanch's daughter from an enemy tribe; for this feat he was given the land that would become Smithtown, bringing his holdings to a hundred thousand acres.

Rights to Gardiner's kingdom were confirmed by King Charles I. In the seventeenth century and later, Gardiner's eastern holdings provided a great haven for pirates and smugglers, and evidence appears to indicate that the early Gardiner heirs were more than simply willing accomplices.

In 1672 a report indicated that a Massachusetts pirate named Joseph Bradish set sail for Gardiner's Island with his loot. In 1692 the governor of Connecticut reported that pirates were anchored off East Hampton and engaging in trade. In another report, a prominent Connecticut citizen was accused of receiving stolen property and selling it in Boston, and it was noted that the shore of eastern Long Island was the haunt of pirates and smugglers. Still another report stated that a pirate ship called the *Sparrow* had taken on eighteen passengers under an agreement made in the Caribbean. The master, Richard Narramore, then carried the passengers to Gardiner's Island, where they disembarked, chests and all. As the story spread, the unnamed men, who were suspected to be pirates, were brought before a magistrate. Christopher Goffe was one of the few accused men who appeared. He confessed that, as suspected, he was a pirate, but he was able to obtain a pardon.[2]

The Gardiner family has maintained its wealth throughout the centuries by the right connections to England prior to the War of Independence and by more secret connections that lasted to the middle of the nineteenth century. While many Whig families were able to avoid losing their lands after the American Revolution, the Gardiners, like their neighbors and often partners who had been Tories, walked a thin line and were not subject to the postwar land grab. Many of these families showed their reluctance to break from mother England, and some of their actions bordered on treason.

The War of 1812 became a second war of independence, as Britain had never ceased treating America as a colony. Her navy regularly impressed American seamen. Her army armed and incited native border tribes against her lost colony. Many families had prospered through their relationships with British firms, and such pro-British Whig families found themselves at odds with President Jefferson. A handful of New England merchant families, who had survived the Revolution and even prospered, proposed that New England leave the Union. Their loyalty was not to their country but to their mercantile interests, which were often shared with British counterparts.

In the decades before the Civil War, America was again threatened with secession, this time from several southern states. One great secret of American history is that the same New England merchant families who had tried to leave the Union earlier were joined by New York merchant families in aiding the breakup of the Union. Despite this treasonous activity, few of the powerful families were held accountable. The Gardiner family was one such family that straddled the two sides of the Civil War.

The Gardiner family, while always flying under the radar of public comment, was a power base in New York and part of the Cotton Whigs. The Whig party was divided on many issues, and the so-called Cotton Whigs allied themselves with the powerful families of Virginia and the Carolinas who by the nature of their business, cotton, remained close to English banks and merchants. When Gardiner interests merged with the interests of the planting families of Virginia and South Carolina, the Gardiner family itself merged with the Tyler family of Virginia.

While American politics has evolved over the centuries, in the nineteenth century it was not unusual for a president to be at odds with his vice president. As the result of compromise within the Whig party, William Henry Harrison and John Tyler ended up on the same ticket. Harrison was regarded as a politician in the mold of loyal Virginia leaders such as Washington, Jefferson, and Madison, and so was against the divisive politics of South Carolina, which was first to threaten leaving the Union. Tyler was part of the secessionist movement in Virginia that was based at the College of William and Mary. Although he was a member of the Whig party, he had no inclination to support Whig policy. He agreed with admitting Texas as a slave state, and he was against abolition. Harrison and Tyler still managed to take the White House, using the slogan "Tippecanoe and Tyler too"; this motto referred to one of Harrison's triumphs over the Indians.

Harrison assumed the presidency on March 4, 1841, and one month later he died. His death was attributed first to intestinal illness and later to pneumonia, though no autopsy was performed. Described as robust, the war hero and sturdy farmer was somehow brought down by a head cold. After his long inaugural speech, which was given in the rain, the apparently healthy president became ill; many believe that his cold turned into pneumonia.

In Victorian times it was not uncommon for doctors to misdiagnose arsenic poisoning as "gastric poisoning," as the symptoms of arsenic poisoning usually started with gastrointestinal disorders including abdominal pain, vomiting, and diarrhea. But both of the president's physicians were suspected of pro-British sentiment. Dr. Frederick May was trained by the Freemason Dr. John Warren. May's son was an outspoken Tory and close friends with Benedict Arnold. The other physician, Dr. William Eustis, was also trained by Warren. He had been fired by President Madison because of his actions in the War of 1812. Dr. Eustis helped plan the defense of Detroit with General William Hull. On the way to Detroit, Hull was ambushed. His supplies gone and morale low, he surrendered Detroit as soon as he reached it. Madison believed the British had been tipped off. When the War Department conceived a plan to attack England's supply base in Nova Scotia, Eustis would not allow it to happen. With Harrison dead, the pro-secessionist Tyler was elevated to the presidency in 1841; John Tyler was the first president of the United States to get to his post without election.[3]

Harrison was the first president to die in office. His suspicious death started what was later called the "Twenty-year Curse" or the "Zero Curse," which postulated that every president elected in a year ending with a zero would die in office. The "curse" lasted 160 years before it was broken by Ronald Reagan. Reagan, however, barely missed being assassinated by the mentally disturbed son of a friend of the vice president. Some said the curse was put on Harrison by Tecumseh, the Indian warrior whom the president had defeated. But it is more likely that the death was engineered.

Caleb Cushing, whose political leanings were influenced by profit potential, was no stranger to political manipulation and subtle bribery. He was a thirty-third-degree Mason, the highest level to which a Mason could rise, and an opium smuggler. His fortunes were tied to the pro-British mercantile smugglers, slave traders, and drug traffickers. Cushing wanted to hold a government office.

Tyler claimed he was not a party man and had accepted his nomination reluctantly. But after Harrison's death, Tyler immediately repudiated most of the Whig platform that had brought Harrison to the White House. As a result, the new president was not popular; in fact, he was derided as "his accidency."

Tyler's first order of business was pushing for Caleb Cushing to become Secretary of the Treasury. The Senate rejected his nomination three times, with the third ballot securing only three votes for Cushing. Tyler then proposed sending Cushing to China. This move was greeted heartily, possibly because it was the farthest place from the seat of government that the devious politico could be sent.

Harrison's death was the first of three during Tyler's stay in Washington. The second death was that of Tyler's wife, Laetitia. Tyler did not spend too much time grieving; instead he opted to unite his Virginia plantation family with a northern merchant family. Julia Gardiner, the spoiled daughter of the wealthy and prominent David Gardiner, was Tyler's target.

After returning from a grand tour of Europe, Julia Gardiner became part of the Washington social whirl, dating several congressmen, including the future president James Buchanan, two Supreme Court Justices, and a naval officer. She met President Tyler at a White House party, and he invited her to return. Although she was thirty years younger than the president, their first date ended with him chasing her around the White House. He wasted no time in proposing to Gardiner, but her mother stood in the way of the marriage. She was concerned that the president was not a good enough catch for a Gardiner. The Virginia farmer and plantation owner simply had no money when compared with the Gardiner fortune.[4]

Tyler was not one to give up. The deaths of "Old Tippecanoe" and Tyler's wife had paved the way down his new path, and a third death would allow Tyler to get what he wanted.

The stage was set aboard the USS *Princeton,* where the navy wanted to display a new cannon, which was dubbed the Peacemaker because of its size. Several important personages were aboard and the gun was fired numerous times. David Gardiner, a friend of Tyler's and the New York State senator at the time, brought his attractive daughter, Julia, to witness the scene. She quickly became bored and invited the enamored president belowdecks for a glass of champagne. The overheated gun was to be fired one more time as a salute to George Washington as it passed his Mount Vernon home, but it instead exploded and killed Secretary of State Abel Upshur, Secretary of the

Navy Thomas W. Gilmer, and Julia's father, Senator David Gardiner.[5]

The fifty-four-year-old president and the twenty-four-year-old Julia Gardiner became secretly engaged shortly after her father's death. They later married privately. The huge difference in age presented more fodder for public opinion and the media, but Julia Gardiner Tyler won the hearts of the public even as her husband was the butt of their jokes.[6]

During Gardiner's "reign" as First Lady, as she called it, she revived the formality of White House receptions, which had gone out of style. She welcomed guests with plumes in her hair and surrounded by twelve maids of honor dressed in white. She also instituted the playing of "Hail to the Chief." Gardiner bore several children with the president: David Gardiner Tyler, John Alexander Tyler, Julia Gardiner Tyler, Lachlan Tyler, Lyon Gardiner Tyler, Robert Tyler, and Pearl Tyler.

As president, Tyler's major accomplishment was repaying the favors of his chief promoter, Caleb Cushing, among the Cotton Whigs. He managed to make Cushing an ambassador of sorts, sending him to China to reap the rewards of the British Opium War. The signing of a treaty with China kept the American opium traders in business—a trade that benefited a handful of New England and New York families.

Tyler was booted out of his own Whig party and had all but one member of his cabinet resign. The remaining cabinet member was Daniel Webster, who was deeply in debt to Caleb Cushing and at his beck and call. Tyler was even impeached for not signing a tariff bill, although the impeachment was eventually defeated. His lack of favor in Washington went so deep that he didn't attend the succeeding president's inauguration. Tyler left American politics to join the Confederate government, making Tyler the first American president to bear arms against the federal government. After his death in 1862, Julia returned to New York and worked to promote the Confederate cause.

The Gardiners survived prosecution for assisting pirates, had survived pro-British sympathies after the Revolution, and survived pro-rebel sentiment during the Civil War. Today the sixteenth lord of the manor still defends his preserve from more modern dangers, such as taxes and disrepair. Gardiner's Island is the oldest family-owned estate of its kind in America. The Gardiner estate is now in the hands of eighty-eight-year-old Robert David Lion Gardiner, who divides his time between estates in Palm Beach and East Hampton. With the exception of having to comply with taxation, he is the lord of his manor, just as a lord from another century. He regularly invites guests to take part in a hunt to reduce the island's deer population.

For the first time in the Gardiner family history there is no direct heir. Robert Gardiner's niece, Alexandra Creel, married into another of America's first families, the Goelets, and will inherit the island. The Goelets have been in America since 1676, and they built their fortune in real estate, along with the Philipse and Roosevelt families. One of the Goelets founded Chemical Bank with a grandfather of Theodore Roosevelt. The Goelets and the Gardiners have been rivals for years, and the last lord of the Gardiner manor has recently been quoted as saying he is not happy to see his ancestral lands end up in Goelet's province. The bitter Gardiner-Goelet feud was covered extensively in Steven Gains's *Philistines at the Hedgerow,* and some very colorful anti-Goelet quotes are on peconic.net, the local newspaper covering the long-standing feud.

While both families maintain a high degree of secrecy, Robert Gardiner recently opened up his life and his struggle to the prying eyes of the media. Historians and reporters alike were treated to a rare glimpse of the island, visiting it aboard a Gardiner estate boat, the *Captain Kidd III.*

THE LIVINGSTON DYNASTY

Robert Livingston, another of Captain Kidd's partners, was for the most part unscathed by Kidd's arrest. The Livingston family would go on to play a major role in the politics of New York and the nation, and its support base was Freemasonry, which allowed members to also operate from behind the scenes. Several early scandals connected them to piracy, theft, and smuggling, but their power, which was always just below the surface, allowed them to grow and prosper to modern times.

Just as Robert Livingston was breathing a sigh of relief that Kidd was in the noose, Livingston's daughter Margaret married a Scotsman, her cousin Samuel Vetch. The new son-in-law brought more notoriety to the family, which apparently was not a concern for the Livingston clan as long as the notoriety was matched by enterprise. The Vetch family and the Livingston family had already been connected by marriage in Scotland. Reverend John Livingston brought Samuel Vetch's father into the Presbyterian Church. William Livingston, the older brother of Robert, had also married a Vetch. Samuel Vetch was despised by many in Scotland, and it is unlikely that the Livingstons and anyone else in Scotland were unaware of his criminal activities.[7]

In Scotland a project had been created to found a new colony in America. The Scotland Company Trading to Africa and the Indies was formed in June 1695 with the goal of bringing to Scotland what the British East India Company brought to England. The subscription books, which allowed anyone with money to buy stock in the company, were rapidly filled with the names of merchants, shipowners, and wealthy individuals from physicians to widows. The plan was to buy ships and bring Scottish settlers to their own colony, which would be in Darien, on the coast of Panama. Little attention was given to the fact that the land was claimed by Spain, and the company was not really in the favor of England.

The project was plagued with disaster after disaster. Ships packed with soldiers and colonists were provisioned poorly and would see forty dead before reaching the New World. When the colonists reached Panama they were nearly starving, as their worm-ridden food could barely be tolerated. More were sick than healthy, and few had the ability, the desire, or the knowledge to build a settlement. One ship hit a rock in harbor, sank, and took with it half its crew. Crew members on other ships attempted mutiny and many simply deserted. By the end of the first rainy season, there were no plantations planted, no fortifications erected, no trade established, and a government of five quarreling men.[8] There were, however, two hundred graves in New Edinburgh.

After ten months the colonists were ready to give up their settlement. Over one third had died. Two ships left the colony to sail to New York City in order to sell goods and buy provisions. Samuel Vetch was on one of the ships. In the East River he tried to seize another ship, an act of piracy that he would explain was his right by charter. Two friends of Robert Livingston came to Vetch's aid. Stephen Delancey and Thomas Wenham were Livingston associates who had built fortunes financing the pirates of Madagascar. Livingston had to maintain a low profile, however, as he was already under suspicion from his partnership with Kidd.

Vetch, like his cousin Robert Livingston, was not likely to pass up a lucrative opportunity. He decided to keep the shipload of goods that was meant to buy provisions for the starving colonists in Darien. Livingston helped him sell the stolen goods.

Of course, Vetch could not return to Darien or to Scotland; the news of the fiasco would cause riots in Edinburgh. Hardly a family below the Highland line would not have the loss of a family member or friend to haunt them as a result of the ill-conceived expedition.

A second voyage saw three hundred of 1,300 dead before reaching the devastated colony. Few made it back to Scotland. Because Vetch would likely be hanged on the sands of Leith along with several other criminals related to Darien, he decided to stay in New York. He married Livingston's daughter, and the magnanimous Livingston gave the young couple as a wedding present a house that was once the property of Captain Kidd.

Samuel Vetch and John Livingston went into the smuggling business together. They bought a ship and named it *Mary,* then sailed to Canada to import French brandies and wines. On their second trip they were smuggling cargo onto eastern Long Island, not far from Gardiner's island kingdom, when they encountered problems. This early version of the "gang that couldn't shoot straight" left their ship beached without anchoring it and then took off, presumably to find assistance. The ship was swept away by the tide to Montauk, where it was seized—complete with cargo, logs, and all the evidence required to bring charges against the pair.

No one was hanged; all were let off simply with the loss of a ship and its cargo. The incident did, however, bring unwanted attention to Robert Livingston, who was still hoping the Kidd affair would blow over. Livingston called in his markers, and Edward Hyde, Lord Cornbury, who took over for Governor Bellomont, had the charges against the younger Livingston and Vetch dropped. He also repealed the Bill of Confiscation, enabling Livingston and Vetch to keep their cargo. Not coincidentally, Cornbury's six-year rule was highlighted by accusations of bribery, mismanagement, and even attending parties dressed in women's clothing.[9]

Samuel Vetch learned from his cousin and soon become a wealthy merchant. Unlike his new in-laws, however, his luck did not last. Fortune caught up with him and he died in debtor's prison in London.

Robert Livingston would do much better.

Livingston's life took an odd turn when he traveled to London to plead the case of the Iroquois tribes in New York. On the way his ship was accosted by French privateers, who had no idea they held at their mercy the backer of the world's most infamous pirate. Their advantage was short-lived, as the sudden appearance of a British man-of-war turned the tables.

The immense amount of land held by the Livingston family was of little value if it could not provide an income. In 1710 the opportunity to change the idle lands to profitable lands came with a new governor. While Robert Hunter was reputed to be honest, he may not have been too smart. He had been warned on both sides of the Atlantic about dealing with Robert Livingston. It mattered little to Hunter, whose task was to provide a place to settle German refugees. After the first winter, the starving palatines were in open rebellion against their landlord. The English government refused them permission to leave, and Robert Livingston admonished his wife, Alida, for wishing to give them bread. A second freezing winter found the settlers fleeing across the Hudson in the hope of escaping their feudal lord.

The eighteenth century was marked by wars between the British and the French and ultimately between the colonists and the British. For the Livingstons the century was marked by uprisings by their tenant families. They used the French and Indian Wars to increase their wealth after being appointed to the lucrative position of provisioning the British troops. When the American Revolution came, the family straddled the fence for as long as possible. Then some members went home to Scotland and others fortuitously gambled on the side of the Revolutionaries.

◈

One of the great-grandsons of Robert Livingston was Robert R. Livingston. He played a pivotal role in politics and in the Freemasons, of which he was the grand master for the New York branch. On April 30, 1789, he swore in the country's first president, George Washington. Livingston had hoped for an appointment to Washington's new government but none was forthcoming; it was possible Washington recognized the Livingston clan as playing both sides. Several Livingstons had left New York for the West Indies. Alida Livingston Gardiner, who was married to Valentine Gardiner, had left for England.[10] Robert R. Livingston kept his own power base behind the scenes. The Livingstons' power grew by dynastic marriages, as one Livingston married John Jay, another married an Astor, and another wed a Roosevelt. But Masonic ties were at least as important.

New York State's most influential and powerful lodge was the Holland No. 8. Jacob Astor was aware of the power wielded by the Masonic lodges in both his home in Germany and in London. When he reached New York City, he used his marriage to a member of the Brevoort family to gain entrance to the Holland No. 8 Lodge. There he made connections with New York's governor, George Clinton, his nephew and later mayor of New York City, De Witt Clinton, land baron Stephen Van Rensselaer, and the Livingston family.[11] De Witt Clinton, in particular, was an ardent Mason, and among the offices he held were lodge grand master, high priest of the Grand Chapter, a grand master of the Great Encampment of New York, and grand master of the Knights Templar of the United States. Clinton's power base, however, would remain the Holland No. 8 Lodge.

When Robert Livingston was grand master of the Holland No. 8 Lodge he founded ten other lodges; still the Holland lodge remained the most powerful. The old guard of New York was firmly in control as the Masonic order and the Holland lodge grew in power. Many would advance their careers through Masonic connections, including Charles King, former president of Columbia University; Cadwallader Colden, grandson of the provincial governor; and John Pintard, the secretary of the Mutual Insurance Company. Masonry rewarded the Livingston family well, and the family did not turn away from the craft even during its unpopular years. Today the Livingston Masonic Library is maintained on West Twenty-third Street in New York City.

New York was a power center for the Livingston clan, but its influence was not limited to that state. Robert R. Livingston was disappointed because he did not receive an appointment in Washington's administration, but during Thomas Jefferson's administration he did join James Monroe on a mission to France. They went to negotiate the purchase of New Orleans, and they were reportedly surprised when Talleyrand, Napoleon's minister, asked, "What will you give for the whole?"—meaning the 825,000 square miles offered for sale.[12] Without permission and without the time to contact Washington, the two men offered fifteen million dollars. Livingston later assumed full credit for the purchase, altering his journal entries to say he was given the offer three days earlier, before Monroe reached France. The government issued a vigorous denial and published Livingston's real itinerary, and the disgrace cost him whatever credit might have been due.

The area that was open thanks to the Louisiana Purchase was an early equivalent of the Wild West. New Orleans was the gateway. Very close to the city was a pirate kingdom second only to the one in Madagascar a hundred years before. The new Libertalia was called Barataria, and Jean Lafitte controlled the territory like a king. From India to the Caribbean, Lafitte's career stood out among pirates. Since his navy was so large it could not sail into any port, his kingdom, with protective estuaries, became his home base. At Barataria the pirate created a marketplace where pirates, smugglers, and legitimate traders could buy and sell silks, wines, spices, furniture, and slaves, all of which had been taken at sea. The pirate market at Barataria became so large it threatened the merchants of New Orleans.

Weeks after the Louisiana Purchase was made official a new governor, William Claiborne, was appointed. He rode in with a military escort to assume his office. The city turned out for the occasion: two thousand Americans, French, Spaniards, Italians, blacks from Haiti and Jamaica, Orientals in silks, Hindus in saris—and the brothers Lafitte.[13]

In a short time the newly appointed governor of the area was goaded into offering a bounty for Lafitte and his brother, Pierre. Lafitte posted his own bounty for Governor Claiborne. When Pierre Lafitte was captured, District Attorney John R. Grymes quit his job. Instead of prosecuting Lafitte he would became the pirate's defense co-counsel. Robert Livingston's brother Edward, an active Mason and the mayor of New York City, left New York to join the defense team. The two defenders were allegedly offered twenty thousand dollars.

Edward Livingston had several reasons for leaving New York, all of which had something to do with money, specifically his lack of it. Livingston's land speculations and other ventures had left him in debt. His position as mayor was not as lucrative for him as it was for past mayors. New Orleans would be the start of a new life. He quickly married a nineteen-year-old French widow, Louise D'Avezac de Castera Moreau de Lassy, whose family was the owner of plantations in Haiti and had been driven out by the slave insurrection. As grand master of New York's grand lodge, Robert Livingston had influence that spread far beyond the state borders. Edward Livingston became grand master of the Louisiana lodge upon arrival.

Jean Lafitte was no ordinary pirate. Said to be a French nobleman whose parents lost their lives under the blade of the guillotine during the Reign of Terror,[14] the swashbuckler was also an educated man who could speak four languages. Called "the gentleman pirate," Lafitte was described as tall, black-haired, and sporting a black mustache. He left France aboard a privateer ship that he would later take from its captain, and he began indiscriminately to raid ships of all nations. Lafitte started in the Seychelles, where he bought a boatload of slaves for trade. On the way to sell them in India he was chased by a British frigate. In desperate need of supplies, he captured other British ships, including one of the East India Company's. The privateer soon had a fleet.

Lafitte's reputation grew to gigantic proportions after he used one of his ships and forty of his men to battle a very large, forty-gun British ship manned by four hundred sailors. Lafitte's forty men, with daggers in mouths and bandanna-clad heads, boarded the ship in a frenzy. Lafitte commandeered a cannon and aimed at the men who remained on deck, threatening them with certain death. They all surrendered.

From the Indian Ocean, Lafitte and his navy sailed to the Spanish port of Cartegena, where he was given a commission. The city had just rebelled and authorized him to attack Spanish shipping. At one point Lafitte's navy had fifty ships and one thousand pirate sailors. From there he built his kingdom in Barataria. Derived from the Spanish word *barato,* the name refers to the part of the winnings a gambler gives to the poor for luck. Lafitte's pirate city had a café, a bordello, a gambling house, and warehouses. He would widen waterways to facilitate ships, dig canals, and even build barges that would sail to the port of New Orleans to sell their merchandise.

Lafitte survived the prosecutions of the governor and went on to join the Americans in the Battle of New Orleans in 1812. Besides having the legal protection of lawyer and Mason Edward Livingston, another noted Mason would come to the pirate's aid. Andrew Jackson rewarded Lafitte's crew with citizenship, and Lafitte tried to settle down. When his crew could not give up their old ways, Lafitte sailed to Mexico and was not heard from again.

The Livingstons, of course, would be heard from again. Today the Livingston dynasty is remembered in the names of locations in New York, New Jersey, and Louisiana. And the family is still active in politics. During the Clinton administration, for instance, Robert L. Livingston, the sixty-third man named Robert in the Livingston family tree, was a candidate for the job of Speaker of the House. He is part of the tenth generation, descended from the first lord of the manor in

New York. Other members of the Livingston clan still own vast tracts of land in New York. Modern-day relations of the Livingstons include the Bush family and Thomas Kean, the former governor of New Jersey, who makes his home in Livingston township, New Jersey.

THE MORRIS FAMILY

The Livingstons were not the only landed family to have made their start in piracy. The progenitor of the Morris family also made his fortune capturing ships and used the proceeds to obtain vast tracts of land. Locale names still exist on the maps of New York and New Jersey that recall the extent of the Morrises' property.

Lewis Morris was a pirate who had a king's commission that allowed him to prey on shipping in the colonies and split his prizes with the crown. His nephew, also named Lewis Morris, was involved in the triangle trade. Between running sugar plantations in Barbados and using the labor of imported slaves to create end products like rum, Morris's lucrative trade gave him an estate back in the colonies. The younger Morris would later be a signer of the Constitution.[15]

The younger Lewis Morris was also part of an unusual rivalry that developed into an important American historical landmark. In the early 1730s Morris served as the chief justice of the three-man Supreme Court in New York. A fellow wealthy merchant named Rip van Dam had become governor and then retired his post. The new governor, Colonel William Cosby, was as corrupt as they come. He demanded that van Dam return his salary as governor and give it to Cosby. The case made it to Morris's court, where he cast the one vote in three denying Cosby his claim.

Cosby, in control of the state publication, the *New York Gazette,* relentlessly went after both van Dam and Morris. Friends of the pair backed a rival newspaper and hired John Peter Zenger as editor to retaliate in print. Cosby didn't like playing the role of editorial victim and threw Zenger in jail. After a lengthy and much publicized trial, Zenger's acquittal started the process that later developed into the freedom of the press. Coincidentally, one of the other two men on the Morris court was merchant and financier Frederick Philipse.

THE PHILIPSE DYNASTY

The Philipse family was one of New York's landed aristocracy. Frederick Philipse was also a pioneer in another way; he built the family fortune supplying pirates with goods and money. He had already been in the business before Fletcher assumed the governor's position, but under Fletcher's rule New York grew as a pirate haven and Philipse profited. And many knew about Philipse's business. A Salem minister named Reverend John Higginson once wrote in a letter to his son, "Frederick Philipse of New York, it is reported, has a pirate trade to Madagascar for near twenty years." [16]

Philipse was well acquainted with Kidd and hired Samuel Burgess, who had sailed with Kidd as a privateer. Burgess was recruited out of retirement to sail to Madagascar with goods for the pirates. Clothing, liquor, naval supplies, and ammunition were the imports of choice on Saint Mary's. These goods were in turn exchanged for slaves, one of Madagascar's only exports.

Another employee of Philipse was the pirate Adam Baldridge, who was for a while one of the pirate kings of Saint Mary's. While his title did not entitle Baldridge to rule in a monarchal way, it did make him the number one fence for items stolen by pirates—a very lucrative position. Baldridge bought goods at attractive prices and put them aboard ships to Frederick Philipse. He would also serve as a travel agent, assisting retiring pirates in making their return passage to England or the North American colonies.

With the pirate king Baldridge on Saint Mary's and Burgess sailing back and forth to New York, the aristocratic Philipse had his own trading empire. The pirate Thomas Tew was also in his employ, and Philipse did little to hide his role in piracy. One of his ships that sailed the Indian Ocean for slaves and contraband and to engage in piracy was named the *Frederick.*[17]

But life would not always stay simple for Philipse. After Kidd's arrest, Bellomont was on the prowl for pirates, and he was not above turning on acquaintances like Philipse. When Bellomont became aware that two hundred pirates were being given passage to New York from Madagascar on a Frederick Philipse–owned ship,[18] he decided money was thicker than friendship. The fee charged to each ex-pirate was an expensive fifty pounds, but presumably that was the tip of the iceberg of their personal wealth; the men were most likely loaded with booty intended to provide for them in their retirement years. Luckily for both Philipse and his cargo, Bellomont would not survive long enough to intercept it.

Next Philipse's number one captain, Burgess, was captured at sea. It was the second time for Burgess, who had previously survived arrest being pardoned by Bellomont. But that was before the backlash against piracy started by the British East India Company and the arrest of Kidd. This time Burgess was brought to London, where he was condemned to death. To his credit, Philipse sent to London his son Adolph, who worked for three years to save Burgess from suffering the same fate as Kidd. Burgess returned to sea, and later lived out his retirement years in London as a consultant for the British East India Company.

Unlike the Livingstons and the Gardiners, the Philipse family's power and wealth was divided after the Revolution. They had started in the colonies as part of the landed aristocracy of the Hudson Valley, which entitled them to the patroon system that granted lands to favorites of the royalty back in England: Pelham Manor for Thomas Pell, Philipsborough to the Philipses, Morrisania to Lewis Morris, Cortlandt Manor to the Van Cortlandts. The families in control of these extremely large tracts leased farmland to tenant farmers, who were often kept in poverty and indebted to their land.

In 1766 the Philipse tenant William Prendergast started mob actions along the Hudson that would affect both the Livingston clan and the other patroon families' holdings. At his trial Prendergast said that he was charged more for his small farm than were all the other Philipse tenants. It didn't matter. He was found guilty of treason and ordered hanged, drawn, and quartered in the feudal fashion of the lords of the Hudson manors. When no one would come forward to perform the execution, Prendergast received a stay and finally a pardon from King George III.

King George disappointed the Philipse family a second time by losing the War of Independence. The Philipses were part of a New York contingent that declared their loyalty to the king and signed the Declaration of Dependence. Frederick Philipse III was arrested by Washington's troops and so he fled his home. Washington confiscated the lands. The Morris family somehow ended up with one third of the original grant. Tenant farmers were allowed to buy the farms on the other two thirds after the Revolution.

Some of the Philipse heirs fared better than Frederick. Like the Livingstons, some fled to England after the war, while others managed to avoid being branded as Tories and stayed in the colonies. Also like the Livingstons, at least one Philipse heir would marry into the Roosevelt family. Another Philipse heir, Jacobus Goelet, started his own landed dynasty that eventually united with the Gardiner family's.

Jacobus Goelet had been raised by Frederick Philipse, the lord of the manor. Peter Goelet, the grandson of Jacobus, established himself in business and in politics during the Revolution. Instead of being arrested or deported, Peter Goelet used his close relationship with those in power to remain in New York and prosper. Goelet's relationship with the city controller, Benjamin Romaine, allowed the Goelet clan to acquire real estate as favorably as had the Astors and other large-scale investors like the Rhinelanders, Schermerhorns, and Lorillards.

Romaine was a failed schoolteacher who found his true calling as an early member of the Tammany Society, which was founded as a fraternal charity for Revolutionary War veterans in 1789 shortly after Washington was inaugurated. Washington's Society of the Cincinnati was for officers only and later for those with aristocratic family lines. The Tammany Society was meant to be for men of all classes, although it quickly emerged as a corrupt organization that helped only a handful to loot government coffers. While the history of New York points the finger at Boss Tweed and others who were the most corrupt, the major beneficiaries, such as New York's first families, emerged with larger fortunes, little criticism, and no criminal or civil penalty for their roles.

Goelet's two sons married daughters of the Scottish merchant Thomas Buchanan and furthered the family's rise. The younger Goelets founded the Chemical Bank of New York at a time when there was an antibanking sentiment in New York. It was nearly impossible to get a charter for a bank, so several companies got a charter for a certain type of business and then later amended the original charter. New York Chemical Manufacturing Company was a small company formed to produce dyes, paints, and drugs. One year after getting a charter for this business it became a bank. Chemical Bank counted several generations of Goelets on the board of directors.

The next Goelet generation would collect fortunes topping the $100 million mark when their lands, including Union Square and Fifth Avenue, appreciated. Families like the Goelets, Astors, and Rhinelanders became "Old New York," as they owned so much property. And their fortune grew with the population of the city.

When Newport, Rhode Island, began to attract the likes of the Astors and the Vanderbilts, the Goelets too built their own mansion. Goelet daughters married well, including the marriage of Hannah Goelet to Thomas Russell Gerry. Goelet-Gerry descendants made ties to the Livingstons, Harrimans, and Gallatins, as well as to British royalty. Robert Goelet's yacht rivaled the yachts of the Astors, the Vanderbilts, and the J. P. Morgans.

In 1870 J. Pierpont Morgan founded his own elite society, which he called the Zodiac Club. Membership, like that in the private clubs to which Morgan's father belonged, was limited to twelve Anglo-Christian white men. Pierpont, J. P. Morgan's father, had claimed the family tree included the pirate Morgan, and to drive home the point he called his yacht the *Corsair* and flew the Jolly Roger. One hundred years after the Zodiac Club was founded, Robert Goelet shared one of the coveted chairs with eleven of the mid-Atlantic's most powerful businessmen.[19]

Despite the dilution caused by marriages, the wealth of the secretive Goelet clan is far-reaching. They have been involved with Guaranty Trust, Equitable Trust, the Illinois Central Railroad, and the Union Pacific Railroad and institutions like the Metropolitan Opera and the Museum of Natural History in New York. Through the Goelet Corporation the family has interests in mining, oil, and gas.

The Knickerbocker Club once represented the highest level of wealth in the city of New York. Because New York is a financial capital of the world, entrance to this club is no longer simply for pillars of New York society such as the Goelets and the Astors. In 1965 the ranks of the Knickerbocker included the Aga Khan, Giovanni Agnelli, C. Douglas Dillon, the du Ponts, the Goulds, the Huttons, the Ingersolls, the Rockefellers, Alfred Sloan, and William Vanderbilt.[20]

PIRATES TO PATRICIANS

When the Knights Templar were disbanded in the fourteenth century, they had at their core a handful of wealthy and noble families that had always acted from behind the scenes. Although the illiterate Jacques de Molay was burned at the stake, the elite core remained alive and well. The majority of the rank-and-file Templars also survived—not in their estates in France but in hiding. They were protected by the heirs of the Norman families in France that held power in Scotland. And they were protected by their sworn loyalty to one another. On land some ex-Templars found work as mercenaries and others in the building trades. They established a system of secret passwords and handshakes and a lodge network that protected them from disclosure and from being unemployed in a feudal world. They were sworn to feed and shelter each other until work could be found.

As there had been a handful of core families behind the Templars, there would be a handful of core families behind the ex-Templars. The best known is the Sinclair family of Scotland. The network of lodges created in the aftermath of the Templar downfall emerged as Freemasonry and the Sinclair family was named its hereditary guardians. Former Templars were employed on land by the Sinclair family as construction workers and on the sea as sailors on the massive Sinclair fleet. The same men who sailed under the skull-and-crossbones flag as Templars continued to ply the seas.

The Reformation played a harmful role in dividing the Catholic Stuarts of Scotland, England, and other elite families who had backed the Templars in France. After a century of displacement and massive warfare, Europe experienced a breakdown in morality. America was populated alternately by whatever religious group was out of favor in Europe. The French Protestants known as Huguenots, the Catholic and Protestant Scots, and Englishmen would meet in America and in some cases continue the wars started at home. Masonry, however, would serve to breach the religious divide.

Masonic lodges provided a refuge for many and were places where the ideas of tolerance and brotherhood prevailed amid an intolerant world. For many the lodge system offered the possibility of breaking out of the caste system. The pirate community went a step further: Democracy in its pure form, brotherhood, mutual protection, and equality existed among the pirates in a way that was rarely seen elsewhere. The Kingdom of Libertalia might have served as a model society if it had not been colored by pirate fiction and tainted by its prosperity being linked to stolen goods. In Libertalia all men had a vote, wealth was held individually, and all provided for the community. The old and infirm were provided for by all. Crime against fellow pirates was rare; not only was each man armed and dangerous, but also each had signed articles that did not allow for such activity. The presence of any man who caused disruption in the community was not tolerated in law or in practice.

At the same time both the Masonic lodge and the pirate life were gripped by the same evils that pervade the human condition. Pride and greed guaranteed that some were at a higher level than others. While equality might exist within an individual lodge, the lodges soon separated, with the sea captains and shipowners belonging to one and the dockworkers and ship's crews belonging to another.

As in the earliest days of the Knights Templar, some core families were able to use and discard the rank and file at will. The pirates who sailed under the same flag as the Templars needed to rely on the elite few who could walk in both worlds. Like the Sinclairs in the Old World, the Livingstons, Gardiners, and Philipses in the New World could operate and profit through their connection to the underworld. At the same time they could retreat to their manor houses while the Kidds and the de Molays bore the blame.

Although the seed of a democratic society had formed aboard the pirate ships and among the Templar fighting units, the remnants of a feudal society remained. Ex-Templars and elite families continued their symbiotic relationship in America in the years to come. Family wealth would be built through secret societies. Profits would be made from smuggling, the slave trade, and even the opium-trafficking business, where the fleets of the China traders would still sail under the skull and crossbones. As in the fourteenth century, the risks were often borne by the many, while the gains were enjoyed only by the few who could exist in both worlds.

PART TWO

The Lodge and the Revolution

◆

FOUR HUNDRED YEARS AFTER the Templar order was outlawed by the papal authority, it was still alive in the form of numerous entities. Despite being fractured by the religious squabbles of Europe, the order still retained many of its goals, which included survival, resistance to the overbearing religious powers of the day, and a conspiratorial brotherhood of self-protection. By the early eighteenth century there were several institutions that could claim direct descent from the original Knights Templar. Among these groups were military orders that could exist in the open and secret societies that survived underground. The secret society of underground Masonry in Scotland was the most authentic remnant Templar group, and it would later call itself the Ancient Lodge.

The underground lodge system had been the refuge of the ex-Templars; for decades it helped many survive and evade arrest. Through the centuries, however, the lodge system became more open, and it gave birth to the more public Freemasonry. The world and the Masonic lodges would then become divided as a result of religion, politics, and economics. No longer would every Mason be welcomed in every lodge.

Europe and Masonry would be torn apart by the revolt against the papacy. The conflicts that had started in Europe found their way over the Atlantic, as did the solutions. The revolt against the Church led to a revolt against the aristocratic system that kept the majority in a peasant caste. This economic revolt gave rise to a middle class in which anyone could participate provided he could find a means. Secret societies and law breaking provided the fastest route to economic prosperity.

Europe was rife with conspiracies great and small. Men conspired to protect themselves from the horrors of the constant wars over religion. They conspired to protect their own industry by keeping competition out. They conspired to break a multitude of trade laws that did little to foster trade and much to enrich the kings. And everywhere there was conspiracy, there were places for conspirators to meet. The lodge system provided that refuge.

Not all conspiracy could be considered bad. Joining a secret society in America provided the means to raise one's station in life, to find work, to belong to a community, and to transcend the religious squabbles of the Europeans. At the same time, it also provided avenues to wealth through breaking the law, and it bred dissent and stirred the mobs against the weak government. Once the hostilities against the crown started, secret societies allowed the colonists to create a spy network and to strike the enemy in the most unsuspecting way.

The American Revolution began as a reaction to Britain cracking down on smuggling. Those whom the British declared smugglers were considered by the Americans simply to be merchants, although these merchants had something in common. Like pirates, the smugglers needed connections to survive. This meant belonging to the right lodges. While smuggling was done by individual merchants, it required a support system that was anything but small. Merchants buying even basic commodities from any of the numerous European possessions in the New World were almost always breaking the law. A system of trust evolved through a secret society: Masonry.

The American Revolution was fought by a network of spies, diplomats, smugglers, Freemasons, and slave traders. Although they were rarely united politically, they did share an interest—and the means to accomplish their interest. Masonic ties allowed conspirators from England, New England, New York, and the Carolinas to find a common ground and make critical moves behind the scenes. One prominent example is Benjamin Franklin, who moved freely through Masonic circles that stretched from London to Paris and Nantes. Franklin was able to stir dissent among the British, bring in supplies from the Netherlands, and ultimately bring the French into the war. From Britain, Franklin enlisted members of a hedonistic entity known as the Hellfire Club, whose orgiastic activities would shock even modern Britain to muster public support against the war and for the Sons of Liberty. Through a smuggling network that operated in the Caribbean from Bermuda and from Europe, American sea captains supplied the Revolutionaries with munitions. Franklin's Masonic connections in France were wealthy slave traders, often Huguenots, who operated through lodge systems that reached everywhere their ships sailed. Friends were also found among the aristocratic class in France, with Masonry again paving the way—even as the royals were ardent Catholics.

In a most audacious move, a wealthy French family bribed the British admiral heading the war effort to deny support to Cornwallis at Yorktown. At the same time the French contingent led by the Knights of the Sovereign Order of Malta supplied the American side. The American Revolution was won not on the battlefield as much as in the secret meetings of numerous conspirators like Benjamin Franklin and his lodge brothers.

With the war won, the architects of the new republic gave birth to a government steeped in Masonic symbolism, while Washington founded an aristocratic society where breeding and heredity were the most important tickets for admission. Strange? Yes, but less so as one understands the maelstrom of the eighteenth-century world, in which the old ways of religious and aristocratic authority were being challenged on a regular basis.

The dramatic changes that affected everyone's daily life created a nation while also fostering a new elite. The new elite, unfortunately, promoted an elitist attitude long after the independence that allowed criminal activity, as long as they were the ultimate beneficiaries.

John Hancock might serve as the best example of a well-connected Mason who became a great patriot for the sake of his own fortune. With one foot in an elite lodge and the other in a workingman's lodge, he somehow was able to present himself as a champion of liberty and a prince of industry. Hancock rode in a well-appointed carriage around Boston clad in the aristocratic purple that was his trademark, yet he would be a hero to the thousands of hardworking dockworkers who depended on him for employment. One could argue that the American Revolution started when a ship belonging to Hancock, the *Liberty,* was seized. The event and the actions that followed connected the wealthy Hancock and his lodge to the working class, who belonged to numerous other lodges, and to Sam Adams.

John Hancock was born into a wealthy and connected mercantile family. He became one of the wealthiest merchants through inheritance from an uncle. He understood from early on that a merchant needed connections, and one very important way to develop those connections was through Masonry. Hancock's uncle became a Mason in an aristocratic lodge in Canada. By being admitted to a lodge in one city he could then attend lodge gatherings in other cities. In Boston, Hancock would attend the meetings of a working-class lodge known as Saint Andrew's.

Masonry was undergoing a great change. The craft in America and England had seen a dilution of its original values, which had included liberty and equality. While liberty was prized by all, equality was not present in the new class system. What would be called "modern" Masonry shared much with the rising mercantile and professional classes that formed the English Whig party in the political arena and a bourgeois class in the economy. With new Masons accepted by invitation and common agreement, individuals in the lower echelons of the changing society—a stonemason, for example—were not always welcome. This was a repudiation of the Masonic ideals, and the effect was that an elite class was allowed to develop and service the careers of its members.

Politics and religion were still inseparable, and the Modern Lodge Masons were pro-Parliament and very much Protestant at a time when the world was still fighting a constant series of wars over the religious leanings and marriages of its kings and queens.

On June 24, 1717, representatives from four English lodges met at the Goose and Gridiron alehouse in London and created the Grand Lodge. By going public the Grand Lodge, also known as the Mother Lodge, ended centuries of underground operations. Instead of being a craft guild where members of the same trades could meet and act to serve one another's interests, no longer was a particular trade required for membership. Masonry in the Grand Lodge style became "speculative" masonry; this modern interpretation eliminated the titles and tools of a working craft and made them into mystical symbols. There were four major lodges in England that went public to create the Grand Lodge. They had been meeting for years, so it was not much of an event at the time. Within two years the number of lodges increased tenfold, but as many as twenty-six had been already in operation.[1]

When these lodges met, they toasted the Hanoverian king and sang patriotic songs. Because this was just a short time after the most recent Scottish rebellion, the Modern Masons hoped that going public would distance them from the Scottish Masons and help them avoid suspicion.

The establishment of the English Modern Grand Lodge as a public institution served more than one purpose: It allowed English masons to publicly distance themselves from Jacobite Masons, and it also may have forced the Scottish and Irish lodges to go public. In a very complicated world where the change of the monarchy would often lead to war, these lodges were ostensibly pro-Catholic and pro-monarchy; in England they were the basis for the Tory party. But at the same time as these lodges were accused of being reactionary, they actually held the finer Masonic ideals to be true.

Although they often fell on the Catholic side of the never-ending religious wars, the Grand Lodge had more to do with Templar tradition than adherence to the papal authority. The Grand Lodge had three degrees: Entered Apprentice, Fellow Craft, and Master Mason. The Scottish Rite Masonry claimed higher degrees and direct descent from the Templar organization.

◈

In 1603 James VI of Scotland became James I of England. James was a Stuart, and his family was connected to the Guise-Lorraine families of France, who had been instrumental in the creation of the Knights Templar. The old Templar sword and the trowel of the master builder, which were so important to the roles born hundreds of years before, were now part of the Stuart heraldry. The Stuart ascension to the throne attempted to undo the losses of both Scotland and Catholicism. Noble Scottish families played a strong role in England's affairs, and two families, the Hamiltons and the Montgomeries, moved to Ireland to start the Ulster Plantation.[2] James I was Catholic and a Freemason, and in the early seventeenth century his status would politicize Masonry. James constantly fought with Parliament, which tried to increase its influence in matters such as taxation, foreign policy, and religion. The Stuart rule would not last the century; it ended with the Glorious Revolution of 1688.

Charles I, the son of James I, ascended the throne in 1625. The Parliament of 1640 to 1641, however, declared that it and not the king had the power to tax. This threat to the king's power might have led to the 1641 rebellion in Ireland against the Protestant rule. While Charles I was actually Anglican, his wife and his Stuart family were Catholic. Parliament saw the Irish rebellion as a conspiracy; they felt the king was using the rebellion to raise troops to form a counterrevolution against Protestantism. Parliament attempted to end the king's power to raise troops, but the king ordered soldiers to arrest certain members of Parliament. Civil war broke out, and it ended with the Stuart king being beheaded.

The alternative to Charles's actions was worse, however, with Cromwell attacking not only Catholics but extremist sects of Protestants as well. His Commonwealth did not last the decade, and, remarkably, the son of the beheaded king, Charles II, was put on the throne. Charles II abolished many of the privileges of the monarchy, but when his Catholic brother, James II, took the throne the old religious bugaboo reared its head again. James was dumped in the Glorious Revolution.

Charles and James had a sister, Mary, who had married the Dutch prince of Orange. James also had a daughter named Mary, who was a Protestant and who also strengthened the family bond with the Dutch by marrying the son of the Prince of Orange, William III. The Dutch House of Orange was united from earlier times with the German House of Nassau, a region bordering on the state of Hesse. It would shed the designation Nassau-Orange and come to be called simply the House of Orange. German families were especially adept at the art of strategic marriages, and after the hard-won struggle to get the English throne, the Stuarts would lose it to the House of Orange.

A new Bill of Rights was established under William of Orange and Mary, but it did not resemble the later American Bill of Rights, as it banned Catholics from the throne. The rule of William and Mary also gave rise to the Tory and Whig factions. The Whig faction was made up of several powerful English and Scottish families and was based in Protestant Holland, which was under the rule of the House of Orange. A brotherhood modeled on Masonry was established and called itself the Order of Orange. It was anti-Catholic, and its legacy lives on today in Belfast, where the no-longer-secret order has one hundred thousand members.[3]

When William died (years after Mary passed away), the daughter of James II, Anne, took the throne. When Anne died, the House of Orange relinquished the throne to the rulers of the German state of Hanover. From that point on the Hanoverians provided England with all her monarchs, though they did change the family name much later to the House of Windsor to appear less German. Anne was succeeded by the grandson of Elizabeth Stuart and Friedrich, Count Palatine.

The Stuarts clung to the belief that they could regain the throne. For the purpose of putting a Stuart heir back on the throne, a new branch of Freemasonry was created by Michael Ramsay, a Scottish mystic and the tutor of the children of James III. His plan was to resurrect the old ideals. He modeled the new branch after the Knights Templar, and for the first time in three hundred years he would publicly claim what many in Scotland and Ireland had kept secret: that the Masonic organization was the direct heir of the original underground organization. One of Ramsay's co-organizers, the Earl of Derwent Water, claimed that the authority to create the Knights Templar lodge came from the Kilwinning Lodge, Scotland's oldest lodge.

The Kilwinning Lodge was actually formed before the arrest of the Templars. It dates to 1120, and by the seventeenth century it was practicing speculative Masonry, meaning it wasn't simply a craft guild. The history of the Kilwinning Lodge is complicated, as it was first independent, then joined, then separated from, and then joined again the Grand Lodge of Scotland.

Following the creation of the new lodge, a series of pro-Stuart Jacobite uprisings of the early eighteenth century began, which culminated in the horrible defeat at Culloden in 1746. To the English, Culloden was meant to be the last attempt by Scotland. After the battle the survivors were hunted down and killed. Their families, too, were prosecuted, and a massive Scottish emigration ensued—much of it to the Americas.

Events in the not-so-United Kingdom affected the American continent in many ways: European wars became American wars, Protestants increased their suspicions of Catholics, and the displacement of populations and religious intolerance caused waves of migrations by Puritans, Huguenots, and Scotch and Irish Catholics. These events also forever changed Masonry. Masonry was linked to the Stuarts in Scotland, as the craft had developed and lodges had met since the ancient days of Henry Sinclair's guardian status. It was not, however, a Jacobite conspiracy, as lodges met in England as well among the anti-Jacobite, pro-Whig, pro-Parliament system that was in power.

In America the Grand (Modern) Lodge was established early. Though accurate records remain undiscovered, one of the earliest appointments was by the Duke of Norfolk, who in 1730 granted to Daniel Coxe of New Jersey the grand master title for New Jersey, New York, and Pennsylvania.

In 1733 Henry Price founded a Grand Lodge in Boston.[4] James Oglethorpe, known in American history as the founder of the colony of Georgia, established and became master of his colony's lodge in Savannah. His family included active Jacobites, and his less than enthusiastic command of English forces led to his court-martial.

By 1738 there were established lodges meeting in Boston, New York, Philadelphia, Charleston, and Cape Fear, North Carolina.[5] They attracted and admitted the merchants and shipowners while excluding the average worker. This was not the intent of Scottish Masonry, which stuck to the principles of an egalitarian society.

In Boston and Philadelphia new lodges sprang up, seemingly without any authority. The most celebrated is the Saint Andrew's Lodge in Boston, which met at the Green Dragon Tavern. It received its warrant from the Scottish Rite Lodge rather than the Grand Lodge, and a fissure was created in American Masonry. The ancient lodges attracted a handful of the merchant class but were made up mostly of craftsmen, artisans, carpenters, and shipwrights. The notable exceptions in the Saint Andrew's Lodge were Dr. Joseph Warren, who became grand master, and John Hancock. Both men served important roles in the early conflicts that ignited the war.

Masons played roles on both the English and the American sides of the conflict. In the confusion, a revolution started by the Boston Whigs operating out of a lodge chartered by a Scottish lodge system found as opposition the Catholic Scots that had remained Tory. As brother fought brother and neighbor fought neighbor, Masons too would fight on either side of the American Revolution.

Masonic influences started the war, and Masonic connections tipped the balance toward the Revolutionary side. When the war was finally over, Masonry played the single most important role in creating the new nation.

Chapter 5
SMUGGLERS, PATRIOTS, AND MASONS

On November 16, 1776, the first salute acknowledging the sovereignty of the United States of America was fired. It might have been fired by France, which was just days away from joining the fighters for the American colonies. It might have been fired by Spain, which was next in line and being wooed by American agents. Or it might have been fired by any number of European countries that wished to see Britain suffer a setback in its conquest of the world. But it wasn't.

The shot was fired by the tiny Dutch possession of Saint Eustatius, an island in the Caribbean that was unknown at that time except to sea captains and traders, and is hardly known today despite the Caribbean's appeal to travelers. The shot was fired in reply to a national gun salute by the American brig *Andrew Doria*. While few have even heard of the tiny island commonly called Statia, it was pivotal in deciding the American Revolutionary War and, as a result, American independence. The Golden Rock, as the island was also called, was the central headquarters of a massive smuggling operation that had gone on throughout the century and that provided guns and ammunitions to the struggling Continental army.

At a most critical time of the American Revolution, the British Admiral Rodney was in command of a fleet of British warships. He had been instructed to rendezvous with Cornwallis at Yorktown, where the British were dug in and waiting for reinforcements and supplies.

Rodney was responsible for bringing help to Cornwallis from his fleet and instructing the fleet in New York to bring more help. Had Rodney reached Virginia, the combined ragtag war-weary Americans and their new allies may not have succeeded.

Rodney decided instead to punish the tiny island of Saint Eustatius. He later justified his action by claiming, "This rock of only six miles in length and three in breadth has done England more harm than all the arms of her most potent enemies, and alone supported the infamous American rebellion." Instead of speeding toward Virginia, Admiral Rodney took his time in attacking and then looting the island's hundreds of merchant ships and stores. The tiny "free" port, the home of smugglers of several nationalities, paid the price for aiding the American cause. It wasn't until 163 years later when the president of the United States, Franklin Roosevelt, a Dutchman by descent who was born into a family that was no stranger to the smuggling business, would honor the Dutch island for firing this first salute. A plaque honoring Saint Eustatius and its governor, Johannes de Graaff, who had ordered the salute, was presented.

It is very possible that Saint Eustatius managed to play two roles: being one of the key supply depots of the war and providing Admiral Rodney with a diversion. The actions of the island may have caused Rodney to miss the most important role he might have played in the Revolution—as well as the ability to emerge from the battle with his wealth and prestige intact. It was no accident that Rodney was not present to save the war.

There is no question that the Battle of Yorktown was the single most critical battle of the ten-year war. After Saratoga was lost by the British, the English public began to lose its appetite for a protracted war. Yorktown cinched victory for the Americans, and it was a true defeat of the British military, thanks in no small part to the French army and navy. It disheartened the English populace and finally tipped the scales in the Parliament. The surrender of Cornwallis accompanied to the tune of "The World Turned Upside Down," played by the military band as the army turned in its weapons, marks the beginning of the end of the war, although the peace treaty would have to wait another two years. It also marks the recognition of American independence.

But the war that ended with the diversion provided by a smugglers' haven also started with an attempt to curb smuggling.

LIBERTY SEIZED

In May 1768 the *Liberty,* a sloop carrying a cargo of wine imported from Madeira, entered Boston Harbor. The captain told the customs agent, Thomas Kirk, that it contained twenty-five casks of wine, but the agent knew that the ship could carry much more cargo than declared. It was, after all, a ship belonging to John Hancock. The customs agent decided to look for himself.

Once aboard the *Liberty,* Kirk was shoved into a cabin by a gang of men who then nailed the door shut. While the agent was locked on board, the ship was unloaded. When Kirk was released he was warned by another captain that his life and property were in danger should he ever open his mouth about what happened. He might have complied, except that the British warship *Romney* had also pulled into Boston Harbor. Kirk filed his report, accusing one of the city's most prosperous merchants of smuggling.

The captain of the *Romney* landed troops, seized the *Liberty,* and towed her out to his own ship. He underestimated the anger of the Boston mob, however. One thousand men made their living because of the ambitious firm run by the Hancock family. They took to the streets armed with clubs. Their first targets were the customs agents. Several were beaten by the mob. One, Joseph Harrison, had his own boat at the wharf, which the mob burned. While the crowd stoned the customs house, the Madeira wine of John Hancock was safely removed from the docks.[1]

It is no coincidence that Boston would become the headquarters of the American Revolution. Boston's economy, and in fact the economy of the entire eastern part of Massachusetts, depended on its maritime interests. The king of England depended on the income he could siphon off the business of trade, and he passed laws that hindered the profitability of trade. As a result Boston was also the epicenter of American smuggling.

The resistance was financed by a handful of men including John Hancock, Josiah Quincy, Elbridge Gerry, James Bowdoin, and Richard Derby.[2] Smuggling served as both the cause of and the solution to the problem. What would be regarded as free trade for the New England merchants was actually smuggling under the laws of Great Britain. The economic life of the colonies depended on breaking the laws. America became so adept at smuggling that it was the primary means of supplying itself for the long war.

Britain had passed a series of laws over the course of the previous hundred years, starting in 1660 when the king put restrictions on certain commodities. Tobacco was the first smuggled item, and later molasses continued a lively business. In 1707 Parliament forbade any commerce that did not sail through Britain and sail out on a British ship. In 1733 the Molasses Act closed the loopholes that allowed the Caribbean trade, as well as trading with the French. Virtually all trade in molasses was illegal under British maritime trade rules, although they were rarely enforced.

A commodity such as sugar cost 30 percent more from a British island in the Caribbean than in a French-controlled island. In fact, the available sugar produced for export in the British West Indies was not enough to keep the Rhode Island distillery business supplied. On the other hand, a ship loaded with lumber from New England would not find enough of a market among the British islands. Trading with the Dutch and French was a necessity made illegal by regulation.

The Molasses Act, which specifically targeted the rum and sugar trade, appeared to New England merchants as intentionally designed to aid the British West Indies plantations at the expense of the New England merchants. But from the English king's viewpoint, he was merely treating American merchants equally. He regarded merchants as ripe for the plucking. In fact, American merchants were possibly better protected at sea than were English merchants at home.

The merchants of the newly formed colonies would steadily accept their positions as smugglers as the law became entirely counterproductive to business. Those who complied were soon out of business; those who defied the law succeeded. For the people seeking freedom from religious persecution, necessity brought such changes. The colonists were already persecuted by the very nature of their religion, so being on the wrong side of the trade laws mattered little.

The Huguenots in Europe had already made a very strong presence in the ranks of the merchant traders. They were often French, but under constant threat of the Catholic monarchy, they were a mobile population. Exiled for years in the Netherlands, they became allied with Walloon-speaking peoples, and together they migrated across the Atlantic.

The anti-Rome reaction that later became known as the Reformation began long before Martin Luther. The Cathar movement in the south of France had been more of a threat to Rome than Islam represented. The Cathari believed in a purity in which man and woman shared in directly relating to God. This purity was made possible without a patriarchal hierarchy of priests, bishops, cardinals, and popes. To the papacy the threat of losing power and the implied threat of loss of revenue produced by Church taxes were more important than the armies of Islam. The purists Cathari took as their symbol the dove, which even in Catholic art represents knowledge. The same Gnostic sentiment was shared by the Knights Templar. Their worship of an alleged severed head called Baphomet was actually an appreciation of wisdom, or *sophia* in the Greek translation. Although under torture some Templars confessed to worshiping a severed head, there is no proof of its existence.

When the pope decided the Cathari would be the victims of a crusade, he had to get support from England; the Templars of France had refused. Ironically, the Templars, who were supposed to take direction only from the pope, fought against their master. The end for the Cathari came at the siege of Montsegur, where Templar knights defended the Cathari until their surrender.

While both the Templars and the Cathari were victims of the Church, the tradition of a more humanistic Cathar religion continued. The blood of the Cathar defenders watered the soil of southern and western France, and when the seed of the reformers was planted three centuries later, it bore the most abundant fruit in those lands. Both the Templars and the Cathari carried their ideas into exile into nearby Switzerland, and this group of cantons became a country that protected the reform movement.

Although Martin Luther of Germany and John Calvin of France, who were both exiled to Switzerland, were better known for the Reformation, it had begun earlier among the populace of France. Hughes Besançon, a preacher, may have gave his name to the people of the Reformation, the Huguenots. They were often more than just spiritual descendants of the earlier attempts at reforming Christianity. The Templar eight-sided cross became the cross of Languedoc and subsequently the Huguenot cross. Combined with the descending dove, the symbolism of the cross and dove is hard to miss.

THE TEMPLE AND THE CROSS

As a large contingent of French Templars had survived in what would become Switzerland, it is not surprising that the Protestant Reformation, under leaders like John Calvin, would find refuge in Switzerland at the same time that the religious revolution was spreading rapidly through France and into England. Within twenty years of Calvin's proselytizing, Huguenots were established in France; in Kent, England; in the Channel Islands; and in the New World. The reaction to the conversion was equally swift. In 1545 Protestants were massacred—often burned at the stake—in twenty-two towns. It seemed like the anti-Cathar crusade was starting all over again. The powers behind the original Knights Templar were often found on both sides of the reform movement. The Guise family, which owned the border state of Lorraine, were militant Catholics. The duc de Guise instigated anti-Huguenot massacres and toppled any peaceful initiatives that the French king attempted.

When Charles IX became king of France, the Queen Mother, Catherine de Medici, controlled France. While she was allied with the Guise family, there was no peace. Through the century the Christian-versus-Christian wars worsened, highlighted by high-level assassinations and ultimately the St. Bartholemew's Day Massacre, where tens of thousands of Huguenots were slaughtered. Finally Henry of Navarre became king. He owed his political survival to the Huguenots but needed to remain Catholic to be king. He could appease both groups by bringing peace and religious tolerance to France with the Edict of Nantes in 1598. Religious freedom was granted in degrees to Christians in seventy-five towns. By this time the port of La Rochelle, once a Templar stronghold, was now a Huguenot stronghold. Reportedly the Catholic mass was not said for forty years in La Rochelle.

The cross of Lorraine and the eight-pointed Maltese cross came to represent both sides of the religious conflict. To the Huguenots the cross with a descending dove represented the freedom to seek God through individual knowledge. To the Catholic orders, such as the Knights of Saint John, the same cross represented the feudal order in which the Church and the king were the masters.

The protection granted under the Edict of Nantes was suddenly revoked a century later, and fifty thousand families fled France for their safety. The Huguenots were a mobile population, but they were also highly organized in lodges or guilds. They would dominate many industries, such as thread and lace making, glassmaking, and cloth manufacturing. With no homeland, many took to the sea as merchants and traders. As merchants they were under threat of both piracy and English customs; many turned to piracy, to smuggling, and to the Americas. The Huguenots were among the largest groups to settle both French Canada and English America. From Nova Scotia to Boston, New York, the ports of the Carolinas, and even south to Florida, Huguenots escaped the volatile climate of Europe.

The colonies of the New World did not always offer the freedoms desired, but religious and social prejudice was minor in comparison to the repressive religious wars of the Continent. Economic repression became the threat to the colonists' newfound prosperity. The series of laws designed to raise the king's taxes or protect his friends, such as the British East India Company, affected the colonies—some more than others.

MERCHANTS AND SMUGGLERS

For Virginia the laws weren't much of a detriment, as the state's products were shipped directly to markets in England. New England in general, including Boston, was self-sufficient in comparison, a mercantilist entity that had the materials and manpower to build ships and trade with the world. The currency of the time reflects just how important trade was. The most common currency in New England was the Spanish dollar, the famous piece of eight. While many currencies traded hands, including money from France, the Netherlands, and Portugal, they were all valued against the Spanish dollar.

Merchants who understood their business profited from the unworkable policies and unenforceable rules. A typical starting point was the British-owned island of Saint Kitts, which specialized in false British documents. On Saint Kitts a captain could pay a cash-only fee to secure the necessary documents showing that his cargo was sold in a British port. From Saint Kitts he would then take the cargo to whichever foreign island paid the best for his commodity.

Trade with foreign nations was so ingrained in New England that smuggling was just a natural consequence. The restrictive laws, enacted one after another, were hardly enforced, as Britain did not have the means. Customs agents in general were receptive to bribes, as were many officials. The numerous ships of the Boston merchants carried restricted items such as gunpowder, paper, and luxury goods along with bulk commodities like sugar, molasses, and spirits aboard the same ships as those carrying legal commodities.

The damage done was twofold. The British presented arbitrary rules that were apparently designed to sacrifice the interests of some to the interests of others. The Americans, an apparently principled people, were developing a deeper disrespect for the law. By the time of the Revolution, smuggling had been a way of life for two generations.

John Faneuil, whose name is immortalized in Boston's Faneuil Hall, was a French Huguenot whose fortune was built on disobeying the laws of the absentee government. He was a Freemason at a time when most Masons belonged to lodges that were composed of people in similar trades. Faneuil's lodge consisted of sea captains and merchants. John Hancock was another merchant, shipowner, Mason, and smuggler.

John Hancock was born in Braintree, Massachusetts, in 1737. He was seven when his father died, so he was sent to live with his uncle Thomas. Thomas, an apprenticed bookbinder, had married into one of New England's wealthiest merchant families, and as a result became rich himself. While he claimed he was in the whale-oil business, he did much better than other legal commodity merchants. The whale-oil business was one of the few legal trading businesses in which a person could sell to Britain and get cash, in the form of sterling, rather than trade credits, which depended on the solvency of other houses.

Thomas Hancock's ships carried foodstuffs to Newfoundland, then took on whale oil in exchange and sailed for England. Others, however, engaged in the same trade, and because of the volatility in the prices of these commodities, the merchants would not always do well. Hancock had a larger house, dressed in a more dignified style than his fellow merchants, and was rapidly building a small navy of trading ships.

Hancock's secret was that he was importing tea from Saint Eustatius. He had his agents in England, in the Netherlands, and on the island that came to be called the Golden Rock. A Hancock ship would sail south to the Dutch port on Saint Eustatius with legally exported items and return with contraband. Hancock maintained a high degree of secrecy aboard his ships to avoid attracting attention. His men were cautioned never to speak of their business, and were not allowed to write home to their wives.

As a smuggler, Hancock was also a visionary. Most likely he received news of Europe through his agents in various ports. When he came to the conclusion that war in Europe would spread to the colonies, he anticipated the profits it could bring from importing arms.[3] During the French and Indian Wars, the poorly supplied British troops came to Hancock's firm to buy munitions.

Hancock's sudden rise in wealth thanks to sound business practices—and illegal trading practices—eventually brought him attention. While his contemporaries were mystified by Hancock's wealth, the governor, Thomas Hutchinson, was not. But finding proof was another issue.

Thanks to the wealth of Thomas Hancock and his firm, his nephew John, whom he adopted, was sent to Harvard and graduated to a partnership in the company. Thomas died in 1764, and John inherited the business. Today the value of his inheritance is estimated at more than $100 million.[4] While not yet thirty, John Hancock was at the helm of a thriving business.[5] He emulated his uncle in every way; he valued his ostentatious home, he rode in a fine carriage, and he made his money in the smuggling business.

One of the goods Hancock smuggled was tea. With the opening of trade in China, Americans, like their British cousins, became addicted to the exotic beverage. The colonists drank an estimated six million pounds of tea per year. In 1773 Hancock supplied one million pounds. It was, of course, good business, but although it was very profitable, it was also illegal. The British East India Company was given a monopoly over the tea business, and as coincidence would have it, Thomas Hutchinson, the acting governor of Massachusetts, was an investor in the company. In fact, he committed all his capital to company shares.[6] In addition, his pay was linked to how much tax he collected on the tea.

The British East India Company was the second largest British financial institution, second only to the Bank of England. It was also near bankruptcy, as it had not managed to addict China to opium yet. The company set the price of tea at three shillings a pound, compared with the two shillings a pound set by the Dutch. The company so important to the British aristocracy then had the British government ban all other tea. It was a move that served only to make smuggling profitable and to pit the governor of Massachusetts against her wealthy citizens, who rose to the occasion.

Hancock remained a member of the Grand Lodge for a year, and when he received his inheritance he returned to a Grand Lodge, mingling with people of similar newfound merchant status. His business, however, depended on the labor of the dockworkers and shipbuilders, warehousemen and carpenters, so he could not separate himself completely from the common men of Boston. Hancock remained close to Sam Adams, who had the ear of the worker populace on which Hancock prospered. Carefully treading his way in both circles was a necessity, and when it came time to putting his workers between himself and the British law, Hancock didn't hesitate.

If Hancock's motivation for rebelling against the crown seemed only monetary, he was fortunate to meet men whose motivations were political.

SAMUEL ADAMS

Sam Adams was born in Boston. His father, Samuel Sr., was a pillar of the community and was called the Deacon. He was a merchant who owned a wharf, he was a brewer, and he was an investor in land and property. His high status did not keep him above renting houses that were used as brothels. However, young Sam had grown up with an aversion to sin; he didn't smoke or drink. Born into a family of twelve children, he enrolled in Harvard at age fourteen and placed fifth in his graduating class of twenty-two scholars.

High standards did not mean great fortune for the son of the Deacon. Samuel Sr. had lost one third of his money in the early 1740s as a result of a currency crisis. Sam Jr., who was studying law at the time, had to leave school. He waited tables. He went to work in a countinghouse but left the position by mutual consent with the owner. He borrowed £1,000 to start a business, but it failed and the debt remained. Adams then went to work in his father's brewery. But it appeared that Sam Jr. was not career bound; he dressed badly, often wearing the same clothes for days. He had no money, and whatever money he occasionally had he forgot to carry with him. He had few prospects.

Adams did have a strong sense of values, in both personal life and political affairs. When he was not allowed entry in the Caucus Club, which dominated political affairs, he started his own. While the Caucus Club appealed to the wealthy shipowners and merchants like Thomas Hancock, Sam Adams's club allowed in the dockworker and the mill worker. Within his circle were the Loyall Nine, who would manipulate mobs, sometimes by simply putting up signs all over Boston to bring out the mobs the next day. Sam Adams was not a Freemason, but his circles overlapped with Masonic groups and his own secretive cells. He manipulated Masons, dockworkers, shipwrights, and shipowners for his cause.

When Sam Jr. was twenty-six, his father died. Sam inherited the brewery, as well as enough money to pay off his debts. He also had enough money to get married; the next year he wed Elizabeth Checkley. But the idyllic life didn't last long. Adams's poor management of the brewery caused the firm to fail.

Adams was elected tax collector of Boston a short time later, a job that would last until he was forty-seven. It was, however, not a pleasant career. He was accused of malfeasance, sued several times, and almost lost his own property at auction. His failing was his inability to collect from many people, as Boston had suffered severe recessions that kept many unemployed, yet Adams would still count them as having paid. His crime, according to one biographer, was being kindhearted, although at the same time he was considered a poor handler of money.

When Elizabeth died, Adams was at least solvent enough to marry a second time. In 1764 he owned a home, received income from the wharf, and had a new wife, two children, and a Newfoundland dog that had acquired a hatred for anyone in a British uniform. If his personal financial status was rocky at best, Adams's political thesis always remained solid. He believed the loss of a single liberty was the first step to enslavement. He would never back down from this ideal, even when other Revolutionary War leaders modified their own thinking after liberty had been achieved. He wrote that every man had the right to life, liberty, and property, as well as the right to support and defend such rights. While most of Boston's merchants were going around the laws of England, Adams believed in confronting the laws. Three years before the *Liberty* was seized in Boston's port, Adams and John Hancock had started a letter-writing campaign to fight the Stamp Act.

The meeting of Adams and Hancock may be one of the most critical events of the war for independence. Hancock provided the money to keep Adams's political clubs afloat while Adams validated the ideals and enlisted the mobs that would make sure everyone heard about them. Following the Stamp Act, an Adams-incited mob from the waterfront attacked the Admiralty Court and attempted to destroy all its records. Then it turned on the home of Justice Hutchinson, who years earlier had outlawed paper money, bringing ruin to many including Adams's father. A Sam Adams editorial the next day condemned mob violence and pointed out the unfairness of the Stamp Act. In the editorial he called the mobs the Sons of Liberty, naming them after a speech in the English Parliament by Isaac Barre sympathizing with the American cause. Chapters of the Sons of Liberty were then started in every city in the North.

When the *Liberty* was seized, Sam Adams again aroused the mobs, telling them, "If you are men, behave like men."[7] He also started a celebration to commemorate three years of resistance to the Stamp Act. Free beer flowed thanks to his brewery. But even as Adams was responsible for inciting the mobs, he and a handful of patriot leaders later negotiated peace. Hancock was acquitted of smuggling charges and the mobs went unpunished. This rebellion, along with a general boycott of British goods in Boston and Philadelphia, led to the repeal of the Townshend Acts, but Britain would still quarter troops in Boston.

Although the situation quieted, the mobs were given plenty of fodder for future riots. While the officers of the British were welcomed in Tory homes, the common man had no room for the common soldier. Bar brawls and street fights were started among commoners, and many British soldiers deserted as a result of the harsh treatment and the hostile daily life.

Two years after the *Liberty* affair, a mob armed with snowballs containing rocks went after the British. The fight resulted in gunfire from the redcoats, and four Bostonians were killed. As was Adams's style, the confrontation was orchestrated; three days before the incident, posters appeared informing that the British would be attacking townspeople. Adams's newspaper had been publishing incidents of boys being roughed up by soldiers and of rape committed by the occupying army. The day of the massacre church bells all over Boston rang to alert people that something was happening. Adams would dub the incident the Boston Massacre, a name that has survived in the history books.

Remarkably, the patriots again brokered the peace. John Adams, who had defended John Hancock in the *Liberty* incident, defended the captain of the British soldiers in the Boston Massacre.

The confrontations worked, but even after repealing the Townshend Acts, the king of England decided not to lose face and keep the exclusive right of the British East India Company to sell tea to America. He would also appoint just which agents could import the tea in America. The colonies responded by boycotting tea. Consumption of tea dropped dramatically. In 1769 the colonies had imported tea costing 900,000 pounds sterling, a figure that dropped to 237,000 pounds sterling three years later. This drop of almost 75 percent did not help the British East India Company, which was nearly bankrupt. The king decided that the tea would be forced on the colonies.

In October 1773 Philadelphia was first to hold meetings and appoint a committee to challenge the authority of the king and the British East India Company. They forced the British tea agents to resign. In November meetings in Boston attempted to force a similar action, but the colonial governor was opposed to their resignation. Three ships sailed into Boston Harbor, and despite the colonists' refusal to unload them, Governor Hutchinson demanded that the city pay the tax on the tea aboard the ships, even if they sailed away unloaded.

Sam Adams addressed a crowd of eight thousand to rally the opposition to the tea tax, but that was just part of the plan. At the Green Dragon Tavern, later called Freemasons Hall, Saint Andrew's Lodge and other groups, some clandestine, would meet. While the Masonic groups were aboveboard and signed in at every meeting, other groups such as the Committee of Correspondence, the North End Caucus, and the Sons of Liberty (with their core group, the Loyall Nine) could not always afford to be so open. The Freemasons, which was an ancient order-chartered lodge, had the largest and most open membership, and often membership overlapped between it and other organizations. The North End Caucus consisted of the wealthier shipowners; the Masons were more a working-class group.

Adams and his Sons of Liberty decided to dress up as Mohawks and board the British tea ships. They cracked open ten thousand pounds' worth of Darjeeling tea and dumped it into the water. The night of the event, which became known as the Boston Tea Party, was a regular lodge-meeting night. Only five members showed up for the meeting, however, signing their names and leaving a notation in the book that the meeting would not be held on account of the lack of attendance. These members were most likely Tories or were at least opposed to the planned activity, and their signatures would possibly serve as alibis. At least twelve of the thirty known "Mohawks" were Saint Andrew's Lodge members, although Sam Adams was not, and twelve more would join the lodge after the Tea Party. At a time when the Modern Lodges were often Whig and Protestant and the ancient lodges were more Tory, Stuart-leaning, and often even Catholic, the ancient lodge of Saint Andrew's defied the classification of American Masonry.

Sam Adams was the one to be contended with, and the king knew it. In a late attempt to stop the resistance, Adams was visited by General Gage, who, on behalf of King George, offered Adams a deal he wasn't supposed to be able to refuse. The choice was to make peace with the king and be paid for backing down or to risk the wrath of the king. Adams's reply was, "Sir, I trust I have long since made my peace with the King of kings." The Sons of Liberty sent New England horsemen south to the other colonies, posting handbills with a skull and crossbones warning them of the British reaction.[8]

Adams, while not a Mason, displayed the traditional ideals of the craft: liberty, fraternity, and equality. Meanwhile Hancock, a Mason, an elitist who favored a class structure even within the craft, was an active attendee of both a modern and an ancient lodge. A third brand of Masonry was also developing in the Americas: the Military Lodge.

THE MILITARY LODGE

Shortly after the Grand Lodge went public in the early eighteenth century, Freemasonry began to grow in both the colonies and the English army. Within the army the "lodge" was now mobile and the paraphernalia of Masonry carried by the regiment. The commander of a unit was typically the master of the lodge, and both officers and common soldiers were brought together by the brotherhood of the lodge. It often allowed the common-born to advance in rank to officers, an option not available before becoming a lodge brother. Commissions of officers were still purchased, but the commander would frequently lend the candidate the funds for his commission.

The Irish Grand Lodge, not the English Grand Lodge, authorized the military field lodges. In 1754 the French and Indian Wars began as a result of French and English hostilities in Europe. The population of the colonies had been growing by leaps and bounds, due to immigration from Scotland and Ireland. The new lands offered an escape from the religious war and from post-Culloden persecution, and provided a way to increase one's standing in the world. Many served in the military specifically for the social advancement, and it was no secret that being admitted into a lodge was the ticket—and not just for the common soldier.

Jeffrey Amherst began his career in the military during the War of Austrian Succession. His military prowess earned him recognition, but by the end of that war he was a middling officer without the prospect of advancement. Although he had been aide-de-camp to General John Ligonier, Amherst was serving as a procurement officer. The outbreak of war gave Ligonier the chance to recommend his protégé for a position, yet Amherst did not have the funds to buy a commission. The funds were loaned by Lionel Sackville, the First Duke of Dorset. Sackville's two sons were very active in Masonry; Charles Sackville founded a lodge in Italy and was a close friend of Sir Francis Dashwood, and George Sackville was a regimental lodge master who would later become the grand master of the Irish Grand Lodge. With the help of friends in high places, Amherst was put in charge of the siege of Louisbourg in Nova Scotia. Amherst's victory at Louisbourg and Ticonderoga and his efforts in attacking Montreal led him to the position of commander of all the British forces in the colonies.

Wherever Amherst served he established a field lodge, and his influence grew because of his military exploits. Amherst was one of the earliest commanders to establish the different fighting methods that would work well in the Americas. Instead of two opposing regiments simply picking away at each other, the new tactics of sharpshooting, camouflage, skirmishing, and scouting were employed in the heavily wooded hills of Pennsylvania and New York. Under Amherst's command many of America's prominent Revolutionary War heroes received their training. These included Ethan Allen and Benedict Arnold, who fought at Ticonderoga; Israel Putnam, who later would be the hero of Bunker Hill; Charles Lee, who participated in the attack on Montreal; and the New York patrician Philip Schuyler.[9] Amherst captured Louisbourg, Ticonderoga, and finally Montreal in 1760 in the coup that would cause France to admit defeat and sue for peace.

Amherst was not the only high-ranking military officer to spread Freemasonry throughout the English forces in America. Under his command was Lieutenant Colonel John Young, who fought at Louisbourg and Quebec. Young had been appointed deputy grand master of the Scottish Lodge by William St. Clair of Rosslyn. In 1757 Young was the provincial grand master for all the Scottish lodges in America and the West Indies. He was succeeded by Augustine Prevost, who became grand master of all the warranted lodges in the British army that were Scottish Rite.[10] From Amherst to Young, Prevost, and further down the command, the Temple and the Lodge systems show how junior officers have been promoted and subsequently put in charge of lodges that would later dominate Canadian provinces.

When the American Revolution broke out, many high-ranking British Masons refused to play a role in defeating the American colonists. Sir Jeffrey Amherst turned down a command. Because the Freemasons fought on both sides of the war and Tory-leaning Masons even attended the Green Dragon Tavern in Boston, it is not possible to reach the conclusion that a massive Masonic conspiracy was responsible for the defeat of the British. However, numerous minor conspiracies swirled that certainly thwarted the British military effort.

Between the Boston Tea Party and the outbreak of war, the groups that Samuel Adams created built up a guerrilla movement that operated from the inner core, the Loyall Nine, and spread to other cells. From there a militia was created and munitions were obtained in secrecy and kept hidden. English intelligence was active too, and soon the English decided to seize the munitions and the patriot leaders. They sent troops into the countryside. The famous "one if by land, two if by sea" warning was given by Paul Revere, a descendant of a French Huguenot family and a master craftsman and a Mason.

War broke out on April 19, 1775, when the Massachusetts militia, alerted by Revere, attempted to head off an advance guard of British troops. This first battle of Lexington and Concord would go down in history as "the shot heard round the world." Three weeks later Ethan Allen and Mason Benedict Arnold captured Fort Ticonderoga in New York to obtain badly needed supplies and ammunition. In June the Battle of Bunker Hill exposed the weaknesses of both sides. The British "won" the battle at a tremendous cost, leading many to question the motives of General Gage, who could have cut off the Americans from reinforcements and didn't, and General Howe, who had let the American forces withdraw intact.

The American forces had their own doubts as well. Men were not brought into battle at critical times, the command structure was a shambles, there was a lack of discipline among the soldiers, and there were inadequate supplies or inadequate means of getting the supplies to where they were needed. Among some of the militia, officers were elected, and at critical moments the soldiers huddled together to decide their plan.

Two days before Bunker Hill, John Adams decided that the colonists needed a "Continental Army" and a commander. His choice for the latter was George Washington. Within days the Continental Congress appointed Washington general and commander in chief of the American army.

George Washington was initiated into Masonry on November 4, 1752, at the age of twenty, in the lodge at Fredericksburg, Virginia. His entrance fee was a steep twenty-three pounds sterling, an amount the average man would be unable to afford. But Washington was not an average man, and although his lodge was an ancient lodge, it still attracted men of greater means. George Washington's life seemed set for that of a modest landowner until 1752, when his brother died. George had looked up to his brother, Lawrence, who had sailed to the West Indies under the command of Admiral Edward Vernon (the namesake of Mount Vernon) to fight the Spanish. When Lawrence suggested George take a seaman's job, their mother prevented him. His brother's family, however, was soon hit with tragedy: Lawrence's three children succumbed to tuberculosis. George went to Barbados with Lawrence in the hopes of alleviating his brother's condition, but the climate change did not help and Lawrence soon died too.

Through inheritance George's landholdings grew to 2,500 acres.[11] Through marriage he would add another 17,500 acres, increasing both his wealth and his social standing. He rose quickly in his lodge as well, attaining the rank of Master Mason within a year. But it was an ancient lodge and not particularly influential.

From his brother George had stood to inherit a military rank, that of the colony's adjutant general. The position was divided into three, and George was forced to lobby for a lower rank. He intended to use the position as a starting point and quickly volunteered for action against the French. On his first expedition against the French he was promoted to lieutenant colonel, and he was made second in command for another expedition. The driven young commander, who constantly set plans and rules for himself in writing, had broken from the rules of his family. He was a natural leader because of his impressive bearing and his understanding that keeping a certain distance encouraged respect from his men. From his earliest time in the military George looked to his Masonic brothers to fill positions of importance. He brought a Dutch interpreter from his Fredericksburg lodge on his next expedition against the French. This Masonic brother, however, would let Washington down after the loss of Fort Necessity.[12]

Negotiating the terms of surrender of the fort was difficult because of the language barrier between the French and American commanders. The interpreter rushed through a document in the rain, and since it was poorly translated, it appeared to frame the English not only as the provocateurs but also as assassins. The French had already claimed the English were the aggressors, and Washington's initial foray was unprovoked. Washington was then put under review and demoted. When he went to war he would go back to the Fredericksburg lodge only once, instead becoming active in the military lodges.

Before long, another engagement in the French and Indian Wars allowed Washington's bravery to shine through and restored his briefly tarnished reputation. The war had spread to Europe and claimed nearly one million military casualties. The loss of pounds sterling was equally distressing to England, which raised taxes. Unable to collect the necessary taxes at home, Parliament turned to the colonies. The series of repressive measures that would lead to the seizure of the *Liberty*, John Hancock's ship, and to the beginning of revolution in Boston had their roots in the actions of the French and English wars from years earlier.

Washington returned home from war to live the life of a country gentleman. He was elected to the House of Burgesses on his third try—possibly because of his engagement to the wealthy widow Martha Dandridge Custis. Her 17,500 acres did much to increase his social standing, and there is evidence that this is what the young military officer sought in a marriage. Just before settling down, he visited another young heiress, Eliza Philipse, for the last time. She was one of the inheritors of a real-estate empire built by the profits earned from supporting piracy. Washington had been courting Philipse for a while before her family's Tory stance distanced them from the Washington family, which was decidedly Whig.

While Boston's ancient lodges often represented the more common working man, Virginia's lodges usually leaned toward the aristocratic elite. Washington himself was no exception. When Washington's stepson John Parke Custis attended Kings College in New York, the boy ate with the faculty—a privilege not granted to any other student.[13]

After Washington was appointed military commander, he immediately set out to create a real army. He asked the men of the various militia groups to commit to an enlistment of one year, only to discover that few were willing. In fact, the entire Connecticut militia decided to head home. Washington wrote, "Such a dirty, mercenary spirit pervades."[14] He then turned to his Masonic brethren for officers. He hoped that the unity found in the lodge system could be brought to the ragtag continentals. According to Lafayette, Washington "never willingly gave independent command to officers who were not Freemasons." At least twelve of the generals in Washington's army were Masons.[15]

Washington first looked for candidates from his own Fredericksburg Lodge, later called the No. 4 Lodge, from which he appointed several of his commanders. General Hugh Mercer of Virginia, who would die of wounds at Princeton, was a Mason in the Fredericksburg Lodge. Brigadier General William Woodford was a member of the same lodge, while Brigadier General George Weedon was made a Mason at the Port Royal Kilwinning Cross Lodge, which was affiliated with Fredericksburg. Brigadier General Paul Muhlenberg, who was a member of the Royal Arch Lodge No. 3 of Philadelphia, was also from Virginia.

The British gave Washington a year to put together a fighting force. Why they had not pursued the weak and nonunified colonials in New England is one of the major questions of the American Revolution. Instead they abandoned New England and made brief inconsequential forays elsewhere in the colonies. Washington anticipated that New York City was where the British would attempt to get serious, and he was right. A massive fighting force of thirty-two thousand troops, the largest the colonies had ever seen, was on its way to New York.

Washington had fortified Brooklyn Heights, only to be faced with a force that threatened to end the war in one fell swoop. While Washington made a mistake by positioning his troops with their backs to the water, fishermen and sailors from Massachusetts rescued 9,500 men by ferrying them to Manhattan. At the same time, General Howe stopped his advance and sipped tea for two hours in Murray Hill at the residence of Mrs. Robert Murray. Washington continued his retreat to White Plains, then across the Hudson to Fort Lee and west across New Jersey. The British followed slowly.

The British clearly had the advantage: a superior land army complete with nine thousand foreign mercenaries, a large navy, ample supplies, a large treasury to buy more supplies, and even a large loyalist population, the Tories, who aided their efforts. The Americans had an inferior force, no navy, inadequate supplies, and no means to buy more. Their own population had divided loyalties, as did their leaders. So how did the Continental army defeat the British? The war was won by the efforts of a handful of men, often bound by Masonic ties and sometimes united by religious events, often operating illegally and almost always acting in a self-serving way. In the end the crowning achievement, victory at Yorktown, was accomplished by an audacious act of bribery that was not atypical of the times.

Chapter 6
FRANKLIN AND THE
MASONIC UNDERGROUND

One of the greatest untold stories of the American Revolution involves the behind-the-scenes intrigues of Benjamin Franklin and his European cohorts. Had it not been for Franklin's efforts to keep the colonials supplied and funded and to bring French and Spanish allies aboard, the war might not have turned out the same. Franklin operated through Masonic groups in England and France, and his partners in the pro-American war effort were more often than not hedonists, occultists, Rosicrucians, slave traders, and spies.

Franklin had made his fortune by a young age, mostly through his ownership of newspapers and *Poor Richard's Almanack*. He was a Quaker but also had occult tendencies. Franklin could be called a pioneer of the New Age, as he meditated every morning and evening, occasionally practiced vegetarianism, and was concerned with life after death and the possibility of reincarnation. He was a self-assured, happy extrovert who popularized hard work and frugality while enjoying the high life and a liberal sexual code. He enjoyed the company of women and wrote about the joy of sex with older women.[1]

Franklin was a joiner and a founder who would start his own political club, the Junto, as well as the Philosophical Society. He planned to create the United Party for Virtue when he was introduced to Masonry. The craft employed the ideals that Franklin valued, and it also attracted him because of its esoteric roots. And being a Freemason had a practical side; Franklin was able to observe how jobs and contracts were awarded to other Masons in Pennsylvania and neighboring New Jersey. While it had no social barriers, the craft did place an emphasis on assisting the already elite gentlemen of the city. How else could a printer's apprentice meet the Penns and Shippens of Philadelphia?

Franklin became a Freemason in the Lodge of Saint John in Philadelphia in 1731. The lodge was made up of the leading merchants of the city; in fact, 75 percent of its members were merchants or sea captains.[2] Franklin jumped in with two feet, using his intellect and his printing presses to promote Masonry, writing pro-Masonry articles, drafting the lodge's bylaws, and printing the first Masonic book in America. Masonry brought him contacts and contracts, and he attributed his being awarded the contract as assembly printer to his "friends in the House."[3] His fortunes soared in the ten years after his initiation.

As an independently wealthy publisher, Franklin was ever the student, "majoring" in philosophy and "minoring" in politics. He rose to master of his lodge and shortly afterward to grand master of the province. He was among the first to speak out against taxation without representation and went to England in 1754 for that purpose. It was Franklin who drew up a plan of union that included a large house of representatives.[4]

Franklin established firehouses, hospitals, libraries, and street lighting. He was occasionally self-serving, and his post office was started in part so his newspapers could be delivered for free. He owned eight newspapers in places from New York to Antigua, including a German-language newspaper in Pennsylvania. In 1748, at age forty-two, he retired from the newspaper business to devote his life to his science and politics, although he never stopped writing.[5]

While Franklin is remembered for his public works and practical proverbs, another side of him is generally ignored. His world straddled both the practical day-to-day existence among the new colonies and the esoteric secrets of science. His connections to philosophers, Rosicrucians, occultists, and especially Masons allowed Franklin to move freely around all sides of the conflict.

THE HELLFIRE CLUB

Among the men Franklin met on his pre-Revolution travels to England was Sir Francis Dashwood. Dashwood was the chancellor of the exchequer and also the founder of his own society, the Dilettanti, and later another semisecret group called the Friars of Saint Francis or the Monks of Medmenham. Neither group bore any resemblance to a religious order. Dashwood's parties were infamous and were said to have included prostitutes dressed as nuns, satanic rites, goddess worship, and orgies.

Dashwood was the son of a wealthy businessman, a Mason who was initiated in Italy at a very early age and who married into aristocracy. Dashwood sat in the House of Commons for more than twenty years and held numerous posts, including chancellor of the exchequer, treasurer to King George III, and postmaster general. This Mason's money allowed him to rebuild his family's ancestral home in West Wycombe in a way that would make Caligula proud—complete with statues of Greek and Roman deities, ceiling murals inspired by ancient Rome, and even a lake created to stage mock naval battles. The west wing of the building was a re-creation of a classical temple to Bacchus, with Dionysus and Ariadne in leopard-drawn chariots. Another room in Dashwood's mansion was designed like a Masonic temple. His pagan theme extended to the garden, with erotic depictions of classical gods and goddesses in stone.

Nearby was the Abbey of Medmenham, which Dashwood also modified into a pagan monument, with a carving over the front entrance advising, "Do as thou will." The dining room, however, with its statues of the Egyptian and Roman gods of silence, advised visitors not to speak about their adventures. His strangest conversion was in excavating a network of caves under West Wycombe Hill, where it is said that his fellow "monks" could pair off with female guests. An underground inner sanctum it is believed to have served as the setting for Black Masses that were part of the entertainment.

Having been initiated in Masonry and dabbled in the black arts while founding one society after another, Dashwood moved within the highest circles in England, which became known as the Hellfire Club.[6] He was, however, too strange for some. Once a member of a druidic order founded in 1717 to revive the Celtic religion (members also included the poet William Blake, a druid and the grand master of a Rosicrucian order), Dashwood was expelled as the stories of the West Wycombe activities spread.

In 1758 Franklin was in England and West Wycombe, and he and Dashwood met to discuss their vision for the colonies. Franklin was admitted into the Hellfire Club, where he mingled with luminaries such as John Stuart, the Earl of Bute; John Wilkes, a radical politician, member of Parliament, and later Lord Mayor of London; John Montagu, the Earl of Sandwich; the son of the Archbishop of Canterbury; and the Prince of Wales.

John Stuart, the third Earl of Bute, was born in Edinburgh and was the first Scottish-born British prime minister. Educated at Eton and the University of Leiden in the Netherlands, Stuart married Mary Wortley Montagu. His status was elevated further when he met the Prince of Wales at the races and became a member of his card-playing clique.

Frederick Louis, the Prince of Wales, was the son of King George II, who was then the ruler of England. George II detested his son, as did the queen, and neither wanted anything to do with him, despite the fact that he was heir to the throne. Young Frederick was small, frail, and ugly, with a low receding forehead, bulging eyes, baggy eyelids, and a flabby double chin. In effect, he was a Hanoverian.[7] Frederick and his wife, Princess Augusta of Saxe-Gotha, were evicted from Kensington. Frederick found refuge in the weeklong orgies at West Wycombe, and Princess Augusta would give birth to George III, the boy who would be king during the revolution in the colonies.

John Wilkes, the young Parliament member, was, like Sam Adams, the son of a malt distiller. He married a much older woman, the heiress Mary Meade, for the convenience her money offered. She owned a large estate at Aylesbury, although Wilkes spent little time there. Instead he lived the lifestyle of many English aristocrats: as a rake and a gambler.

Wilkes soon lost his wife's fortune and then separated from her and turned to politics. Despite his active participation in the Hellfire orgies, he came to hate the English king and the Earl of Bute. When the earl was made prime minister, a large number of members of Parliament were unhappy, as Bute was considered incompetent. Wilkes in particular turned on his old friends at the Hellfire Club and went public, speaking out in Parliament against the monarchy and for a constitutional government.

In his most famous speech, published in issue 45 of the *North Briton,* a journal he distributed, Wilkes declared: "The prerogative of the crown is to exert the constitutional powers entrusted to it in a way, not of blind favor and partiality, but of wisdom and judgment. . . . The people too have their prerogative." Interpreting the last line as an invitation to revolution, the king had Wilkes imprisoned in the Tower, although his Parliamentary immunity soon earned his freedom. After returning to Parliament, Wilkes continued to write, and his later writings, which mixed obscenity and power, earned him expulsion. In England and America, however, Wilkes was viewed as a hero.[8] In 1774 he was elected Lord Mayor of London. The active Freemason served as a secret British representative of the American Sons of Liberty and raised money for the Continental Army, which would be passed through Franklin.

Another member of the Hellfire Club was the Earl of Sandwich, John Montagu. Educated at Eton and Cambridge, well traveled, and an active member of the Royal Society, Montagu was also a rake and a gambler. He is rumored to have refused to leave the gaming tables even to eat, instead placing meat between slices of bread and thus inventing the sandwich. His personal life was as tragic as his public life was full of accomplishments. His wife, Dorothy, left him while she was suffering from progressive mental illness. His mistress, Martha Ray, was a popular seventeen-year-old singer when they met. Montagu shared his home with Ray for seventeen years, until the singer was murdered by a deranged clergyman who wanted to marry her.

Montagu had several military appointments including Lord Admiralty of the English navy. He was responsible for modernizing the navy, but his navy still lost the Revolution to upstart American fighters and their French allies. Montagu was almost immortalized when he sponsored the expedition of Captain Cook, who discovered the "Sandwich Islands" in the middle of the Pacific. The islands would later undergo a name change, however, to Hawaii.

Sandwich met Dashwood in 1740 and became a member of the Dilettanti and the Order of Saint Francis. Sandwich met Benjamin Franklin when he headed the navy, and they became fast friends, as both enjoyed the parties at their mutual friend's West Wycombe home. With Montagu in charge of the navy, Dashwood in charge of the English mail system, and Franklin heading the Committee of Secret Correspondence, the men were an odd threesome.

At such an early period of the mail system, *postmaster* would also mean "spymaster," as the chief postman had access to all the mail. Franklin had been in England for years as an agent of Pennsylvania and later as spokesman for America, and he was brought up on charges and ordered before the Privy Council at the time England was receiving news of the Boston Tea Party. Franklin was charged with attempting to create an American republic, but he suffered only the loss of his office as postmaster for the colonies. The spy was also being spied on, his own mail being opened and read.

FRANKLIN IN FRANCE

The contributions of Franklin and the anti-Tory support in England cannot be overestimated. From behind the scenes a propaganda war was launched to keep English public opinion divided. When American intelligence got wind of the hiring of Hessian mercenaries, Franklin went into action. He worked with Jefferson to fight the Hessians on two fronts. In Europe Franklin penned a letter allegedly written by a German prince to his American commander, arguing that the British figures for the Hessian dead were too low, and that he was being cheated out of his payment for each of the dead soldiers. He encouraged the officer to allow the wounded to die, rather than send home crippled and thus burdensome wounded. In America Jefferson distributed notices offering Hessian deserters land grants in the colonies. In the end, more than five thousand Hessians deserted.

It is possible that friends in high places—and in low ones—helped Franklin avoid being hanged as a traitor. He soon established his Revolutionary War headquarters in Paris. Franklin and family did not traffic with the common French people; instead they were wined and dined, entertained, and boarded by the aristocracy. The high-born of France and England were well acquainted with each other and the backstage intrigues would frequently cause embarrassment to those involved. One of Franklin's acquaintances, Caroline Howe, was the sister of General Sir William Howe, who had fought at Quebec and was rumored to be getting a command in America.[9] Another brother, Admiral Lord Richard Howe, was already the commander of the British navy's efforts in the colonies. General Howe's sister brought Howe and Franklin together, a move that led later to accusations against General Howe.

Franklin understood the value of the people who plied the seas in trade. They were an all-important means of supply and communication, they were generally supportive of the cause of liberty, and because almost all of them routinely broke the ever-changing series of trade laws, they operated in secretive brotherhoods. Masonry ruled the seas, and even Franklin needed an entry to gain the trust of the merchants.

In France such connections were made through Sieur Montaudoin of Nantes and Dr. Jacques Barbeu-Dubourg of Paris. When Franklin reached France, he headed straight for the Masonic stronghold of Nantes. The busy port was controlled by merchants, and few had any intention of following the rules that hindered trade. They communicated through a series of codes that kept outsiders from penetrating their cabal. Nantes was also a slave-trading port—France's largest—and the triangular trade that brought slaves and munitions to America depended on the Caribbean merchants, who were often Americans.

The relations between French and American smugglers would be very important in the fight for independence. The French slave traders were heavily armed and often carried letters of marque that allowed them to take a British ship. Franklin's new friends were valuable assets to the American cause; Dubourg bought the badly needed supplies, which were carried on Montaudoin's ships.

In Paris, Franklin's wartime acquaintances were all Masons, and they helped gain him membership in three Masonic lodges. The most prestigious was the Lodge of the Nine Sisters. Franklin was rapidly admitted into the lodge, which was a nest of political activity. The lodge had committed itself to the politics of the reform of French society. One of its goals was to provide an alternative education system, which would take control from the Catholic Church. Public lectures were given on history, religion, and science at the lodge-sponsored College of Apollo. One Masonic writer even credits Franklin with creating the Apollonian Society to further his goal of uniting science and religion. Later revolutionary zeal caused the college to rename itself the Lycée Republicain. Members included the duc de La Rochefoucauld, who translated the American Constitution into French,[10] Captain John Reinhold Forster, who would sail with Cook, and the philosopher Voltaire. Franklin, in fact, would be present at the initiation of Voltaire into the lodge in April 1778. Dr. Edward Bancroft, a friend of Franklin's as well as an agent for Lord Auckland, the head of the British spy network, was another member. After the war, John Paul Jones was admitted into the order.

The intrigue that assisted Franklin in building his support network in France defies full understanding. At once the high-ranking Masons of the Lodge of the Nine Sisters appeared to be both pro-Church and anti-Church. Many of the members met at the salon of the wealthy and eccentric Anne-Catherine de Ligniville d'Autricourt Helvetius, who was despised by John Adams and was also the target of Franklin's amorous interests. Her salon was regularly attended by members of Catholic religious orders and by men of business and science. Such an ambiguous circle would have similar government and religious leanings.

Franklin, ostensibly a deist (a nonallied believer in God), was active with the aristocracy in France who had desired a gradual move from the monarchy. The most suitable form of government, they believed, was a constitutional monarchy that maintained a king, as well as a strong relationship with the Catholic Church.

The headquarters for this intrigue was at Saint-Sulpice in Paris. Here met the priests who would later be ostracized because they refused allegiance to the Revolutionary (anti-Catholic) state. Instead, they allied themselves with the Knights of Malta, who also found themselves threatened by the mob state and later by Napoleon. A curé of Saint-Sulpice would one day be the confessor to the wife of the Marquis de Lafayette, Marie Adrienne d'Ayen de Noailles. Lafayette had fought for freedom from the tyrannical monarchy in England but found new problems at home after the war. His refusal to take the oath of the new government became a dividing line that forced the Lafayette family to take a stance. They sided with the Catholic Church and paid the price.

Many aristocrats and Church leaders literally lost their heads as a result of the Revolution, which was as much against the Church as the monarchy. But Saint-Sulpice and its secret Company of the Sacred Sacrament survived. After the French Revolution, an order of the company called the Ladies of the Sacred Heart enjoyed the support of the d'Ayen family. Their duty was a constant devotion to the sacred sacrament, an unveiled host. Every hour a sister would replace the last sister in the perpetual vigil. Even this order of sisters was forced to operate in secrecy.

Such steadfast devotion to the mysteries of faith contrasted with the practical realism of men of science, but this was not an issue to Masonic cabals like the Nine Sisters and religious centers of influence such as Saint-Sulpice. Whatever Franklin's opinions might have been, he kept them to himself. He had a role to play, namely the securing of supplies for the struggling colonies. For this reason Franklin also joined the Lodge of Saint Jean of Jerusalem, the Loge des Bons Amis,[11] and a mysterious conclave called the Royal Lodge of the Commanders of the

Temple West of Carcassonne. Such connections were invaluable, and helped procure badly needed supplies that were then shipped on Mason-owned ships such as the *Jean Baptiste,* which was named for Masonry's greatest saint. Ninety percent of the gunpowder used by Washington's army originated in France.

Through the efforts of Franklin and his Masonic collaborators in Europe, other traders and even pirates joined the American war effort. When the participation of the French merchants became known among the merchant underground, the Dutch were quick to follow. As a nation they had lost their command of the seas and their colonies to the English. The Crommelin House of Amsterdam was more than happy to tweak the nose of the English king and make a profit securing gunpowder for the Americans.[12] To maintain the appearance of neutrality, Dutch ships sailed directly to the tiny island of Saint Eustatius, where they would unload their cargoes of ammunition and tea for the American ships. When British ships posted themselves in the Netherlands' waters and British spies uncovered their mercantile plots, the Dutch used Portugal as a go-between. Goods were shipped to Portugal and then reshipped to the Caribbean. The British soon understood the problem, but they had no solution. Rather than risk a further breach in relations and face a war at home, they sat back and watched as Dutch ships were repainted, changed flags, and transported their cargoes to the Americans.

The British had larger problems than stopping the trade; the country was concerned about the revolution and the war spreading to other colonies. It may have been only the relative distance from the original American colonies to some of England's other colonies that kept the revolution from spreading. The West Indies, Canada, and the isolated outpost of Bermuda all had their own interests, and their loyalty was never a sure thing.

The Masonic underground that united one smuggler with another bound Americans to their English cousins on Bermuda. Men like John Hancock needed to maintain a certain amount of secrecy in order to maneuver around the customs ships of the English, as well as the series of constricting laws. Masonry provided the protection of a wide-ranging brotherhood. To be able to make connections in the far-flung islands from Bermuda to Barbados, a ship's captain or merchant needed to connect to those he could trust. The Masonic brotherhood that existed on the high seas allowed many to straddle religious and political conflicts and survive. The Tuckers of Virginia and Bermuda are one example of how duplicity, questionable loyalties, and blatant crimes didn't impede prosperity—providing the right connections were in place.

THE TUCKER CLAN

The history of Bermuda is very much linked with American history. Discovered first by the Spanish in 1503, the Isles of the Devil, as they were called by Juan de Bermudez, remained unsettled for a hundred years. King James I awarded a land grant to the islands to the Virginia Company. In 1612 a group of sixty Englishmen became the first settlers. From the earliest days of settlement the economy was based on smuggling and piracy, tobacco trading and whaling. Freemason lodges on Bermuda recently celebrated their two-hundred-year anniversary, but the craft was established on the island for at least fifty years before the Lodge Saint George officially received its warrant in August 1797. The Earl of Strathmore, the grand master of the English lodges, had appointed a provincial grand master for the islands around 1544. Lodge Saint George is, however, the oldest continually working Scottish lodge operating outside of Scotland. The prevalence of Masonry is visible even today where the Customs House at Saint George resembles a Masonic temple more than an official government building.

With an estimated one third of all trade in colonial Bermuda considered smuggling, it was no small wonder that very strong connections existed between the American colonies and Bermuda. In 1775 a small delegation from Bermuda attended the Continental Congress in Philadelphia. Bermuda remained loyal to the crown, but that did not stop the residents from providing assistance.

The Tucker family of Bermuda and Virginia represented the leadership of the resistance movement. The Tucker dynasty traces its history from the Norman invasion of William the Conqueror. Seven hundred years later, as Britain expanded its role in the New World, the clan again played a role in the invasion. The Tuckers landed in Charleston, South Carolina, Virginia, and Bermuda, where they rose to power and privilege.

Colonel Henry Tucker was the agent for Bermuda during the American Revolution. In July 1775 the Continental Congress gave permission to trade foodstuffs for gunpowder. Washington told the congress that his army would desperately need the gunpowder, while residents of Bermuda desperately needed food. In August of the same year two patriot ships rendezvoused with Colonel Tucker's men. The Bermudians helped the Americans break into their own Fort William to steal one hundred barrels of gunpowder, which were quickly loaded on Bermuda whale ships and then transferred to American ships. The gunpowder thieves were never apprehended, as England was afraid the populace was looking for an excuse to join the American cause. It also helped that Colonel Tucker's son was the governor of Bermuda, and despite his potentially treasonous actions, he remained governor well after Britain lost her colonies. In addition, the grandson of Colonel Tucker, Henry St. George, became the chairman of the British East India Company.

During the Revolution, American diplomat Silas Deane had recommended that the island of Bermuda be used as a supply port and a harbor that could keep America's very small navy provisioned and protected. In exchange, the Bermudians would receive food. The island provided the Americans with fast ships made of Bermuda cedar. St. George Tucker was a Virginia relative of the Tucker clan with strong business ties to the island, and he suggested a takeover of Bermuda to George Washington in 1780.[13] St. George would serve at Yorktown as interpreter for Rochambeau; his help was apparently more valuable off the battlefield, however, where the French commander needed help in meeting women.

The combined efforts of the Tucker family in the Revolution, which may have been considered treasonous from a British standpoint, did little to tarnish Tucker's prestige. The Tucker House in Saint George, which was named for Henry Tucker, the colonial treasurer and Governor's Council president who purchased it in 1775, is a part of the Bermuda National Trust and a current tourist attraction. The Tuckers' prestige and connections helped them to survive almost any scandal. "India Henry," as Henry St. George Tucker was known, spent six months in jail for an "attempted rape" committed while he was chairman of the British East India Company.[14]

John Randolph, the son of the prominent Virginia statesman (also named John), and his wife, Nancy, were charged with the murder of their infant child. Related to the Tucker clan, they too had the charm of surviving any scandal. The Randolph "dream team" of lawyers included Patrick Henry, Alexander Campbell, and John Marshall.[15] The Randolphs were acquitted of the murder.

In America the Tuckers married well. In 1778 St. George Tucker married the widow of John Randolph (of the Jefferson-Randolph clan). He received 1,300 acres on the Appomattox River. Ann Tucker married Lyon Gardiner Tyler, son of the president and heir to the owners of the pirate refuge at Gardiner's Island.

Wherever the Tucker family was prominent, it imported Scottish Rite Masonry. In Bermuda the Tucker clan was instrumental in bringing the Scottish Rite Freemasonry to prominence over the Grand Lodge Masons. In Charleston, where belonging to the right lodges was the ticket to mercantile wealth, Scottish Rite ruled. And in Virginia, where the secessionist movement orbited around the College of William and Mary, the Tuckers, the Tylers, and others who played key roles in the Confederate side of the Civil War were prominent Masons.

It may have been Scottish Rite Masonry that allowed the individual Tuckers to avoid the ultimate penalty for treason against the British from their Bermuda base during the Revolution and again in the Civil War. For example, Nathaniel Beverly Tucker, serving as the U.S. consul in Liverpool, used his office to start constructing Confederate ships for use against the government that paid him. During the war he was part of the "Canadian cabinet" that instigated draft riots in U.S. cities. Tucker would even be indicted for playing a role in the Lincoln assassination.[16] But somehow the charges were dropped, and when Tucker returned to the United States, he served with the Pennsylvania Railroad as a lobbyist.

From Medmenham to Nantes and from Bermuda to Boston, the men who were the forces behind the Revolution were not always motivated by pure or singular interests. Of questionable morals and unquestionably law breakers, many of these men were at least as corrupt as those they fought against. The power of elite groups as well as rank-and-file Masons, however justified, served to forever change the political landscape of the eighteenth century.

Chapter 7
THE MERCHANTS OF WAR

While it is surprising that those who played major roles in the war abroad had to turn to Masons, occultists, slave traders, and smugglers for support, it was hardly different back in the colonies. Men like Sam Adams, George Washington, and Patrick Henry would risk life, liberty, and property for the cause, but the motivations of others were not as pure. When war with England became a reality, many American merchants lined up to make their fortunes. People who built fortunes from the importation of arms and supplies included New York's Livingston clan, Marblehead's Elbridge Gerry, Philadelphia's Stephen Girard, Boston's Thomas Cushing, and Virginia's Benjamin Harrison.[1]

Benjamin Franklin put together what became known as the Secret Committee. Gaining an appointment to it was getting a license to steal, or at least to overcharge. The Secret Committee was supplied with an immense amount of funds from the newly formed Congress, and it was made up of merchants who knew the ropes and were not above breaking the laws for their own gain. These men were responsible for keeping the colonies supplied. The first chairman of the Secret Committee was the business partner of Robert Morris, Thomas Willing. The first contract went to his own firm, which raised an outcry from the other merchants and members of the new Congress.

Despite the criticism Morris, at age forty-one, became the greatest supplier of military goods in the war. He was born in Liverpool, the son of a Chesapeake merchant. After his father's death he joined the firm of Willing and Company; he later became a partner. The firm of Willing and Morris had a fleet of merchant ships in the West Indies, which meant they participated in the underground economy that thrived under a mass of complex and ever-changing rules and regulations. The partners both had reputations for being clever and honest, as smuggling was not considered a dishonest act. While Franklin realized that the combination of the firm's experience in the Caribbean trade and their network of agents around the world made Willing and Morris capable of transacting the business, Congress estimated that the firm would be making an exorbitant gain at the same time. Morris, in fact, wrote to an associate remarking that he stored powder until prices improved before delivering it to Congress.[2] Merchants did not see any moral dilemma in making a profit while defending the country.

It did not help that the very first assignment went badly. The commissioned ship, the *Lion,* reportedly could not find any goods to be bought in Europe and returned empty. It was highly suspicious that a seasoned captain would return with an empty hold from such a long voyage. Morris offered to return the thirty thousand pounds sterling (eighty thousand American dollars) advanced by the Congress, but instead a new assignment was given.[3]

The second assignment went better. Ammunition and powder were bought in England, shipped to Saint Eustatius, and then sent to the colonies. The firms taking the contracts were entitled to $2\frac{1}{2}$ percent on both the exported goods and the imported supplies. It was actually a very small commission considering the risk that the ship's owners were taking. This did not stop the committee from handing the contracts to their own firms, to friends, and to family. Robert Morris was quick to learn which angles could maximize profits and minimize losses—such as shipping the firm's goods alongside goods that Congress was paying for aboard American warships. Morris and Willing are not on record as ever having paid the freight for their company's exports of indigo and rice to France. Having Congress pay the insurance for the entire cargo of the ships was an opportunity Morris could not pass up.

Franklin, with his great experience as a Philadelphia business leader and his connections with English and American merchants, was quick to recognize the talent and administrative abilities of Morris. Congress would soon come around to accept Morris as the best man it had.

It comes as no surprise that other members of the committee, which included Silas Deane of Connecticut and Robert R. Livingston, John Alsop, John Dickinson, and Francis Lewis of New York, gave the assignments to themselves or to friends. The Browns of Providence increased their slave-trading fortune by war profiteering. Samuel Otis, Thomas Cushing, and Elbridge Gerry of Massachusetts also participated in profiteering. Arthur Lee, a Virginia planter, was the biggest critic of the commercial side of arms procurement, in part because he mistrusted merchants. His brother William, however, took part in the double-dealing with speculations of his own. But the greatest amount of mud being slung at the profiteers was directed at Silas Deane.

DEANE AND LAFAYETTE

Silas Deane was born in 1737 in Groton, an early seaport town on Long Island Sound. His father was a blacksmith. Deane, however, managed to put himself through Yale and was admitted to the bar. Teaching school in Hartford while also practicing law, Deane's career path took a dramatic turn when he settled the estate of Joseph Webb. Whether it was opportunity or love, the young lawyer met and married Webb's wealthy widow, Mehitabel. Her family was active in the West Indies trade, and Deane gave up teaching and the law. Instead he began making voyages to the West Indies and learning the trade. After his first wife died, he married Elizabeth Saltonstall, the granddaughter of a governor and daughter of a general. While her family had also been active merchants, their political influence was greater and the opportunist Deane went into politics. A member of the new Congress and a merchant, Deane was in the right place at the right time to get assignments as a munitions supplier.

When Deane lost his congressional seat because of a dispute with fellow Connecticut delegate Roger Sherman, Deane's close friend Morris found a better assignment for him: He went to Europe as an envoy to the French and a merchant, and his mission was to enlist the French in the American cause, or at least to procure supplies for the war. By some accounts Deane exaggerated his accomplishments with the French, but he did well in the war supplies department, where he was entitled to a 5 percent commission. At home his enemies grew and Congress not only failed to pay his commissions but also charged him with misappropriating funds. His letters to a British correspondent suggesting a negotiated settlement of the war earned him the accusation of treason. When Deane finally left Europe to return home, he was gripped with a violent abdominal attack that led to his death within hours. It was believed that he was poisoned by the British double agent Dr. Edward Bancroft.

Whatever truth is in the accusations of Deane's detractors, he deserves credit as well. Early in the war Deane contracted for thirty thousand rifles, four thousand tents, thirty mortars, and clothing for the troops. He was responsible for the introduction of more than one young French aristocrat to the American cause. One of Congress's problems with Deane was his giving of contracts to French officers who desired high ranks and believed they were getting them by enlisting in the American cause. One such officer was Marie-Joseph-Paul-Yves-Roch-Gilbert du Motier, the Marquis de Lafayette. Born in 1757, Lafayette's father was killed in the battle of Minden at the age of twenty-seven by a battery commanded by the English general Phillips. Lafayette was only two at the time, but he was destined to get revenge. Twenty-two years later he commanded a battery in Richmond, Virginia, and bombed a house where General Phillips reposed.[4]

The future major general was raised by his mother and grandfather, but they too met an early demise when Lafayette was thirteen. He was, however, one of the wealthiest men in France and had advisers who looked after his numerous holdings. At fourteen he was committed to an arranged marriage with his 12 1/2-year-old cousin, Marie Adrienne d'Ayen de Noailles, and they soon set up home in Paris.

De Noailles's family was equally noble and of ancient lineage. Her grandfather was the Maréchal duc de Noailles, which gave him a hereditary right to maintain his own cavalry regiment. Lafayette and his brother-in-law, the Viscount of Noailles, met for dinner in August 1775 with the Duke of Gloucester, who was the brother of King George III. In a candid moment the duke announced that the insurgency in America could actually escalate and provoke France to start new hostilities against England. The marquis and the viscount called on a third relative, the comte of Segur, who married into the d'Ayen family, with their plan to join in the fray. The trio, dubbed the Three Musketeers by their family, quickly rushed to the home of Silas Deane to enlist.

The young marquis had the rank of captain of the reserves when he sailed to America. Described as an overgrown boy stuffed into a handsome uniform, he was pudgy, red-haired, and already balding and had a long nose. He supposedly proclaimed, "The moment I heard of America, I loved her; the moment I heard she was fighting for freedom, I burned with desire of bleeding for her." Such sentiment, as well as a shipload of munitions and supplies, endeared him to Congress and especially to General Washington. Washington and Congress may have also been endeared to the family that Lafayette brought with him: His brother-in-law, Viscount Louis-Marie de Noailles, also came to the colonies and was second in command to one of France's legendary fighting units, the Soissonnais. Lafayette was commissioned a major general, one of the highest ranks in the Continental army. When he was wounded at Brandywine, Washington instructed the surgeon, "Treat him as if he was my son."[5]

The meeting of Washington and Lafayette began a long friendship, and Washington lived to repay the favors. When the marquis's ideas on liberty and equality backfired in a faction-driven madness that is called the French Revolution, only funds from America bought Lafayette's release from prison.

Although Lafayette served with distinction and earned the respect of the regiment he was given to command, not all such foreign volunteers were welcomed. Massachusetts was a closed society that admitted few to its cliques. While New York City was an open society at the close of the eighteenth century, Boston was always English. Prejudice against

Irish and Italian immigrants would arise later, but in the colonial period simply being from Scotland was a barrier. Masonry would overcome that hurdle.

JOHN PAUL JONES

John Paul Jones is an odd hero. He was born John Paul in Kirkcudbright, Scotland, in 1747, at a time when there was not a world of opportunity awaiting those who stayed home. His father was a gardener who was married to a housekeeper, and they were both employed on the estate of William Craik. Many believed John Paul's real father was James Craik, the son of William. Craik and John Paul's mother, Jean, got married a day apart to other people, and Craik provided Jean with a cottage to start her new family. Even biographer Samuel Eliot Morison points out that Craik's activities "suggested" Jean's relationship with him was as more than housekeeper.[6] From birth a cloud hung over John Paul because of his unclear parentage. At age fourteen he started his career aboard a ship engaged in the Barbados trade of rum, sugar, and humans. By age seventeen he was a third mate on a blackbirder, the term for a slave ship, having proved himself able at sea. He would sail aboard slavers for another two years before quitting the "abominable" trade. It was not as much the morality that assaulted his sensibilities as it was the smell. A slave-trading ship that confined sometimes hundreds of men and women in its hold without sanitary facilities could be smelled for miles away.

Upon sailing home from Kingston, Jamaica, the master and mate of Paul's ship died, so he brought back the ship on his own. In doing so he earned the appointment of master, a great achievement at the early age of twenty-one. Paul did all he could to live the part. He tried to drop his rural Scottish accent and he learned to read and write well—in fact, better than his peers. He dressed the part of an officer and sought out the company of other officers. He also enforced discipline.

At five foot five inches tall, command did not always come easy for Paul. Over the course of his career, he would more than once single-handedly quell a mutiny. Discipline, however, had its risks. On an early voyage as captain, Paul ordered the son of a wealthy merchant whipped three separate times. The man pressed charges, of which Paul was acquitted, but later died aboard another ship heading back to Scotland. The father then pressed further charges against Paul and had him arrested. Again Paul was cleared, but he came to understand the value of connections.

Within days of his release from the Tolbooth jail, Paul applied and was accepted to the Saint Bernard Lodge of Freemasons in Kirkcudbright. As a member of that lodge, he was welcome to visit and sometimes find accommodations in other lodges around the world. He also made connections in the lodges that would advance his career and even save his life.

Three years later, Paul was again charged with murder. His version was that the leader of a mutinous crew was about to hit him with a club when he ran the man through with his sword. The incident occurred on Tobago, where the small population of whites was mostly Scottish and the lieutenant governor was a friend. However, the young captain chose to flee. He disappeared for two years and then turned up in Virginia with the new surname Jones. Most likely he hid in Edenton, North Carolina, where he had a hometown friend, Robert Smith. He then moved to Virginia, where Robert's brother James, also from Kirkcudbright, was a shipowner and an officer in the local Masonic lodge.

With a new name and a new life, Jones found safety and acceptance in Scotchtown, Virginia. Smith was a partner in a shipping firm with Joseph Hewes, who would become Jones's patron throughout the Revolution. Another friend was Dr. John K. Read, who was related to Ben Franklin's wife and was also active in Masonry. Jones knew Patrick Henry and would compete for the hand of Dorothea Dandridge in marriage. When war broke out, Jones called on Hewes and another Kirkcudbright Mason, David Sproat, for an appointment in the first American navy.

Before meeting the enemy, Jones had many battles to fight. He encountered hostility from the New England bluebloods who resented a Scotsman; in fact, they resented anyone who was not a Saltonstall or a Winthrop who rose above his caste. Incompetents such as Dudley Saltonstall, brother-in-law of Silas Deane, who was descended from the Winthrops, received command instead of an upstart like Jones. It was only after others proved their incompetence that Jones received choice ships. Another battle was finding men. The American navy paid less than it did to sailors aboard the privateers. When a prize was taken, a privateer sailor could get twice the share.

Jones overcame his first hurdle by lodging with Boston Masons such as Thomas Russell and Abraham Livingston and Portsmouth Masons like John Wendell. Wendell was a member of the very important Saint John's Lodge of Portsmouth and introduced Jones. Jones in return hired Wendell's son, David Wentworth Wendell, cousin to both John Hancock and John Adams, as a midshipman. Repaying Abraham Livingston would be tougher, as Livingston "ordered" twelve cases of claret, a Chinese tea set, tableware, decanters, glasses, almonds, anchovies, capers, and olives from Jones's voyage to Europe.

The second hurdle was overcome by "impressing" sailors, forcing them into service at pirate hideouts like Tarpaulin Cove in the Elizabeth Islands. It didn't win him friends, and in fact almost caused his arrest in Providence until he pulled his sword on the local sheriff.

Jones made his career in Europe, shocking England with attacks on her ports and ships. Timing is everything, and Jones's timing was excellent. France was beginning to question the American chance at independence when news of Jones's exploits hit. When Jones landed in France he was the toast of the town and was accepted in France's most prestigious Mason group, the Lodge of the Nine Sisters. Benjamin Franklin and Voltaire were also brothers of this mysterious group, which met at Saint-Sulpice.

Jones spent his time in France accepting medals, dining with his new Mason brethren, and shopping for war supplies and tableware. After having denied Virginian Arthur Lee passage home because of his enormous baggage and retinue of servants, Jones made a new enemy. Once home he had to answer to charges of delaying the needed war supplies. His hero status allowed him to answer in an abbreviated style, avoiding mention of anything but the condition of his ship.

◈

The war was then being fought on several fronts. Washington's Continental army went from one defeat to another, retreating across the rebel country, while the British took advantage of the loyalist Scottish Tory factions in the south to demoralize the American forces. In Europe, American agents like Franklin and Deane labored behind the scenes to find America friends. And at home a handful of wealthy elite took advantage of their appointments to build fortunes.

BENJAMIN HARRISON

Benjamin Harrison was a Virginia aristocrat whose family had prospered most likely from both being politically connected and being one of the first families in Virginia. From 1632, when the first Harrison landed, the family was represented in Virginia's governmental body, the House of Burgesses. By the time of the Revolution the Harrisons' property, called the Berkeley Hundred, was a kingdom within the state. A one-and-a-half-mile road bisecting the property wound past tobacco fields and slave quarters before reaching the great Harrison mansion. Benjamin Harrison was by this time related to every aristocratic Virginia family, including the Lees, the Carters, and the Byrds. Besides being a signer of the Declaration of Independence and a governor of Virginia,[7] he was also a secret partner in the Willing and Morris firm.

In 1776, with the war just starting, Harrison the planter and Willing and Morris the merchant traders bought most of the American tobacco crops. The prices were low because everyone believed shipping the product to Britain for sale would be impossible at a time when a war was happening. But Morris and Harrison understood that at the same time that prices were falling in Virginia they were rising in England. Tobacco represented half the value of America's exports, and the stakes were huge. Morris hired ships from New England, Deane insured them, remarkably, in London, and they set sail. They did not have to go far; the free-trade market in Saint Eustatius was the market. This helped make Morris extremely rich during a time when he was competing against the Secret Committee, on which he served.[8]

Harrison fathered seven children, including William Henry Harrison, who became the ninth president. William's record in the War of 1812 and the family's patrician status helped him gain notice. The publicity surrounding his involvement in the small skirmish called Tippecanoe might have gotten him elected, but Harrison wasn't really a war hero. He had marched his thousand-man force against a Shawnee village half the size in a punitive measure. Despite his force being twice the size and his army losing more men in battle than did the Shawnee, Harrison claimed victory. The media took his word for it, and he was considered a hero. His campaign for the presidency was not going so well until he came to Richmond on a stop. There a pickpocket being hauled off to jail yelled "Tippecanoe and Tyler too," which became Harrison's campaign slogan. Harrison was soon elected America's shortest-term president.[9]

Harrison's administration lasted only one month, as he became the first of two presidents to cross the Cotton Whigs. Both Harrison and Zachary Taylor died of stomach distress after very public events. Harrison's death, first declared to be from a stomach ailment, was later blamed on his catching a cold during the inaugural address. Taylor's death was blamed on his eating cherries and drinking milk. Both deaths conveniently paved the way to significant policy changes in Washington.

The family wealth and status remained, and the great-grandson of Declaration signer Benjamin Harrison, who was also named Benjamin, would become president. At the time, Harrison's party was divided. At its convention the party went through seven ballots without a leader. At the critical moment James Blaine, who has been credited with putting the previous president, Grover Cleveland, in the White House, sent a cable from Scotland that read, "Take Harrison." Because he was perceived as a man who could be manipulated, Blaine got the job of Secretary of State. Benjamin Harrison, like his grandfather, would deliver his long inaugural address in a March rain, but he survived. His accomplishments are few. His pet causes were high tariffs, banning Asian immigration, and overthrowing the government of Hawaii in order to annex the territory.

ELBRIDGE GERRY

Elbridge Gerry was one of the Marblehead aristocracy. In a time when and a place where merchant shipping paved the way to wealth, Gerry's father was a wealthy and politically active merchant shipper. His mother was the daughter of a British merchant. Marblehead was known more as a fishing port, and a great deal of the Gerry business was shipping codfish to Barbados to be used as food for the newly imported slaves. Before the war Marblehead rivaled Salem in importance, and Gerry was one of its richest citizens.

As a man of wealth who was dependent on trade, legal or otherwise, Gerry did not agree with the growing anti-British feeling building in Boston. He was outraged by the Boston Tea Party and left his low-level political job as a result. Under the influence of Sam Adams, however, Gerry returned to politics. But like Hancock, his motives were often designed to increase his pocketbook. He served as the chairman of the Committee of Supply, a post that suited him perfectly. In addition, he sat on a congressional board that regulated finances. When Congress was stingy in doling out money to suppliers like Gerry, he walked out. He became considered the "soldier's friend" for his demands for better equipment and supplies, although he did nothing in the debate for soldiers' pensions. During the war Gerry could not have been luckier. The British closed the harbor of Boston, yet somehow they left Marblehead alone. Marblehead's importance soared as patriots around the colonies donated goods for Boston and Gerry shipped them.

Haughty and aristocratic, Gerry was never popular among the

Massachusetts voters. His interest had always been in his own wealth and property. The night of the British march against Lexington and Concord, Gerry hid in a cornfield in his nightclothes. Before the Battle of Bunker Hill he tried to persuade Dr. Joseph Warren, the president of the Provincial Congress, from joining the battle.[10] Warren said to Gerry, *"Dulce et decorum est, pro patria mori,"* meaning "it is a sweet and glorious day to die for one's country." Warren then went to his death. Gerry didn't.

Although he was publicly for independence, Gerry had his doubts about signing the Declaration. Benjamin Harrison joked with Gerry about the danger of signing, saying his own weight would ensure a quicker death at the gallows than the slender Gerry's.[11] Gerry may have taken this to heart, as he was absent when the Declaration was signed; he put his signature on the document months later. Gerry's strongest effort in the Provincial Congress was getting the Congress to issue letters of marque. This allowed shipowners like him to legally capture British ships and profit from the goods seized.

To keep himself and his favorite politicians in office, Gerry redrew the lines of various districts to manipulate the effect of the vote. One district was drawn to resemble a salamander, and the term *gerrymander* entered the vocabulary.

THE CUSHING FAMILY

The Cushings represented the American aristocracy. Thomas Cushing was an active merchant and a political ally of Sam Adams's father. Cushing, whose nickname was Death's Head,[12] saw no need to separate politics from profit. As a businessman he attempted to serve both "gods." He gathered intelligence information on the Tories but was sometimes reluctant to share it. He was equally reluctant to elevate the conflict, and checking the "violent designs of others" was his goal before the war.

The men in charge of supplying the military might today be accused of allowing themselves excessive commissions and profits. In the eighteenth century it was almost expected that these men and their friends would use their posts for personal gain. While Cushing and Gerry made fortunes in the war effort, those who supplied them thought nothing of marking up goods 500 percent. The smaller merchants saw little wrong in selling to the British as well, and in overcharging the French, who had entered the war to save the colonists' efforts.[13]

The Cushing clan raised self-interest to the most treasonous levels. After making profits during the war, the Cushings, led by Caleb Cushing, acted in a step-by-step method to defeat the interest of the United States and to enrich themselves. Caleb Cushing's mentor was John Lowell, who served as an agent for many of the wealthy British forced out of Boston. He would go on to play a leading role in New England's Essex Junto, which attempted to incite the region to secede from the newly formed United States because the merchants did not like the policies of Jefferson. Shortly after going to work for Lowell, Cushing married the daughter of a leading member of the secessionist movement.

Cushing became a power broker and apparently would stop at nothing to turn a profit. He was a one-man Masonic conspiracy. As a thirty-third-degree Mason of the Scottish Rite, he used his influence to enrich himself, bring his country to war against China and Mexico, and finally lead the United States to the breakup of the Union. Publicly Cushing was an abolitionist, yet at the same time he fought for the annexation of Texas, which most of the northern states feared would tip the balance in the conflict. Cushing, as a Cotton Whig, saw no problem in a divided Union if trade with England was secure. That trade depended on cheap cotton as a key export; cheap cotton depended on cheap labor. Soon after it became obvious that President Harrison had no intention of furthering the cause of annexation, he was dead. Not everyone believed it was from natural causes.

A book titled *The Adder's Den* was published in 1864. The author, John Smith Dye, claimed that the agents of the pro-slavery South had poisoned Harrison to put Tyler in the White House. Harrison had been a farmer, had served in the army, had marched through wilderness for months at a time, and had fought as a soldier. It would seem unlikely that spending two hours in the rain could lead to his death. After the suspicious death of President Harrison, the accidental president John Tyler appointed Caleb Cushing to be Secretary of the Treasury. Cushing, however, was not liked or trusted, and the Senate rejected his nomination. Tyler then appointed him as a commissioner to China.

Cushing's family was made wealthy by the opium trade in China. Shortly after the British began a war against China to impose its right to sell the country opium, Caleb Cushing ordered American ships to enter Canton with guns blazing to further humble China. His next act was to push for war against Mexico. Admitting Texas and other states to the Union as "slave states" helped slavery to continue. New England and the Brahmin families depended on the South's ability to provide cheap cotton. The cotton could then be spun into textiles in New England's mills, of which Lowell was the preeminent force.

When support was needed to rally certain Southern states against the abolitionist movement, Cushing dispatched other New Englanders to the South. Albert Pike, from Cushing's home base in Newburyport, Massachusetts, was sent to Arkansas. He too would be raised to the thirty-third degree in the Scottish Rite, and he played a key role in formation of the Ku Klux Klan. Another friend, John Quitman of New York, was sent to Mississippi, where he started Scottish Rite Freemasonry and a secessionist movement.

After the war against Mexico, Cushing invited his Mexican war generals, including Jefferson Davis, to Massachusetts, where he informed them that he wanted Franklin Pierce to be president. Zachary Taylor had been the hero of the Mexican War but had alienated the Cotton Whigs by opposing the extension of slavery into California. Nevertheless, he was elected. After sixteen months in office, Taylor participated in the decidedly Masonic dedication of the obelisk known as the Washington Monument. He allegedly became sick after eating cherries and drinking milk and died shortly afterward. Again a war hero who had survived both the travail and the rigors of war was brought down by a simple problem.

Cushing still played a strong behind-the-scenes role in the

Buchanan White House, and once war became inevitable he supported Lincoln. Despite the fact that he had planted men in the South to lead the way to secession, Cushing's duplicity was never enough to keep him out of government.

STEPHEN GIRARD

Stephen Girard started his career as a pilot of a French ship in the Caribbean trade. His first voyage was aboard the *Pelerin* to Port-au-Prince in Saint Domingue. This slave port was one of the capitals of the triangle trade. Slaves were brought from Africa to work on the sugar plantations. Sugar was the return cargo, having been produced there for almost two hundred years, when the Portuguese built many of the mills. The pilot was the man in charge of the trading, and he was often given carte blanche by the ship's owner to make a profit in any way he could. Selling the sugar to the American colonies brought higher prices because the trade had been outlawed by the British.

Girard made six such voyages before being promoted to captain. On his last trading voyage from France he decided he had done poorly, as commodity prices had dropped. Instead of returning to France with a less-than-profitable stake for his backers, he simply sold the goods and kept the money. With the ill-gotten proceeds he took on a cargo of sugar and brought it to New York. There he joined Thomas Randall in the New Orleans trade, but it was the British blockade that would finally plant Girard in Philadelphia. The City of Brotherly Love was especially warm toward its Masonic brothers, and Girard, who had become a Mason in Charleston, quickly joined his city's lodge. The lodge would serve as an old boys' club for merchants like John Wanamaker and ship captains like Girard.

An ugly man with one bad eye, Girard married a penniless Irish maiden, Mary, at age twenty-seven. Five months into the marriage he caught her cheating with a British colonel. His brother visited and left him with a black concubine called Hannah, whom he would name in his will. His wife was committed.

During the Revolution the wealthy merchant and shipowner added to his fortune by acting as a privateer for the American side while also trading with the British. Girard had taken an oath of allegiance to the colonies, but his allegiance had been first and foremost to himself. His treasonous trade with the British, his participation in the slave trade, and his later role in the opium trade made him the fourth richest American ever.[14]

After the war Girard hired a new eighteen-year-old mistress. His wife, who was still in the asylum, gave birth to a daughter he never would meet.

Girard's fortune grew, as he was a pioneer in the China trade. Biographer George Wilson says, "He eventually derived more profits from the China trade than any of those who were in on the ground floor."[15] When the British were banned by the Chinese government from smuggling opium into the country, American ships such as Girard's took up the trade. Girard raised capital through a British banking house, Baring Brothers, to finance his entry. From both legitimate trade and smuggling Girard became one of America's richest men. During the War of 1812 he put up half of the sixteen million dollars the country needed to get through the conflict, charging his country a 10 percent commission.

At age seventy-seven Girard hired his fourth and last live-in maid and mistress. He lived four more years. His will provided generously for those who worked for him; housekeepers, servants, and sea captains all received lifetime incomes. Girard's Masonic lodge received twenty thousand dollars. The orphans of Philadelphia received a school to house and educate them that remains to this day. Today Girard's living will is still more than two hundred million dollars.

◈

The American army marched from one defeat to another and was forced to subsist on minimal rations and without proper uniforms or even shoes. At the same time the American procurement effort was in the hands of Cushing, Gerry, Girard, and other profiteers who thought nothing of cheating and overcharging their own side. The British side, however, had no shortage of self-serving and inept politicians and military leaders who managed to steal defeat out of the jaws of victory on several occasions. The responsibility was then left to the French, and in particular a small circle of French aristocrats and Masons, to tip the scales.

Chapter 8

THE BRIBE
THAT WON THE WAR

The story of how one French aristocrat may have been responsible for the American victory has never before been told.

The American Revolutionary War is an illustrious tale of victorious moments. The first was the remarkable turning point at Saratoga, which served as the catalyst for bringing in America's potential allies. The second was the surprise crossing of the Delaware at Christmas, where the ragtag starving American army defeated the well-trained, well-equipped Hessians. The climax came at Yorktown, where the Americans and their new allies, the French, surrounded the army of General Cornwallis.

Students of the war, however, see another side. They see the few victories weighing against the multiple losses of the Americans through Brooklyn, Manhattan, and White Plains; the English chasing Washington from one defeat to another; the starvation and deprivation of untrained continentals, and their subsequent desertion and mutiny. The army of freedom fighters was half destroyed in battle and nearly finished off by starvation and sickness, but the colonies were still populated by many who were not loyal to the new cause. Tories dominated the population of eastern Long Island, where the British army was able to buy cattle. New Jersey was mostly Tory and provided food for the English army while Washington starved across the river in Pennsylvania. Tory landowners dominated the Carolinas, their loyalty often to their personal pocketbooks, which were closely tied to England. Many Americans, while loyal to the cause of liberty, still put their personal fortunes first, denying food to Washington's army and refusing the Continental as a currency.

Despite the state of the economy, the constant defeats in skirmish after skirmish, and the loss of most of the American army to disease, capture, and desertion, the outcome of the war was an outstanding victory. The serious student might be led to wonder just how this was possible.

There is a third side of the story that might seem even stranger. Sir William Fraser once said, "The Battle of Waterloo was won on the playing fields of Eton." His statement refers to the school where England's future leaders were trained. It may be valid to paraphrase Fraser when discussing how the Revolutionary War was won: The battle of Yorktown was lost on the playing tables of a London gambling house known as White's.

HIGH SOCIETY IN LONDON

At a time where the sun never set on Britain's empire, London society may have been at its most decadent. It was the largest city in the world and England, of course, was the master of the ocean. While the poor starved in the streets, the upper crust of society delighted in heavy drinking, wild gambling, practical jokes, and bawdy behavior. As the world's largest port city, there could be as many as eight thousand ships in the Thames at any one time. The number of drinking houses and brothels to serve the thousands of sailors and officers was staggering. The upper classes distanced themselves from the lower classes even in partaking of London's vices.

From an establishment called Shakespeare's Head, a Covent Garden tavern popular with sea captains and directors of the British East India Company, John Harris published a list of the better prostitutes and where their services could be found.[1] But for those at the pinnacle of London society, there were gentlemen's clubs.

The fashion of eighteenth-century London gentlemen was to

belong to one or more of the gentlemen's clubs. Many of them moved from place to place; others were anchored in a specific tavern or hall. A handful of the clubs were as spectacular as modern-day casinos, and becoming a member was everything to the aristocratic class. Almack's, Brooke's, and White's were among the top clubs. Almack's had a large ballroom that could accommodate seventeen hundred of London's fashionable dandies. Gaining admittance was important to London's young social scene, and the Duke of Wellington was once turned away because he arrived in trousers rather than the required knee breeches. Women were admitted at Almack's, and it became a marriage mart for London's most eligible.

The main attraction of the gentlemen's clubs was gambling. At a time when the average wage earner was paid a pound a week, it was not uncommon to see ten thousand pounds sterling on the table. Brooke's and White's were strictly men's clubs, and the chief amusement was gambling. They kept an open betting book where one could wager on anything, and seats at the card tables were occupied all night. Whist, loo, faro, and hazard were the favorite games, and the size of the wagers ruined many of England's young elite.

White's and Brooke's would occasionally attract members divided by politics, and in the years before the American Revolution Brooke's was regarded as a Whig club and White's a Tory club. White's members included the Duke of Devonshire and the Earl of Rockingham. Brooke's members included Charles James Fox, Lord Robert Spencer, and Sir Joshua Reynolds.

Charles Fox may epitomize London's macaronis. Born with the proverbial silver spoon, Fox's wealth brought him election to the House of Commons at the age of nineteen. At the time of his election he was traveling throughout the Continent, so he did not suffer the boredom of a campaign. In fact, according to his own letters, he was laid up with a bout of the clap in Nice. Back in London, Fox would spend days hopping from Brooke's to White's to Almack's to other clubs, where a bad night might cause a loss of ten to fifteen thousand pounds and a good night might see its return.

While the Fox family fortune supported such excess, the same could not be said of all of the young dandies who made up the Saint James Club scene of London. A massive gambling debt incurred at the gaming tables of White's in London led to the bribery of the one man whose role would be so pivotal in the final outcome of the Revolutionary War: Sir George Brydges Rodney.

Born into a Somerset family that traced its lineage for twenty generations, Rodney studied at Harrow. Like many other naval commanders of his day, he left school at an early age, twelve, to train in the navy. But prestige and profit did not always go hand in hand. An elegant, handsome figure, Rodney was a rake and a gambler without any of the inherited wealth to pay off his losses. The young dandy lost his family's fortune on the playing tables of White's.

Even worse than his losses were the debts he incurred. Rodney planned to go to sea in order to share in the booty that was promised to the commanders. In one early action in the West Indies he was able to partially repair his finances. While the income bought him time, the sea would disappoint him as much as the gaming tables of White's. Rodney spent his remaining funds to get into Parliament, but even this campaign failed. His debts were all too often to men in office, and his connections soon became a detriment to his career.

Unable to stay away from White's or regain his finances, Rodney was forced to flee London and his creditors. While in exile in France he heard that he had been picked to head the British navy. But he owed French creditors as well, and was told he would have to pay off his debts before he left. The prospects were gloomy indeed. Even if he found enough money to get out of France, he could still be thrown in a debtors prison in England before he even saw a warship.

Taking command of the navy was the light at the end of Rodney's tunnel. In his darkest hour Rodney was approached by a representative of one of the wealthiest families in France. Rodney would be provided with enough money to satisfy his monumental debts, but what was required for such a favor was equally monumental.

MASONIC BROTHERS FROM ABROAD

The winter of 1777 to 1778 was particularly hard for the American army under Washington's command. Many soldiers had little more than blankets to keep out the cold, as their shirts and pants were in tatters. Shoes were a luxury, and many soldiers lost their feet and legs to the cold. Often those on sentry duty stood in their hats to keep their bare feet warmer. The food was so scant that the Thanksgiving treat was four ounces of rice cake.[2] At the same time, German farmers in nearby Valley Forge were driving cattle to Philadelphia for the British.

Washington himself had to contend with the constant excuses of Congress when he pleaded for food, clothing, funds, and medicine. And a handful called the Conway Cabal plotted against Washington. The army was undernourished and poorly clad and had been forced to retreat from one defeat to another for years. It appeared that if victory were to be had, it would be a miracle. That miracle finally became a reality with the arrival of assistance from Europe.

The efforts of American agents in Europe brought the French on board as allies. Early in 1778, while Rodney was hiding in Paris, the French had signed an alliance to join the Americans. They would not actually declare war against England until July, however. One of the first conflicts featured the French navy and the English fleet near the island of Ushant. The two forces were equal, but the English were used to winning. When the French fleet was forced to retreat, the two English commanders somehow confused their signals and also retreated. In a move that was very reminiscent of the numerous land battles fought in America, it appeared that the English refused to press the advantage.

Because the battle was so close to home for the English and the failure was so public, the citizens rioted in the streets of London and both commanders were court-martialed. Each blamed the other for the failure to exact a victory.

The English army appeared unable to press its advantage on land, as well, although the public was less aware of what occurred across the Atlantic. There had been worse blunders. After the war Sir William

Howe, Sir Henry Clinton, and Lord Charles Cornwallis were blamed for incompetence. The famous story of Howe sipping tea while letting the defeated Continental army escape Long Island is one that most likely plagued him. But Howe was competent. He had served with Amherst, who had taught the American commanders and Howe alike the values of guerrilla fighting. He was a knowledgeable battle-hardened commander who had fought at Montreal, Louisbourg, and Quebec before the American Revolution. Howe did make serious mistakes. He had allowed Washington, whose army spent the night in the rain without tents and low on ammunition, to escape Long Island. And this was not the last time Howe allowed the American army to escape. He followed Washington across New Jersey, where desertions reduced the small force to less than ten thousand. With victory again simply a day away, Howe allowed Washington to cross into Pennsylvania.

When winter came, Howe's army was camped within twenty-five miles of the Americans, but Howe had no desire to shiver through winter in a camp. Instead he headed back to New York City, where his mistress, Elizabeth Loring, kept the general warm. Her husband had been sent by Howe to Boston to watch over the prisons. A London newspaper accusing the general of ineptitude was brought to Howe. He decided to turn in his resignation, and while he waited for it to be accepted, he and Loring enjoyed dinners, concerts, and ballroom dancing in Philadelphia. When Franklin was asked by the French if Howe had taken Philadelphia, Franklin replied that Philadelphia had taken General Howe.[3]

Sir Henry Clinton was a military man as well. He started his career at the age of thirteen in the Coldstream Guards, where he was commissioned as a lieutenant. He also distinguished himself in battle and rapidly rose through the ranks to become a major general in 1772. When he took over for Howe, he was more interested in being in New York than in commanding his troops in the field. After the war Clinton was called on to explain his failure as a commander. He blamed Cornwallis and the other generals, even going as far as writing a book about his actions. He claimed that three times his army was in danger of starving, although compared to Washington's forces, starving was a relative term. With twelve thousand pounds to cover his salary and expenses, Clinton's provision orders included brandy in ten-gallon lots, beef, veal, mutton, fish, sweetbreads, and eggs.[4] He held four houses in New York City, which, he claimed, were used for hiding because his life was in danger, and he also had a mistress in the city.

Cornwallis was a very well-trained military commander born into a wealthy and prestigious family. His grandfather had been awarded a baronetcy by Charles II, his father was the first Lord Cornwallis, his mother was the daughter of Lord Townsend and was related to Prime Minister Robert Walpole. Charles Cornwallis likely chose the military at an early age. He enrolled at Eton, where the younger classmen were the object of harsh treatment by older classmates. Cornwallis, a tall man, thrived at Eton and went on to be tutored by a Prussian officer. He bought an officer's commission in the Grenadiers Guards. At age eighteen he took a tour of Europe with his Prussian tutor and then enrolled in the Military Academy of Turin. It was one of Europe's finest, and the young officers combined military strategy with ballroom dancing in their curriculum. Over the course of Cornwallis's career, his training helped him serve with distinction in the Seven Years War, in Ireland, and in India. After he married he took a brief respite from the military and enjoyed the estate lifestyle with his bride. He was favored by King George III but at the same time counseled against the harsh measures exacted by the king against his colonial subjects. Cornwallis's loyalty was never in question, however, and when war broke out he volunteered for his command against the American rebels.

Cornwallis lost heart soon enough. His wife at home in England had taken ill, and his commanders, Clinton and Howe, disappointed him. Cornwallis had outflanked Washington on Long Island only to watch Howe allow his escape. Cornwallis beat the Americans at Brandywine in 1777 and Monmouth in 1778, and was then sent south. Clinton, with Cornwallis as the field commander, effectively stopped the resistance in the South, so Clinton headed for New York, leaving Cornwallis in charge. The war heated up as Cornwallis fought several major battles and worked his way north. From New York Clinton ordered Cornwallis to find an area where his army could position itself to be supplied. He chose Yorktown, which turned out to be a fatal decision as the French, by sea, and the Americans, by land, surrounded him. Eight days under siege ended the war. Cornwallis's actions in the Revolution did not hurt his career for long, however, and he went on to serve with distinction in India and to quell rebellion in Ireland.

Baigent and Leigh's *The Temple and the Lodge* examines how the effect of Mason fighting Mason may have hindered determination. Howe had served with Amherst, where most of the officers were brothers in the craft. Twenty-nine of the thirty-one regiments under Amherst's command had field lodges. Cornwallis served in two regiments that had military lodges. His brother Edward had served as well, and was the founder of a lodge in Nova Scotia. Clinton served as aide-de-camp to Ferdinand, Duke of Brunswick, one of the most influential Masons of his day.[5] Three seemingly capable British commanders chose to avoid making the coup de grâce at every turn, instead simply continuing the war until, like America's Vietnam War, the soldiers in the field and the citizens back home despaired of ever seeing victory. If conspiracy is the secret behind defeat, then the final battle of Yorktown was the stage. Nevertheless, there is no evidence that Cornwallis had planned for anything less than victory. But there is evidence that one man would serve to destroy the chances of the British.

BEHIND THE SCENES IN FRANCE

As the efforts of the Americans Franklin and Deane in France paid off, a French fleet and French soldiers headed to America. When the American effort was exhausted, France stepped in to provide most of the troops, the arms, the food, and the money to fight the final offensive of the war.

The commander Rochambeau was one of the first and most important figures of the French effort. He was quickly followed by the troops of Count William Deux-Ponts, who led a regiment from the

Saar Valley; the Viscount de Noailles, from whose regiment in France Napoleon would later emerge; Count Mathieu Dumas, who would become a hero at Waterloo; the Marquis Claude-Henri de Saint-Simon; and the Duke de Lauzun. All had been enlisted through the diplomatic efforts of Franklin and Deane and had supplied clandestine aid before France officially committed to war with England.

Rochambeau and his troops were ferried by seven transport ships to Rhode Island in July 1780. They stayed for a brief time, with the well-funded army enjoying the good life, but they were shocked with the allies they came to save. The Americans overcharged them for supplies, openly traded with the British who blockaded their coast, and on occasion shot at them. The first French troops did not see any action until Yorktown; however, when it came time for action, the French impressed both the Americans and the English with their order and discipline.[6]

General Jean-Baptiste-Donatien de Vimeur, the comte de Rochambeau, was a career military man with a mission. He, like Lafayette and others, wanted to see the rebels break their ties with the monarch of England. When the French king Louis XVI signed a treaty with the Continental Congress, his first act of assistance was to supply America. His second was to send over a six-thousand-man army called the Expédition Particulière under Rochambeau's command.

Rochambeau had entered the military at age seventeen and fought at the siege of Maastricht in Holland during the War of Austrian Succession, in a French expedition against Minorca, and during the Seven Years War. Rochambeau was fifty-five when he brought over three regiments to fight the decisive battle at Yorktown. One unit was the Deux-Ponts. Under the command of Rochambeau, this thousand-man unit was recruited from Germany. It was a typical unit in that the officers were often adventurers. Many sailed aboard the French fleet accompanied by their wives and children, and at least one officer, Baron Ludwig von Closen, brought his servants.[7]

Other military leaders who commanded troops in America were interested in the social experiment that became a new country. Saint-Simon's cousin became the founder of French socialism. Like Lafayette, the duc de Lauzun was very interested in the New World's social experiment. His desire was to be present at the birth of a new age, to fight for the cause of liberty. Like many French nobles, the contradiction of the noble class fighting for democracy did nothing to dim his enthusiasm. Lauzun was from an ancient family that had titles from the time of the Crusades. As was tradition in such a titled military family, adventure called first. At age thirteen Lauzun became an ensign in the elite French Guard. At eighteen he married into another French royal family. Lauzun went to Corsica and proved himself in battle. He was rewarded with the title of colonel of the Légion Royale. But peace bored him, and he was among the first to volunteer to aid the American cause.

Lauzun sailed from France as part of the fighting force that joined Rochambeau. Lauzun's cavalry and infantry joined the ancient regiments of the French military, the Bourbonnais, the Deux-Ponts, the Saintonge, and the Soissonnais, and they marched to Yorktown.

Lauzun's Legion, as it was called, was made up of men from various European countries. Most had come from the Alsace-Lorraine corridor between France and Germany; others came from Sweden, Italy, Poland, and Russia. They spoke eight different languages, and by tradition they would curse in Hungarian. They were volunteers, and often adventurers; many were from noble families, others were rakes and thieves. They were the predecessors to another French fighting force, the French Foreign Legion.

For the duc de Lauzun, the American Revolution was just one more adventure. His exploits in both the battlefield and the boudoirs of Europe were legendary. He was said to have made love to every woman he met in France and Newport, Rhode Island, where he was first headquartered. His men followed his example, and despite their prowess against the British they also achieved the dubious distinction of fighting the most duels among themselves, typically over women. Lauzun continued to have great adventures after fighting in America, including becoming Marie Antoinette's lover. While Lauzun was aware of his rank and his importance—he was even privy to Rochambeau's and Washington's discussions of strategy—he may not have been aware that his presence in the war was the single most critical factor in its outcome.

◈

While the Marquis de Lafayette, the duc de Lauzun, Count William Deux-Ponts, Count Mathieu Dumas, the Marquis de Saint-Simon, and the other nobles eagerly awaited battle, their supreme commander, Rochambeau, debated strategy with Washington. Washington thought that a move to recapture New York would advance the war effort. Rochambeau argued that a decisive victory against the English in the Chesapeake Bay would end the war. Rochambeau's logic won, and the focus was turned on beating the one commander who was a serious contender: Cornwallis. Rochambeau and Washington marched to Virginia to catch Cornwallis while both the Americans and the English were depending on the navy to arrive on time.

After the Battle of Guilford Courthouse, the forces under Cornwallis's command were low on supplies. At Yorktown, Cornwallis spent three months digging in while waiting for his rendezvous with Admiral Rodney. The British fleet commanded by Rodney was supposed to be the most important factor in the outcome of the showdown between the British army and the combined forces of the Americans and the French. Supplies and reinforcements were to be brought by Rodney; this was the reason Cornwallis hadn't marched farther north.

Rodney had other plans. Instead of sailing north when he had the advantage over the French, he launched a vicious attack on tiny Saint Eustatius. While Cornwallis's army had its head in an ever-tightening noose that could be relieved only by Rodney's ships, supplies, and fresh troops, Rodney stayed to loot Saint Eustatius. His army spent valuable time confiscating everything from almost every citizen of the tiny island. In fact, he instructed his men to go as far as looting graves, claiming that valuables had been buried.

Meanwhile, Washington and Rochambeau used the three months well, coordinating their cross-country march and the arrival of the

French fleet. Lafayette used a small force to block an English retreat, Washington and Rochambeau rushed to cover five hundred miles, and Admiral de Grasse sailed up from the Caribbean with twenty ships and three thousand fresh troops.

François-Joseph-Paul, the Marquis de Grasse-Tilly and Comte de Grasse, had joined the fleet of the Knights of Saint John of Jerusalem, also known as the Knights of Malta, at age twelve. This was the original order known as the Hospitallers of Saint John of Jerusalem, and was established even before the Knights Templar. While both orders were ostensibly Catholic, the exposure to different faiths may have had a lasting effect on the Templars, who supported the Cathari during the papal crusade and were accused of heresy. The Hospitallers had no such crisis of faith, but they needed a reason to exist after the Crusades. They took refuge in the Mediterranean, where they waged endless wars against the Barbary pirates to protect Christian shipping.

After six years of training, de Grasse was attached to the French navy. Like his fellow Knights of Malta, de Grasse had an interest in the American cause of liberty. He was joined by nineteen other knights in the effort. After the war, fourteen joined Washington's Society of Cincinnati.[8] Admiral de Grasse became part of the French Revolution, retiring when the excessive bloodshed stained the cause of liberty.

Admiral de Grasse had overnight become a key figure in the Revolutionary War.[9] With a fleet of twenty ships, he sailed from France in March. His fleet, including the *Ville de Paris,* the largest warship in the world, guided a convoy of 150 merchant ships carrying supplies for the war. De Grasse reached Martinique in late April and sent thirty ships with troops and supplies to Rochambeau. The resupply included the infantry of Marquis Claude-Henri de Saint-Simon, and the ancient regiments of Agenais, Gatinais, and Touraine. De Grasse's fleet found action almost immediately after landing the merchant ships.

In late April, de Grasse encountered the British navy. This first brief action was later described as indecisive, but the British lost six warships, which had a lasting effect. De Grasse had outmaneuvered the fleet of Admiral Hood, which was under the command of Admiral Rodney.

Hood blamed his early loss on Rodney's incorrect positioning of his ships; it was Rodney's second mistake but certainly not his last.

Five weeks later Rodney again ran into the French fleet. On June 5 Rodney's navy reached the French fleet, counted twenty-four ships and five frigates, and chose to do nothing. Rodney had the advantage of size, yet he failed to pursue de Grasse, allowing the French admiral to head north to Virginia. But Rodney was aware of the crucial importance of French naval and military support in determining the outcome at Yorktown. Still, he failed to give priority to stopping or even slowing the French assistance. The most critical engagement of the war was decided on which side was more prepared for the battle. The American and French side needed Admiral de Grasse; the British side needed Admiral Rodney. There is ample evidence that both naval commanders were aware of their importance.

Admiral de Grasse was scheduled to rendezvous with thirty American pilots who were necessary for navigating Chesapeake Bay. De Grasse supplied his food stores in a hurry and chartered fifteen new merchant ships to carry food. Not wishing to wait for letters of credit, he paid for the supplies with his own money.

While it seems that Rodney had failed to understand the implications of his delay, his actions prove otherwise. He dispatched a warning to Admiral Graves in New York, stating that the French navy was on the way. He told Graves that both fleets needed to link up to prevent the French navy from supplying Rochambeau and Washington. The first message was intercepted; the second arrived days after the French fleet had already destroyed part of Graves's fleet. Rodney even wrote to his wife that he would attack the French if given the opportunity, and that the "fate of England may depend upon the event." Given the evidence of Rodney's letters, it is shocking that he chose to then split his forces and sail home with his loot from Saint Eustatius. This final action can hardly be deemed a mistake; Rodney deserted his post. At the same time that he abandoned his mission, Rodney warned his charge, Admiral Graves, of just how important it was to bring the fleet to Yorktown. Rodney's actions, combined with the lack of timeliness of his warnings, contributed to the American and French victory.

Historians have pointed out that Rodney's errors may have been attributable to problems with his health. But the true cause of the victory at Yorktown is that Admiral Rodney allowed himself to be defeated on purpose. In doing so, he ensured the French-American victory, which was allowed to repay a monumental debt.

THE MOTIVE

As mentioned earlier, in 1774 Rodney fled to Paris to escape debtors prison.[10] The gambler was still in Paris in 1778 and still an admiral, though he did not have a post. Rodney had been put on a half salary by his superior, the Earl of Sandwich. The Earl of Sandwich, when not at the gambling tables himself, served as Lord of the Admiralty. The earl was also a friend of Benjamin Franklin's through their shared adventures at Wycombe.

After nearly four years in exile, Rodney was informed that he was being recalled to active duty. It was an opportunity to rebuild his fortune and his career, but because of new debts incurred in France, the down-and-out admiral could not return to England to accept his command. Even worse, he could not rebuild his fortune without the command.

Then, seemingly out of the blue, a French noble and commander of the French Guard offered to help Rodney. The Maréchal duc de Biron offered Admiral Rodney the money needed to pay off his debts and assume his command. Some historians call it a loan; others call it a gift. In either case, the implications are staggering.

It seems that at least one of the two parties was committing an act that could be deemed treason. While Rodney's reasons were evident, one must wonder, What was the French commander's motivation?

When the offer was made, the duc de Biron's nephew was Armond Louis de Gontaut, the duc de Lauzun. It is unreasonable to think that the duc de Biron actually wished to help Rodney take his post; in doing so the duke would be aware that he might be contributing to his nephew's defeat or even death. Apparently the well-timed loan or gift to Rodney was the one way the duc de Biron could ensure his nephew's success. The loan was a bribe. And that bribe won the war.

Rodney upheld his part of the bargain. When he could have pursued the advantage, he chose to wait. When he could have stopped the French fleet, he chose to defend Tobago. When he could have raced to Yorktown, he decided it was time to punish Saint Eustatius. Finally, he simply headed home.

THE WORLD TURNED UPSIDE DOWN

Rochambeau and Washington continued to tighten the siege around Yorktown. Lafayette had been reinforced with the fresh troops of Saint-Simon. Meanwhile, four thousand British troops sat in New York Harbor and Rodney's partner Graves waited. When Rodney's message arrived, the Brits set sail. It was then two days after the surrender at Yorktown; when the British fleet was informed of Cornwallis's defeat, they simply turned around.

After losing the war, Britain would go through a long series of blaming people. While others pointed their fingers at their fellow commanders, Rodney seemed above the fray. The reason was that before any charges of incompetence, cowardice, or treason could be leveled against him, he returned to the West Indies to become a hero.

Despite the surprising victory at Yorktown, it would still be more than a year before Britain ended the hostilities. Clinton in New York still had a standing army during this lull, and Rodney returned to pursue the French fleet. He sighted the French fleet under de Grasse sailing for Jamaica; the same French commander that he avoided meeting prior to Yorktown he now chased. For three days Rodney followed the French fleet until he was in position in the passage between Dominica and Guadeloupe known as the Saints. He had thirty-six ships against the French fleet of thirty-three, and the battle was a standard line battle in which ships form a line and fire directly at each other. A fleet captain, Sir Charles Douglas, recommended Rodney break the line after the French left a gap in their formation. But this was against the *Fighting Instructions,* the British navy's rules of engagement, and it was a gamble that could result in a court-martial or even a firing squad if it failed. Rodney was not even sure his captains would follow such an order.

Years of gambling, however, inspired Rodney to take such a great bet, and he won. Five ships followed him and he circled several French ships to fire upon them from both sides. His other captains also exploited gaps in the French line. Even the *Ville de Paris,* the world's largest fighting ship, was overtaken, abandoned by its crew, and set on fire by the British. Of course, this had no effect on the outcome of the war in the colonies. It did serve to make Rodney a hero, however, and so his motives would not be challenged after the war.

The deal made between the duc de Biron and the indebted Admiral Rodney worked out very well for both men. Admiral Rodney had his fortune back, and despite abandoning Cornwallis at Yorktown, Rodney was still regarded as a war hero for the naval battle he chose to win. The duc de Biron's nephew was safe, for the time being, and was now regarded as a hero in a war against England. However, the duc de Lauzun's status would not save him from the terrors of the French Revolution. He would go to the guillotine, but not before offering his executioner a glass of wine. The deal that allowed Rodney's gambling debt to be repaid also allowed America to win independence.

Chapter 9

ONE NATION UNDER THE GREAT ARCHITECT

Even though the war ended in February 1783, it would still be almost ten more months before the peace treaty was signed in Paris. The new nation then turned to winning the peace.

From the very beginning of American history it was evident that a handful of Masons would exert a powerful influence both in the open and in secret. The Declaration of Independence was drawn up by the non-Mason Thomas Jefferson. It was first signed by a Mason, John Hancock, and on its first vote on July 1, 1776, the document was approved by nine of the states—a clear majority. The next day the vote reached twelve, with the New York delegation not voting. (John Adams had predicted that July second would forever be celebrated as the day of independence for the American colonies.) On the fourth New York voted and the Declaration was signed by the president and the secretary of Congress, not by Hancock or any of the other fifty-six signers, which would come later. When the Declaration was signed, up to forty-one of the signers were Masons, even though not all of these Masons were publicly acknowledged as such. Among Masons July 4 was held as a sacred day. It marked the rising of Sirius, which in ancient religions was related to the god Thoth, who brought knowledge to man. It was also considered the guardian to the goddess Isis; as such it was the most important star in the sky, and at least seven major Egyptian temples were oriented to it. The Fourth of July was now sacred to the new nation, as well.[1]

The Constitution was also drawn up by several influential Masons—including Washington, Franklin, and Randolph—and by non-Masons John Adams and Thomas Jefferson. All of them had been influenced by the philosophical movement that swept Europe and included Sir Francis Bacon, Rousseau, and Voltaire. The Founding Fathers, however, had ambiguous feelings toward the secret societies that spread these philosophies. Washington was known never to willingly promote a non-Mason in the military, but John Adams, on the other hand, wrote several anti-Masonic tracts. Adams believed Masonry was one of the greatest moral and political evils, and regarded it as a conspiracy of the few against the many.[2]

Jefferson was not a Mason, although his attendance at Masonic meetings has been documented. There is some evidence of his flirtation with Rosicrucianism, including some Rosicrucian codes that were found among his writings.[3] There is stronger evidence that Franklin was connected to the Rosicrucian group that was centered in Germantown, Pennsylvania. And certainly there is no shortage of evidence of Franklin's numerous Masonic affiliations.

Of the forty men who signed the Constitution, many were already Masonic brothers and others would become Masons afterward. Masonic lodges claim that nearly all the signers at least participated in lodge activities, but most historians agree that several were not Masons, including Madison and Jefferson.

The Illuminati group was the most secretive and possibly the most conspiratorial entity in Europe, but members did not make headway in the colonies the way the Masons did. Washington spoke out against that group, condemning them as "self-created" and unrelated to Freemasonry.[4] But Washington could trace his own family's aristocratic roots, and despite his efforts on behalf of a democracy, he was an elitist who would create the Society of the Cincinnati, which admitted only those with aristocratic backgrounds. This elite society caused widespread fear of a new aristocracy, and even fellow Virginian Thomas Jefferson immediately distrusted the institution. Washington later stepped back from the aristocratic leanings of the group.

On April 30, 1789, George Washington was inaugurated as president. The oath of office was administered by Robert Livingston, who was the grand master of New York's Grand Lodge. The marshal of the day was another Freemason, General Jacob Morton. Yet another Freemason, General Morgan Lewis, was Washington's escort. Washington, the master of the Alexandria lodge, took his oath of office on the Bible from Saint John's Lodge of New York.[5]

THE NEW ORDER OF THE AGES

Soon the nation's new capital was laid out. The location was in a wilderness more suited for hunting grouse than for administering the new country, but it had its advantages. Washington feared that New York would serve as a bad example and allow the money men like Hamilton to control the country, and he did not want to place the capital there.[6] Jefferson enjoyed the proximity of the new capital to Virginia. The city was blueprinted in a Masonic plan, designed by the French Mason Pierre-Charles L'Enfant, who had volunteered to fight for liberty. He was close to Washington and a member of the Society of the Cincinnati. The ceremony commemorating the laying of the Capitol's cornerstone was strictly a Masonic event. Washington served as master, wearing the apron and sash of his lodge. Members from lodges all over Maryland and Virginia were in attendance and accordingly dressed in Masonic regalia. The ceremony itself was a Masonic ritual performed with baptism by corn, wine, and oil to signify nourishment and refreshment. Masons were also called on to design, plan, and build university buildings, state houses, bridges, and war memorials, which they then consecrated with their corn, oil, and wine blessing.[7]

The Capitol building and the east–west axis of the new city were oriented in a complicated way to correspond with the arc of the sun. The dome of the Capitol is "a symbol of the half-arc of the visible heavens . . . where the equinoctial and solstitial points meet."[8] The tradition of incorporating arcane geometry and esoteric symbols continues to modern times. In May 1974 Senator Joe Biden of Delaware made an official inquiry into the astrological symbols on the ceiling of the Senate post office and the Civil Service Committee Room.[9]

The Great Seal of the United States was designed at the same time. It had been proposed that Franklin, Adams, and Jefferson design the new seal, but their suggestions of heraldic devices, twin goddesses, and the illuminati eye of God in a triangle were rejected. Two new design committees would be employed before the designs were acceptable to all. The final Great Seal is also full of arcane symbolism.

The bald eagle is said to represent Scorpio, who is associated with death and rebirth. The eagle holds a scroll that depicts the thirteen-letter motto *E pluribus unum,* meaning "one out of many." Some believe this motto represents one nation arising from the thirteen colonies, but others believe that it refers to the concept of one God over all gods—a Masonic tenet. The reverse of the seal is a truncated pyramid, a common Masonic symbol. The pyramid has thirteen steps, one for each colony. Its face has seventy-two bricks, representative of another number that is sacred in religious writings from the *Rig Veda* to works of the Babylonian *Berosus* to the Finnish *Kalevala.* The pyramid without its cap is said to be the loss of wisdom by humanity because of the long reign of the Church over knowledge. This symbol first appeared on colonial money. The seal also depicts the all-seeing eye, which was a cult symbol that can be traced back to ancient Egypt. Many believe the eye represents the goddess Isis, who is also regarded as a personification of knowledge.

Another thirteen-letter motto, *Annuit Coeptis,* is taken from Virgil's *Aeneid* and is a prayer to the pagan god Jupiter to bless the new undertaking. In Virgil's work the prayer is *annue coeptis,* which contains twelve letters, but the spelling was purposely modified to give the phrase thirteen letters.[10] In addition the Great Seal contains the words *Novus Ordo Seclorum,* meaning "the new order of the ages."[11] This phrase too is taken from Virgil, and in modern times the New World Order has ominous meanings, although its Masonic meaning was a breakaway from the religious intolerance of Europe.

The eighteenth-century Masonic architects of the American nation did not stop using arcane symbolism with the Great Seal. The modern one-dollar bill includes the same Masonic symbolism of an unfinished pyramid topped by an all-seeing eye. The all-seeing eye was on American currency as early as 1778.

A MASONIC FAITH

There are numerous claims regarding just how many of America's Founding Fathers were actually Masons. Washington and Franklin were documented and active members of Masonic organizations, while Jefferson and Adams were not. They all shared a common belief, however—a variation of faith known as deism.

Adherents of deism believed that a superior power created the world and established nature as his law. Masons believed the supreme power was the great architect of the world, and his law was reflected in and revealed by science. The G symbol, which is so often debated, may simply be representative of the science of geometry. Deists, especially the eighteenth-century followers, held in contempt the wars between Christians in which people were killed over minor points of doctrine. Men of science, treated with suspicion by the Church, also held dear the respect Masonry held for science. This new religion, the deist religion of the Masons, found a conciliation between God and science, and the G symbol was revered as a sign of this progress.

The ranks of American Revolutionaries that held deist beliefs included George Washington, Benjamin Franklin, Thomas Jefferson, Thomas Paine, Ethan Allen, James Madison, Alexander Hamilton, and John Quincy Adams.[12] Paine was one of the most outspoken, and his *Age of Reason* is an anti-Church treatise. Washington attended the Episcopal Church but usually left before the communion. Jefferson regarded Christianity as a tyranny over the mind of man. Franklin, as a member of the Nine Sisters Lodge, was a brother to Voltaire, who, along with Jean-Jacques Rousseau, is given the credit for being the leading proponent of this "natural" religion.

Deism did not require a structured religion, nor did it oppose adherence to one. Although Franklin still called for prayer at the Constitutional Convention and Hamilton opposed it, both were Masons. Masonry allowed its members to transcend the divisions of religious pettiness and unite with each other. At the same time, there was a dark side to Masonry.

Like organized religion, Masonry preached equality and practiced elitism. The American government itself was formed not so much as a democracy as a hierarchal organization that could bar representation. For example, the right to vote was typically limited to men of property.

Those "inalienable rights" declared in 1776 were not a desire of all people. When Thomas Jefferson and George Mason pushed for a Bill of Rights for individuals, they had to overcome the staunch opposition of men such as the elitist Alexander Hamilton. George Mason believed slavery to be a crime and an abomination, but there were many opposed to any attempt at ending that institution. But Mason was joined by Virginians Richard Henry Lee and James Madison in overriding Hamilton, and the Bill of Rights was accepted.

Masonry had been born in the feudal Dark Ages when a small portion of the population had life-and-death control over the people in their realm. Liberty and equality were ideals that were not always shared by those higher up the food chain. The great American gamble achieved a result that somehow eluded countries that chose to follow its example.

Writers like Franklin and Jefferson had seemingly declared that challenging government by violent means was acceptable. Revolts ignited throughout Europe and South America and were mostly led by Masons. In some countries, new republics were formed quickly and without violence, such as in the Netherlands, in Switzerland, and among the various states of Italy. In Italy, the grand master and thirty-third-degree Mason Giuseppe Garibaldi fought to unify Italy and place another Mason, Victor Emmanuel II, on the throne.[13] In Russia Freemasons were the primary leaders of the Decembrist Revolt, which was planned in Masonic lodges. In Latin America, Freemason revolutionaries included Simón Bolívar, José de San Martín, and Benito Juárez.

In France, where Rousseau and Voltaire inspired freethinking and Masonic ideals, the revolution took bizarre and bloody twists, turning the country into a mob bent on murder and destruction. Sadly, many of the champions of the American cause suffered dearly, including the marquis de Lafayette and the duc de Lauzun.

In America, elitist concepts and an "end justifies the means" philosophy allowed a handful of men to steer the membership of lodges. The product of such organization would rear its ugly head in massive organized criminal activity. From the slave trade to Asian opium smuggling, the elite would prosper while the rank and file took the risks for them.

PART THREE

From the Sacred to the Profane

◈

IN THE CENTURIES THAT FOLLOWED the arrest of the Knights Templar and the dissolution of their order, the secret society became a powerful force in world events. No longer was the secret government as organized as it had been prior to 1307, but despite its fractiousness, its power had not diminished.

Several European countries and states were in direct control of the knights of various surviving ex-Templar orders. Portugal, Spain, and the not yet united German states serve as examples. In other countries, most notably Scotland, the orders exercised control over the military. The soon to be united cantons of Switzerland preserved both the military tradition and the institution of banking that had descended from the Templar organization. Banking, international trade, statecraft, merchant guilds, and even the average worker's job would soon come under the influence of organizations that were typically closed to outsiders and often above the law.

While these secret societies, which included the Knights Templar, had rebelled against autocratic government, the power and misrule of the Church, and the hostility of the organized religions to science, they were becoming the new establishment. As such they would be as corrupt and powerful as those they sought to change.

Piracy and smuggling were more often the province of the wealthy and powerful than of the colorful individuals that history portrays. The same is true of the institution of slave trade and the trafficking of drugs. In both cases, the religious orders have played a role in the creation of these institutions, and lodges and merchant guilds continued the trades well after they became illegal. The toll that the slave trade and drug trafficking took on the world is well known. The fact that both institutions were controlled by a handful of wealthy individuals whose names were often carved in marble in libraries and at universities is America's darkest secret.

The so-called pillars of society were such a force to reckon with that even the president of the American nation was disposable when his programs threatened the profits of those with more organized power. While there is no denying the assassination of Lincoln was a conspiracy, at least two other presidents would fall victim to the cabals that desired to control the government as well as they controlled the most profitable trades.

Chapter 10
THE SLAVE TRADERS

Antigua was barely out of sight when Captain Hopkins, the leader of the brig *Sally,* realized there was a problem. The small crew was getting sick with the flux, a disease later known as dysentery. The weakened state of the men was alarming, as belowdecks in the hold was a live cargo that outnumbered the skeleton crew. The cargo was a boatload of African slaves who had been captured or sold into slavery in Africa, branded, and then delivered to a coastal port for export. Beaten, underfed, and bound in chains, the slaves usually were placed aboard a British ship for the transatlantic passage. Many did not survive the journey. Those who did survive were then placed in holding pens in another port. There they were fed and bathed, as the smell of confinement was enough to make the neighboring farmers complain. The slaves were then brought to market to be resold to an American trader, beginning the process of confinement at sea yet again.

When the crew was outnumbered by as much as a hundred to one, it was never safe to allow the Africans on deck. The condition of the *Sally,* however, was becoming desperate. Captain Hopkins decided to take a chance; he allowed a handful of his slaves to be brought topside in order to augment the efforts of the crew. The Africans quickly realized they had the advantage, and they began freeing the others in an attempt to take the floating prison. The captain was armed and quickly killed or wounded several slaves and began ordering the others to jump overboard. After eighty men were forced into the Atlantic, order was restored.

The owner of the ship, Nicholas Brown and Company, was quickly notified of the loss, which it had the foresight to guard against with insurance. The Newport Insurance Company, the Bristol Insurance Company, the Mount Hope Insurance Company, and other large companies that dominate the New England economy got their start from marine insurance. One modern insurer, Aetna, recently issued a public apology for its role in insuring the lives of slaves. While that does not sound unlike modern life insurance, the difference is that the slaves were being insured as property.[1]

A myriad of rules on just what could be collected from the insurers often put a burden on shipowners. A cargo of very sick Africans rendered worthless by their passage was not covered. One enterprising captain decided to throw his sick passengers overboard, as cargo lost at sea would then be covered. The Supreme Courts in Louisiana and North and South Carolina regularly heard cases in which a shipowner's claims were denied because of mitigating circumstances. In Aetna's policies, such exclusions included slave suicide, slaves being worked to death, and slaves being lynched.

In 1781 the slave ship *Zong,* which was owned by two prominent merchants from Liverpool, carried 440 slaves from São Tomé. The captain, Luke Collingwood, erred in his sailing directions and the voyage took longer than expected. When disease hit the ship, sixty slaves died and almost half of the ship became sick. The captain ordered 132 slaves thrown overboard in order to capitalize on the insurance. The insurance company, Gilbert, et al., turned down the claim and the owners of the *Zong* brought the insurers to court. The shipowners argued that cargo was thrown overboard to save the rest of the goods, making their claim legitimate. The *Zong's* owners won. Even the judge was surprised at how easily the jury accepted the concept that sacrificing the slaves was no different from if they had been animals.[2]

In New England owners of slave ships took any means available to hedge their bets; they organized and invested in the marine insurance companies that would provide for such losses.

Nicholas Brown and Company was also in part responsible for the early development of another New England business: banking. The company played a role in establishing the Providence Bank, which allowed it to finance its own ships, and out of this institution the modern Fleet Bank, one of the country's largest banks, developed.

The Brown family began its ascent to fame and fortune in the New England whaling business, in which ships sometimes had to be out at sea for years with the goal of transforming whales into spermaceti candles. Needing funds for his business, Nicholas Brown fitted out the first Guineaman—a name given to mean a slave ship trading with Africa—the *Mary,* for the slave trade. In 1736 his son Obadiah Brown signed on as the supercargo, or head trader, on what would become Providence's first venture into the slave-trading business. Obadiah soon came into his own and fitted out another ship, the *Wheel of Fortune,* to join in the trade. The young man then brought the entire family into the business and developed a colony-wide reputation. Virginia planters like Revolutionary War statesman Carter Braxton wrote to the company requesting to participate in a joint venture with the Browns.[3]

For the Browns, wealth led to greater power, and John Brown became a congressman representing Rhode Island; fellow slave trader James De Wolf represented the state as a senator. Profit from the trade brought all the trappings of wealth. When former President John Quincy Adams visited the Browns' home he called it the "most magnificent and elegant mansion that I have ever seen on this continent." Today the house still stands at Fifty-two Power Street in Providence, where it is operated by the Rhode Island Historical Society,[4] which would like the family's slave trading mentioned as little as possible.

The fact that the Brown family fortune was made in the slave trade is a matter of historical record. In August 1797 John Brown became the first American to be tried in federal court for violating the Slave Trade Act. Brown's legal maneuvers and favors from cohorts did not save him from reaching the court, as his brother Moses was the person pressing charges. Moses had seen firsthand the horrors of the slave ship and subsequently quit the family business and became its greatest opponent. His efforts stopped the importation of slaves into Rhode Island, and he helped enact a federal law against it. A bill freeing the children of slaves and completely banning the trade would have succeeded, but William Bradford of Bristol removed the clause on the ban. His rum business depended on the slave trade. The business of his son-in-law, James De Wolf, depended on it more. John Brown died in 1803, before the trade was banned forever.

The profits from the slave trade helped the Brown family reach immortality. Near the Power Street house stands Brown University. Because the Browns were such great benefactors, the school originally known as Rhode Island College showed the family the ultimate gratitude by changing its name to Brown University. Although Brown University is the great monument to the profits of the Browns' slave trade, a lesser known monument to John Brown is the Fleet Financial Group of New England. Brown was one of the founders in 1791 when it was called the Providence Bank. It merged with Samuel Colt's creation, the Industrial Trust, and underwent a name change to Industrial National Bank. In 1982 the Rhode Island bank changed its name again to Fleet Financial. Finally it merged with the Bank of Boston to become the seventh largest financial holding company in the United States.

NEW ENGLAND AND THE SLAVE TRADE

There are many secrets surrounding the slave trade. The profits from dealing in human cargo built a great deal of American, and particularly New England, industry. The trade brought together a handful of tightly knit families bound by Masonic ties and intermarriage. The same families still have inherited fortunes and inherited power that dominate the economic landscape. While being a Mason was often a necessity to get hired by a shipowner or a shipbuilder, the lodges that the workers were welcomed into were not the same as the lodges that the owners joined. An elite layer had once again risen to the top of society, just as it had in the feudal period.

The French Normans did not invent the feudal system. The elite

Normans, however, did thrive by controlling every aspect of the economy. They exported this type of economy to England, Scotland, and Ireland, where Norman overlords impoverished and evicted entire populations in order to establish their estates. They brought the feudal economy to Italy as well, where Norman armies had wreaked more havoc than the Celts had a thousand years before. The same Norman families that had amassed huge estates had created the Knights Templar, which became Freemasonry. Yet liberty and fraternity within the organization had its bounds; membership in the powerful lodges was centered first on the aristocracy, and only when industrial society replaced the feudal economy would a professional class come to power within the organization. The rank-and-file trade lodges, in turn, remained at lower levels in both public society and Masonic society.

Entry into the upper crust of society could be accomplished by marriage, but more often members of one shipowning family married members of other shipowning families. Only the captains of the ships had a chance of being upwardly mobile, as they shared in the profits of their voyages. The captains started as members of the lodges that included dockworkers, carpenters, wrights, and sailors. Unions, which came much later, did not invent the closed shop. The unions, however, built on the concept of the union hall and joined together in quasi-Masonic groups like the Knights of Labor. Being admitted was the all-important first step. Being accepted by the captains who did the hiring was the next step. For this a laborer had to be considered trustworthy and focused on the goals of the captain and his masters, the shipowners.

The geometric terminology employed by Masons was just as important as a secret handshake. Being regarded as "on-the-level" or "on-the-square" meant that a prospective hire was a lodge member. This showed the owners that they had the employee in their control as surely as if they were feudal lords in fourteenth-century France or Scotland. Being included meant having a job and surviving the harsh economy of the eighteenth and nineteenth centuries; being excluded could mean being homeless.

The irony is that where the populace had played such a critical role in igniting a war of independence and creating a democratic society, the elite were still able to retain their roles as the power behind the economy. Masonic principles of brotherhood and equality were lost as the Masonic organizations gave a handful of masters the ability to control their organization.

Americans today have a particular view of history that grants New England the moral high road. The Pilgrim myth tells how the Pilgrims landed, made friends with the Native population, and soon invited them to celebrate Thanksgiving after a particularly harsh year. The Pilgrim reality was that the Pilgrims landed in the wrong place, fought among themselves, nearly starved to death, and were rescued by a Native population. The Natives—not the savages later portrayed in books and films—instructed the Pilgrims in the science of agriculture. The survivors then repaid their hosts by subjecting them to a land grab that would not stop until the "savages" were confined to reservations.

The Puritan culture is thought to have steered America into creating a democracy, but religious freedom and tolerance were not hallmarks of the early Massachusetts colony. Citizens were placed in stocks for dancing, sent fleeing to other areas because of minor religious differences, and frequently burnt as witches not for any religious reason but instead to settle feuds with neighbors. While it cannot be denied that New England, and, one could argue, Boston, was the cradle of American democracy, the region soon became the high command of the Federalists, who replaced the values of the Revolution with those of a merchant-class elite that introduced slavery, furthered smuggling, invented child factory labor, and nearly overturned the Bill of Rights in a short-lived attempt to end dissension.

The American dream was tarnished by the unbridled power and unquenched thirst for money that led those we now call the Boston Brahmins into slave trading, opium trading, and labor abuse. In this Brahmin-like class, members preserved their status through Masonic societies that excluded the average worker and through intermarriage between New England elite and occasionally aristocratic English families. The elite class had access to both financial and political power because of the enormous wealth the trade brought. The same elite class exists today.

The basis for many of the fortunes of today's political leaders can be traced to a handful of Founding Fathers. They built fortunes in criminal conspiracies that were as illegal and immoral then as they are now. They plowed the profits into factories and railroads. When their empires were threatened, they became politicians and lawmakers. And along the way they decided that there was value in public relations, and so they endowed schools from Brown to Harvard, Princeton, and Yale.

THE SUGAR PLANTATION

The world of the Cabots, Lodges, and the rest of the Boston Brahmins would never have existed if not for the slave-trading Brown family and a more powerful but lesser known family, the Perkinses. The Browns developed their empire on the slave trade, on banking, and through the most remarkable act of industrial piracy, the textile industry. The Perkinses went even further. By starting as slave traders, they took New England to its highest level of wealth by introducing the region to the opium trade. The Perkins family united the Whitneys, the Tafts, the Roosevelts, the Cushings, the Appletons, the Bacons, and others in the criminal enterprise that would form the bedrock of New England and American wealth.

It is little wonder that the Perkins family roots were in the slave trade, specifically in Saint Domingue, an island where in the late eighteenth century thirty thousand white planters and their soldiers controlled a half million black workers. Control was maintained by harsh treatment, and this control made Saint Domingue wealthy. While it was ostensibly governed by the French, the island was made up of eight hundred sugar plantations that were often owned by Americans. The island, which would one day become Haiti, was responsible for two thirds of all France's overseas trade. Saint Domingue outranked all the agricultural exports of the Spanish Indies combined. Commerce with the mother country employed a thousand ships and fifteen thousand sailors. Cotton from Saint Domingue kept the cloth mills of France in operation. Historians estimate that in France, one person in five depended on the overseas trade for employment. This staggering wealth was the envy of all the European countries.[5] The Haitian plantations maintained a higher degree of profit than any other island in the Caribbean. One third of the plantations returned to their owners 12 percent each year, compared to an average of 4 percent in the British-owned islands.

The media of the day often supported business against its detractors, as happens today. While Adam Smith wrote of the superior treatment of plantation workers by the French, it was a fantasy, and the mortality rate of slaves proves it.[6] One survey shows a plantation going through four times its original slave population; this means that the act of killing 80 percent of one's workforce through harsh treatment was somehow acceptable in sugar plantation economics.

Workers were poorly housed and underfed. The food for slaves was often the stock fish brought in on the four thousand or more American ships that registered in Saint Domingue. The American ships were mostly from New England and returned with sugar and molasses. The American ships also traded slaves. Industry in New England and France prospered as those who engaged in slave trading plowed their profits into the factories, the railroads, and the mines.

In order for a small population to control such a large population, violence was commonplace. For a minor infraction, whipping and the application of salt and pepper on the wounds was typical. Branding, mutilation, and death were typical as well. A runaway slave could expect to be hamstrung. The act of eating sugarcane was punished by being forced to wear a metal muzzle. Women could be raped without recourse. Documented cases exist in which disobedience was curtailed by nailing a man by the ear to an object. And in one case a slave's ears were cut off, cooked, and forced upon him as food.

Common slave tortures included spraying the slave with boiling wax or cane syrup, sewing the lips together with wire, binding men glazed with molasses in the paths of ants, and sexual mutilation. Death was a blessing to many, and hundreds committed suicide to avoid being burned alive or hanged by the planters and their overseers.[7]

The Perkins family plantation might have been typical of any Saint Dominguan plantation. Although lucrative for the owners, it was a living hell for those forced to work for them. In the *Memoir of Thomas Handasyd Perkins,* Thomas Perkins spared future readers the details of the sugar plantation business and his participation in the slave trade. Instead his memoirs simply mention that the Perkins brothers had a "house," or company, in Haiti, but found the climate not agreeable and so returned to Boston.[8]

The "climate" Perkins referred to was a revolution of the black slaves against their white overlords, in which two thirds of the whites were killed or forced to flee and one third of the blacks were killed. It was the third in the series of revolutions starting with the American Revolution, which then spread to France and to Saint Domingue. The Perkins family and its heirs survived the carnage and became pillars of New England society.

The slave trade was not invented by the Perkinses or even by the New England merchants. Instead it had existed in Europe, Africa, and Asia for thousands of years. Europe's involvement in the African trade, however, did grow and thrive after coming under the control of the post-Templar military orders.

Chapter 11

RED CROSS
AND BLACK CARGO

Modern history attributes the beginning of the European slave trade in America to the Portuguese. The Knights Templar, reincorporated in Portugal as the Knights of Christ, were under the control of Henry the Navigator, the Portuguese grand master who saw an economic opportunity developing as the *reconquista,* the reconquest of the Iberian Peninsula, pushed the Arabs out of Iberia. Henry didn't invent the institution of slavery; it was already thousands of years old when he became master of his order. But Henry did modernize slavery so that he could incorporate it into his quest for new lands, just as he had incorporated the trade in a number of other commodities. He licensed slavery. He developed a system in which the trade would grow and he could collect royalties from it. Yet slavery as an institution is as old as civilization. Prince Henry and the Knights of Christ "improved" the trade and institutionalized the business, but neither Henry nor the Knights can shoulder the blame for inventing slavery.

Aristotle wrote that humanity is made up of slaves and masters. Plato, who believed no honest man could ever be rich, saw nothing dishonest about the slave trade and believed only in regulating its role in the marketplace. Pre-Christian Rome employed slaves in galleys and the proverbial salt mines, where they worked under horrid conditions. Roman Christianity did not question the slave trade, as yielding to Caesar's decisions was still the rule. The barbarian Alaric raided Rome with the aid of forty thousand captured slaves. Later Anglo-Saxons and Vikings traded white slaves who had been captured in raids and war. In Ireland slave girls were an actual unit of exchange or currency, and were valued more highly than male slaves.[1] In an early version of enlightenment, Venice was one of the first city-states to ban slavery, in A.D. 960.

THE MILITARY ORDERS
AND THE SLAVE TRADE

Slave trading prospered all the way through the spread of Islam. While Europe participated in the age-old institution, it used mostly white slaves from European lands that had been conquered rather than African slaves. The Arabs simply made the slave trade more international. When the tide turned against Islam, the Italian merchants and then the fighting crusader orders stepped into the trade. In fact, Italian shipowners had a reputation for simply selling a boatload of passengers to an Arab trader. Such acts led to Templar ships being considered safer from the passengers' viewpoint, as the Templars were more likely to protect their pilgrim passengers. Later the Templar orders and the Knights of Saint John joined the slave trade to fund their operations.

In Iberia, the Arabs used black slaves to cultivate the land and to fight against the Christians. During the *reconquista,* much land was given to the military orders, including those of Calatrava, Alcantara, and Aviz of Spain and the Knights of Christ in Portugal. Estates were also given to the Cistercian order of monks, who saw no moral conflict in cultivating the land with slave labor.[2] With the Arab invaders mostly pushed out of Europe, the Templars' chief business became business. When the Templars were suppressed, the order underwent both a name change and a management change. The Knights of Christ re-created the Knights Templar at their worst. They became an international business cartel with the approval of the government. Henry and his intrepid explorers understood the opportunity to profit by taking over the lucrative slave-trading business. They then licensed the trade for royalties, and ships of the order and ships owned by others but licensed through the order soon plied the seas from Angola to the Slave Coast, buying or stealing slaves from the Arab merchants.

Henry the Navigator had the benefit of being highborn. As the third son of King John I of Portugal and Queen Phillippa of Lancaster, Henry was given the title of grand master of the Knights of Christ. The Knights were one of four military orders in Portugal, all of which were the remnants of the Knights Templar, which had been disbanded by the efforts of the king of France and the Catholic pope. While the French knights were arrested, tortured, and burned at the stake, the Portuguese knights simply changed their name and were born again with the blessing of Pope John XXII. The knights kept their wealth, their status, and even their regalia: a red cross on a white field.

Although he was called the Navigator, Prince Henry did very little navigating. He did, however, pilot his order from a castle in Sagres, Portugal, where he gathered all the nautical wisdom of his day. He improved on the nautical instruments, gathered maps and perfected the art of cartography, developed new vessels such as the caravel (a small, graceful, two-masted ship built to navigate shallow seas and make long-distance crossings), and trained would-be mariners to sail.

Henry's navigators, possibly with the aid of ancient maps, soon rediscovered Atlantic islands such as the Azores and Madeira and then set their sails toward Africa. In 1441 Henry's first caravel reached Africa—and returned with black slaves. The trade was not new to Africa. Black tribes had enslaved each other for thousands of years. The Islamic Berbers and Arab Moors then took over the trade.

The costs of outfitting a fleet and a world-class university at Sagres were great, and the sugar trade with Madeira and the slave trade would defray some of the high costs of maintaining both. Henry also had agricultural projects, dye works, soap factories, fish pools, and coral fisheries, but he was still forced to borrow money.[3] Where Henry's ships pioneered the rest of Europe followed. Lions were brought to Ireland. Parrots and monkeys were carried to Bruges. The king of Denmark was given the tusks of an elephant, and an entire expedition was launched with the goal of capturing a live elephant. The expedition was never heard from again, but Europe's fascination with Africa only increased.[4]

Anticipating the future criticism of capturing, buying, and selling human beings, the Knights of Christ was given spiritual jurisdiction of Guinea, Nubia, and Ethiopia. As "Master of the wealthy Order of Christ which had inherited the riches of the Temple," Henry now had a mission.[5] Europe's entry into the African slave trade became official and was placed under the elite order that not only still exists but also flourishes today, with the president of the Republic of Portugal as its current grand master.

If the Portuguese were responsible for bringing the black slave industry to Europe, the Spanish were more than equally responsible for expanding the trade. Columbus had finally sailed for America in 1492 after years of negotiating for a sponsor. The marriage of Isabella, queen of Castile, and Ferdinand II, king of Aragon, united much of Spain. In the conquest of Granada, which unified a great deal of what is now modern Spain, the government was quick to employ what we would today call ethnic cleansing. The Islamic conquerors were first to go. Next were the Jews; they had thrived under a more tolerant Islamic rule and were allowed to be educators, merchants, and bankers. The third target was the heretics. Even before the 1492 capture of Granada, the Inquisition was in place, its goal to drive out pagans and Christian heretics alike. By 1492 Dominican tribunals were operating in eight major cities. Christians and *conversos,* the converted Jews, were regularly consumed by flames in city squares. August 2, 1492, the day before Columbus left Spain, was the final deadline for all Jews to convert or leave.

When Spain ran out of people to expel, it sent an expedition to the Canary Islands. There the Spaniards met a culture they called the Guanches. With an armed expedition, the Spaniards went to war against the isolated people and eliminated the entire population of two hundred thousand.[6] The Canary adventure served as a blueprint for what would happen in the Americas.

THE MYSTERIOUS CHRISTOPHER COLUMBUS

Columbus himself is of interest more as a man of mystery than as an explorer. His first biography, written by his son Ferdinand, questions even their surname. Columbo, meaning "the dove," was a chosen name, says Ferdinand, as it was the symbol of wisdom and of Saint John the Baptist. Saint John was sacred to the Templars.[7]

Columbus's first service outside commercial expeditions was for the Good King René. Little was written regarding the Columbus–René d'Anjou connection. The book *Holy Blood, Holy Grail* claims that René was a grand master of the Priory of Sion, the secret organization that was behind the formation of the Knights Templar. Certainly René was involved in some very select chivalric orders, including the Order of the Crescent, the Order of the White Greyhound, and l'Ordre de la Fidélité. It is not known whether René played a role in introducing Columbus to the secret orders. More likely the circuitous route that led Columbus to a connection with the resurrected Templar order was through marriage.

In 1477 Columbus sailed north to Iceland, where the Vikings had settled hundreds of years before, and used the area as a way station between Greenland and the Americas. He sailed to Ireland, where in Galway Bay "flat-faced" natives, leading Columbus to believe they were Asians, had washed up dead. These were possibly Inuit from Greenland or North America. Columbus also sailed to the port city of Bristol, England, which was once a stronghold of the Knights Templar and later a stronghold of the English slave trade.

Columbus was more than well read; for his time he was a scholar extraordinaire. At his bedside was a book titled *Imago Mundi,* by Cardinal Pierre d'Ailly, which Columbus had read and reread and whose margins he had filled with notes.[8] He also read Marinus of Tyre, who had divided time into twenty-four hours. Columbus found support from Strabo and Pliny, who estimated the world at one-third less than its true size. And the adventurer read Aristotle and Seneca, who believed the Indies were just a few days' sail from Cadiz.[9] In *Medea* Seneca wrote, "An age will come when Ocean will break his chains, a huge land will be revealed."[10] Columbus also owned a copy of the *Book of Ser Marco Polo* and an Italian translation of Pliny's *Natural History*.[11]

Like the other famous Genoese explorer John Cabot (born Giovanni Caboto), Columbus married well. After being shipwrecked in Portugal, he settled in Lisbon and attended mass at the Church of All Saints. The Moniz-Perestrello family had come from Genoa a hundred years before and settled in Portugal to work as merchants, traders, and adventurers. By the time Columbus reached Portugal, the family had achieved wealth and status. It had also endowed the Conventos dos Santos, where Columbus met the widowed Felipa Moniz. Doña Felipa was twenty-five; Columbus was twenty-seven. Within a year they married.

How the son of a weaver married into a family of the Knights of Christ is a mystery that has never been solved. Moniz's father, Bartholomeu Perestrello, was trained by Henry the Navigator at Sagres Castle and had taken part in the exploration of the Atlantic islands. He was given the title of governor, or *capitano,* of Porto Santo, where he received the revenue from all trade and commerce. His son later inherited the title, the position, and the revenue.

Columbus and his new bride honeymooned on Madeira, accompanied by his new mother-in-law, Isabel Moniz. Her family also had a long distinguished history with roots in the Algarve. Although marriage into the Moniz-Perestrello family brought Columbus status, Isabel Moniz gave Columbus something even more appreciated by the explorer: the books and charts of her husband. The successive discovery and rediscovery of the Canaries, the Azores, Madeira, and the Cape Verde archipelago revealed an ocean full of islands just as Plato had written.[12] Armed with the knowledge of geography that was available to the few who could read, as well as the maps and charts of the Atlantic known to a few and protected by the secrecy of the Knights of Christ, Columbus sailed west.

The New World was not as Columbus expected. First, it was not China, then called Cathay, or anywhere else in Asia. There were no spices, which were at that time as valuable as gold. There was some gold, but it was around the necks of the particularly warlike Arawak tribe, who first greeted Columbus. In search of gold they were convinced could be found somewhere else, Columbus's expedition searched the Caribbean Sea.

Along the way they discovered that the Taino natives of the larger Arawak group on the island of Canoa, a province of Hispaniola, had seagoing vessels that could hold forty-five people. The Spanish called these dugouts "canoes," but they were actually as long as a European galley and eight feet wide.[13] In comparison, the three ships on Columbus's expedition held ninety people total.

An Arawak group known as the Lucayans were active traders who sailed to Guatemala for beads, jade, and quartz, which they used to make pottery. The natives were also capable of smelting gold, silver, and copper.

The natives discovered the "thunder reeds" of the newcomers, from the wrong end of the rifle barrels. In March 1495 in Hispaniola, the island later split between Haiti and the Dominican Republic, the first battle was pitched between the Spanish people and the native population. The island's population would be reduced from 250,000 to 500 by 1558.[14]

NEW WORLD SLAVE TRADE

Spain's complicity in the slave trade started with Columbus bringing slaves from the New World to Spain. At first it was a handful of Taino natives, who were brought to Spain almost as a curiosity. By the time of Columbus's fourth voyage, the Spanish might have brought as many white or Moorish slaves as blacks. In 1505 fifteen black slaves were brought to Hispaniola,[15] but shortly afterward the native population was reduced by smallpox at such an alarming rate that replacement workers were needed. The Spanish viewed a black as being worth the labor of four native Caribbeans and with better resistance to disease. The early Spanish slave trade may have been half white and half black. Jewish captives in the continuing war against Moorish cities and

Muslim slaves were sold in the Valencia market. Black Africans would accompany the Spanish explorers both as slaves and as free men. In fact, on the Cortés exploration of Mexico, Juan Garrido, a free black born in Spain, was given the distinction of being the first European to plant wheat in Mexico.[16]

The Native American population collapse soon opened the floodgates, and licenses were granted even to the Catholic holy orders to import slaves—sometimes by the hundreds. Bartolomé de Las Casas, scion of an old French family in Spain, saw firsthand the destruction of life that Spain was causing among the natives and recommended that blacks be put to work in America instead.[17] Soon both white Europeans and black Africans were making the dangerous crossing to work as slaves for the new ruling class of the Americas. Two hundred and fifty thousand white Englishmen were transported against their will to work on the plantations of the Caribbean.[18] Their treatment was as harsh; their survival was short.

When slavery is discussed today, race is usually emphasized. But slavery, as horrible an institution as it was, would not become a racial issue until after the American Revolution. Prior to this time slavery more often involved peoples who were captured or subjugated in warfare; as such it may have taken on a cultural focus, but it was not along the lines of color. Whites enslaved whites, blacks enslaved blacks, and the conquering armies and navies of Islam enslaved Europeans and Africans as opportunity allowed. The blame for slavery cannot be placed on any one particular group, as the practice was nearly universal.

The early slave trade was an effort of the Old World as a community. The Portuguese and then the Spanish licensed the trade. The sea captains of Genoa bought the licenses. The banking and merchant families from France to Flanders lent the money that paid for the licenses and mounted the expeditions. Slavery was an equal-opportunity exploiter; everywhere, the powerful could enslave the less powerful. The early trade was a matter not of capturing slaves, but rather of buying them. The Africans themselves were an integral part of the trade; remarkably, Prince Henry's slavers even found a market for black slaves among black chiefs, who accepted the slaves in payment for ivory and gold.[19]

The Wolof tribe of Senegal understood that in Africa a horse had the value of seven men. They also understood that in Europe, Salic law set the price of a slave as equal to one horse. The Wolof, who were rich in slaves, soon became rich in horses, and they were no less complicit than the Europeans who came to buy. The Songhai empire in Senegambia was at least as sophisticated in trade, currency, and social status as the Portuguese. Their markets were as developed and often older than those of the traders who came to buy.

The 1520 through the 1540s saw the trade grow to heightened proportions. *Conversos,* or Jewish families who claimed conversion to escape death, found their way to the Netherlands, and then to the New World, where some would play a large role. Jesuits too owned slaves, traded slaves, and ran plantations. From the northern European Danes and Dutch to the Iberians and Arabs in the south, the business was conducted for the profit of those who could build and buy the ships and capture, sell, or employ the slaves.

When the Americas were invaded by the Spanish conquistadors, an early use for forced labor was in the silver mines of Peru and Cuba. The Indians had worked these mines before but not under the harsh conditions imposed by the Spanish. The cruelty of the conquerors led to a much greater mortality rate among the natives. Because the slave owners felt the Indians died too often, blacks were brought in to replace them. The black slaves were destined to work the sugar plantations first in Santo Domingo and then in Puerto Rico. Between 1529 and 1537 the Spanish crown granted 360 licenses to import slaves to Peru alone, and most of these licenses went to Francisco Pizarro and his family. The other licenses were doled out to friends of the crown, who often sold them to bankers. Selling the licenses was as lucrative as actually buying slaves in Africa and crossing the ocean to sell them in the New World.

Although every ethnic group and numerous countries participated in the slave trade, perhaps most of the blame can be laid on the doorstep of a few elite countries. Those who could afford to exploit others did, and in whatever form possible. Often the people who could afford to exploit others had powerful connections. The remnant crusader organizations were still in the best position to participate in these activities.

The Portuguese ex-Templar order, the Knights of Christ, started the trans-Mediterranean trade of Africans to finance its explorations. They later brought the trade across the Atlantic. The Spanish crown, acting through a host of military orders, licensed the rights to explore, conquer, and subjugate foreign peoples and lands. Once an empire was in place in a new region, the government took upon itself the right to sell licenses granting others the right to buy and sell slaves. These licenses first went to the elite families who financed and led for-profit expeditions to the Americas.

THE FRENCH ENTER THE SLAVE TRADE

France was separated by the destructive wars between the Catholics and the Protestants, but both sides would soon follow in the Caribbean sugar and molasses trade. Both Catholic and Protestant participated in the slave trade as well, though usually from different ports. While the French Protestants, or Huguenots, conducted business through a more modern system that gave great power to individual mercantile leaders, the Catholic military orders that survived acted as one great company, like the Knights Templar had before 1307.

Saint Christopher, the first Caribbean island to be colonized by France, was bought by the order of Saint John of Jerusalem in 1653.[20] The order soon added the islands of Tortuga and Saint Barthelemy to its holdings. The knights, however, did not enjoy the slave trade. The slave trade was a physically dirty business and most likely less profitable than the order's mainstay of piracy. The order soon transferred ownership of its Caribbean islands to the French West India Company.[21] After the order paved the way for French participation in the Atlantic trade, individual companies run by Catholics or Huguenots filled the vacuum.

France was still a Catholic country and followed the lead of the pope in Rome in justifying the trade. Edicts beginning with those of

Alexander II in 1493 and the Code Noir of the French king Louis XIV in 1685 instructed that slaves be baptized aboard the slave ships. Somehow the convoluted reasoning allowed the conquerors and slave merchants to believe they were "saving" their victims. They were either killing the "heathen godless pagans" or converting them. But the combined military and religious conquest had an unintended result: The religions of the Africans, as well as their own elite "lodges," were brought to the Americas.

SECRET AFRICAN SOCIETIES AND THE SLAVE TRADE

While the elite European military societies played their part in buying slaves, transporting them, and selling them to American planters, elite African societies played another role. Secret and elite societies may have even run the other side of the business, procuring slaves to sell to the Europeans. In *The Serpent and the Rainbow,* Wade Davis describes captured victims of the western Yoruba being brought down the Niger and delivered into the hands of the Efik. The Efik were ideally suited at the mouth of the river to meet the Europeans. The slave ships that anchored at the river's mouth were required to pay a duty to the Efik chiefs in exchange for slaves. Order was maintained by a secret society, the Egbo, or leopard society.

The Efik chief, called an *obong,* often was the head of an Egbo group that maintained discipline through fear.

The weapons of the Europeans were guns first and organized religion second. The weapons of African societies were similar; first the victim population was conquered and enslaved by force, and later it was subjected to religion. Religion in early Africa was most likely grounded in superstition, as it was in the rest of the world, but it was different in that it utilized more drugs. One of the weapons of subjugation was the Calabar bean, a source of datura, a psychoactively violent herb.[22] The use of such psychoactive drugs was carried to America to maintain order. On the surface it appeared that the elite of the New World required only their weapons and the martial powers of the military and the military orders to maintain order. But religion did serve a purpose; in addition to keeping order, it provided justification for the act of conquering the American Natives. And it provided an excuse for the cruelty of enslavement.

The slaves—blacks and Indians alike—did not, of course, simply forget their own religious beliefs. Their religions, which were often the products of numerous nations, regions, and languages, blended with the Catholic iconography. The result was a multitude of new hybrid religions built on a base of pagan beliefs. The religion of the saints became Santeria in Cuba and Puerto Rico, obeah in Jamaica, vodun (voodoo) in Haiti (Saint Domingue) and later in New Orleans, Curanderismo in Mexico, and Candomble in Brazil.[23]

The glue that Catholicism was supposed to have provided for society was actually supplied in a way for which the Church and the slave owners were not prepared. The same shamans and members of secret African societies who survived the passage brought their own cohesive structure to the New World. On the islands of Hispaniola, Jamaica, and Cuba these groups escaped into the mountains, led by religious leaders and their core elite. They inspired others to escape and join, and they roused enough fear in others that secrets were kept. Assassinations were even conducted by group members who could move around invisibly. The voodoo-inspired revolution that chased the likes of the Perkins family back to Boston was as deadly as the terror of the French Revolution.

The white traders and planters brought Freemasonry across the Atlantic. Just a few years after lodges were established in the northern colonies, they spread south. The first Caribbean lodge was established in Jamaica in 1739. The prosperous island of Barbados had a lodge of its own the next year, and by 1749 Saint Domingue too had its own lodge. The French in Saint Domingue allowed blacks into their lodges at a time when the growth of vodun was at its greatest. The rebellion that brought whites and blacks to New Orleans from the Caribbean introduced both the European lodge system and the vodun secret societies into the United States. The American vodun religion, with its symbolism, ritual clothing, and mysterious doctrines, appears to be an amalgamation of African, Freemason, and Catholic influences.

The black slave insurrection was led by Jean-Jacques Dessalines and Toussaint-Louverture, both active Masons. Toussaint-Louverture had declared independence for Saint Domingue in 1791, and although France's emperor, Napoléon Bonaparte, attempted to suppress it, there were thirty thousand whites among 465,000 black slaves. The population had seen an increase of forty thousand blacks in the three years preceding the revolution. The independence movement eventually succeeded under the leadership of Dessalines, who then renamed the French part of the island Haiti, an Arawak name. Between 1791 and 1794 there was a reign of terror as revolutionary blacks had their own version of Robespierre, Boukman. Boukman used a network of voodoo priests and the mystery of voodoo ritual to incite the revolution. Under Boukman's rule, whites were raped, tortured, and killed; plantations were pillaged; and property was burned. In three years ten thousand whites and an unknown number of blacks fled, mostly to Louisiana. Ten thousand whites were killed, which was one third of the population.

HUGUENOTS IN THE TRADE

As Catholic France paved the way, the Huguenot slavers and smugglers played an even bigger role in the commercial activity of the new American colonies. From the same ports that the Templars once held in the fourteenth century, like La Rochelle, the sixteenth-century Huguenots organized into secret groups from which they supported each other against often larger enemies. These groups were organized through a series of Masonic lodges.

Much of the English and Scottish participation in the slave trade, in smuggling, and even in piracy was organized in lodges and cells whose members protected one another. Masons enjoyed protection that extended to the highest levels in power. Although slave trading today is statutory piracy, it used to be the prerogative of the English crown. The Duke of York organized the English monopoly of the trade, and the largest shareholders were the members of the royal families—who were often at the pinnacle of the secret societies.

The Protestant French did not always have the same blessing from the royals as did their English competitors or the Catholic slavers. The Huguenots were among the last to enter the slave trade, but they caught up quickly. In 1691 a Huguenot in the service of the French Senegal Company became the governor of Saint Domingue.[24] At home in France three ports—Nantes, Bordeaux, and La Rochelle—ended up in control of 70 percent of the slave-trading business.

Nantes, which is up the Loire River from the Atlantic coast, soon controlled 50 percent of the trade by itself, thanks to the tightly knit, intermarried Protestant families of Michel, Luynes, Boutelhiers, Drouins, Bertrands, Grou, and Montaudoin.[25] Islands in the Loire provided suitable harbor for importing cotton and other goods, the final product of the trade that started with African slaves. The house of René Montaudoin emerged as the single largest company, controlling the majority of the trade in Nantes, the largest slave-trading city. The family business outfitted 357 ships in the eighteenth century, almost double the amount of the Luynes family, the next closest competitor.

René Montaudoin was a member of the Royal Academy of Science and also a Mason. His home base, Nantes, was a Masonic stronghold imbued with the ideas of Voltaire and Rousseau. Montaudoin became close friends with Benjamin Franklin and helped supply the American cause against the British. But the rights of man had little application in the principal business of Nantes—the buying and selling of humans.

The role of the French Masons in the slave trade is a prime example of the divisive goals of Masonic groups and of the elite themselves. In 1789 there were more than six hundred Masonic lodges in Paris. They ranged from the craft worker and social groups to the more restrictive lodges with nobles, priests, and even brothers of the king. Prominent lodges included the leaders of the Enlightenment. The Lodge of the Nine Sisters was one such lodge; founded by the astronomer Lalande, the lodge was joined by Condorcet, Chamfort, Houdon, Danton, and Benjamin Franklin. They adhered to no religious doctrine outside of the deist belief that there is a supreme architect of the universe.[26] They acted against the Catholic religion, however, and were instrumental in expelling the Jesuits from France. They were pledged to mutual assistance and religious toleration, which conversely allowed them to control the slave trade and force the Catholic religion on slaves.

There were also liberal Masonic groups whose membership included Lafayette, his in-laws the Noailles, Mirabeau, the duc de La Rochefoucauld, and the duc d'Orleans. Lafayette worked to end slavery and experimented by buying two Suriname plantations from the Jesuits and educating his own slaves in preparation for their freedom.

Perhaps the greatest irony is that the Masonic-inspired revolution backfired against the membership's nobles and elite. A decade before the Reign of Terror would count thousands of heads lost to the guillotine, Masonic-linked families like the Montaudoins came to the aid of the new experiment in democracy.

René Montaudoin's family enterprise might have provided an example to the American captains of the slave and textile industries. Montaudoin donated money to build the Nantes hospital and plowed much of his wealth into factories where cotton was processed. Members of the De Wolf family of Bristol, Rhode Island, were classic imitators, financing the textile industry of New England with the money earned in the slave trade.

Although the motive of the French in the slave trade was primarily profit, their actions took on political and religious overtones. The French Huguenots had numerous enemies, and the Catholic Church presented the greatest threat. French Freemasons brought blacks into the lodges as a way of keeping the groups from becoming Catholic. When Britain went to war with American colonies, France saw an opportunity to hurt its long-term enemy.[27]

THE ENGLISH SLAVE TRADERS

The English were latecomers in the exploration of the New World. After a very brief effort employing John Cabot to sail the coast in 1497, the English waited more than a hundred years, until the time of Queen Elizabeth I, before conducting further exploration. Elizabeth was surrounded by a court of adventurers and alchemists, who advised the queen to participate in the conquest.

Elizabeth's reign began shortly after the death of the Catholic queen Mary I. Mary's death had ended a tense struggle between Catholic and Protestant factions over the throne. Elizabeth's father, Henry VIII, had an unusual propensity for marrying and then dispensing with his wives. One of them, Anne Boleyn, was Elizabeth's mother. Boleyn was accused of the crime of fornication and was beheaded, making Elizabeth illegitimate. That status was not important to the family of the Duke of Northumberland, who wanted a Protestant ruler. The duke and his group attempted a coup to put Elizabeth on the throne instead of Henry's other daughter, Mary. The so-called Dudley Conspiracy ended badly for the twenty conspirators; they were sent to the Tower, some to be executed and others to be imprisoned. Elizabeth, however, remained physically unharmed, but the affair made her almost paranoid.

A few weeks after Mary's death, on a precise day (January 15, 1559) picked by Elizabeth's astrologer, Dr. John Dee, Elizabeth was made queen of England. She had been drawn to the occult since childhood, and it was one commonality she shared with her father. Her long-term friend and rumored lover Robert Dudley introduced Elizabeth to Dee. Dee had been hired by the Duke of Northumberland to teach science to his two sons.

Dee's reputation as a sorcerer grew from his school days, when in the middle of a Greek play at Cambridge he displayed an ability to levitate a large scarab. The year he graduated, he was imprisoned as a sorcerer. The short imprisonment did not hurt his chances at gainful employment; he soon found himself a favorite of Elizabeth's court and was given a home called Mortlake.

At Mortlake the cabalist, alchemist, and mathematician amassed a library of four thousand volumes, the largest in England. Dee's library would be used by two of England's greatest chroniclers, Hakluyt and

Holinshed. To Dee there was no divide between science and magic. He displayed a magic mirror that mystified all but would not allow anyone to reveal what he or she had seen. A maid reported that she had seen a cloud of bees swarm downstairs from his chambers, plainly familiars of the doctor.

Dee introduced Elizabeth to Francis Kelly, who claimed to be able to transmute metals into gold. Elizabeth hired him to avoid taxing her subjects.

Dee persuaded Elizabeth that she was entitled to enormous areas in the New World based on claims that the Saxon version of the Greek conqueror Alexander, King Edgar, had made. Her Majesty was also a direct heir of King Arthur, according to Dee. Dee convinced Elizabeth that Britain had a destiny to rule as Britannia and that as an island the country needed a great navy. He told her that the Americas were to be the new, Greater Britannia, the virgin continent for the Virgin Queen. Now the quest was on for the new Avalon. Having been confined to her palace, Elizabeth lived her life vicariously—intellectually through Dr. Dee, emotionally through the men Dee brought to her.

In 1577 Dee wrote *The Perfect Art of Navigation* and dedicated it to Christopher Hatton, who financed the maritime adventures of Elizabeth's court. Elizabeth gathered together Sir Francis Drake and Sir Walter Raleigh. Drake changed the name of his ship to the *Golden Hind,* which was the heraldic device on Hatton's family crest. Drake was then set loose to plunder the Spanish Main and claim lands for Elizabeth. He brought her an emerald-studded crown, a diamond cross, and a share in the 235,000 pounds' worth of plunder from Spain. Her share alone exceeded her annual royalties.

Drake is regarded as one of the greatest English sea captains of all time. His exploits as a navigator brought Britain into the world-encircling role of Britannia, the empire. Drake declared northern California to be Nova Albion, and claimed it for Elizabeth. His exploits as a privateer—a pirate with permission—helped finance further voyages and added to the coffers of the English kingdom. The Virgin Queen was quick to catch on to the ways of the world. She licensed trade, conquest, and piracy. The risks were small, unless one includes war with Spain. The Spanish were indignant over the raids on their shipping and encroachment on their new lands, and so they threatened to invade England. Elizabeth's chief conjurer, John Dee, put a hex on the Spanish Armada, which is believed to have brought bad weather and the English victory. Elizabeth gave licenses to Dr. Dee, who at one time had the patent to all American lands north of 50 degrees latitude. The queen also licensed explorers John Davis and Walter Raleigh to find a northwest passage to China and India.

Sir Walter Raleigh was a maverick. Alternately in and out of favor with the queen, Raleigh was renowned for his bravado, energy, and intelligence. For Elizabeth and the glory of Britannia, Raleigh searched South America for the legendary treasure of El Dorado. He believed that a source of gold was not far from the Orinoco River, which he called the River of the Red Cross, a reference to the Templars. Raleigh believed he was meant to play the role of the Red Cross Knight, a figure in the *Faerie Queene* by Edmund Spenser.[28]

Raleigh did go down in history as the first to briefly attempt colonization in the New World, which failed. He at least managed to imprint the queen's name on the New World, on the state of Virginia.

John Hawkins, a cousin of Sir Francis Drake, introduced the English to the African slave trade. Other English captains before him had been to Africa, violating the exclusive trade claimed by Spain and Portugal. But Hawkins was given express permission by Queen Elizabeth to trade for slaves. Hawkins's backers included his father-in-law, Benjamin Gonson, the treasurer of the navy, and Sir Thomas Lodge, the Lord Mayor of London.[29]

Hawkins had no qualms about capturing the slaves himself or buying or stealing them from the Portuguese. His first voyage was a mild success, but his subsequent voyages made great profits, and for this he was knighted. His new crest included a female African figure.

Chapter 12

MASTER MASONS AND
THEIR SLAVES

From his castle in New York, Frederick Philipse looked down the Hudson River, his highway to riches. From New York ships owned by the Dutch-born entrepreneur sailed around the world. Philipse had come to America in 1647 and immediately recognized that the laws were not brought to bear on those who held the wealth. He started by selling gunpowder and rum to the pirates.[1] Then he moved on to providing financial backing for the pirates' voyages. Finally he graduated to become one of the pioneers of the American slave trade. It soon became a family business, with Philipse's son Adolph arriving in America from Madagascar on a ship full of slaves. With the money from piracy and the slave trade, the Philipse family bought what was once a Yonkers plantation and established more than one mansion on the Hudson. Despite his business interests, Frederick Philipse achieved respectability and wealth. He held political office and was a long-standing member of the Council of New York.

While many of the early colonists came to America seeking religious freedom, many also sought economic opportunity. Loosening the ties that bound society created opportunity. Not every freedom-seeking immigrant needed to exploit others to better himself. But for every Sam Adams there was a Caleb Cushing, and for every Thomas Jefferson there was a Thomas Perkins. The institutions and alliances made in the Old World prevailed in the New World. The system of an elite group that controlled the masses had existed from feudal times, and although it was altered by mercantilism the system still predominated. Men like Abraham Lincoln would carry the banner for equality and individual rights while others would perpetuate the status quo.

There is no dividing line to say where English slave trading ended and the American trade began. Tracing the start of slavery in what would become the United States, Hugh Thomas, author of *The Slave Trade,* found a letter from the Reverend George Downing of Harvard that was written to his cousin John Winthrop, governor of Connecticut. The letter suggested importing slaves into New England and held British-owned Barbados as an example of the profits of slavery. George Downing's father, Emmanuel Downing, of Salem, also wrote to Winthrop suggesting the same. New England merchants had discovered that the trade was a lucrative business, even though the area itself had little need for imported labor. Massachusetts had only about a hundred slaves in the seventeenth century. But ships owned by Massachusetts firms would move tens of thousands of slaves for profit.

The most successful American slave traders had relationships in Europe. As the slave trade grew in Europe, the English port of Liverpool went from a fishing village to a first-rate seaport. Four families dominated the trade; the wealthiest was Foster Cunliffe, who had four ships that sailed for Africa each year. His wealth grew from the trade and he was elected mayor. The American headquarters of the Cunliffe trading business was at Oxford, Maryland, where Cunliffe's American agent was the father of Robert Morris, the chief financier of the American Revolution.

Just as many American fortunes are founded on the slave trade, opium running, and smuggling, so are many of England's. The slave trade grew in leaps and bounds in Britain and two cities, Bristol and Liverpool, became hot spots for the trade. Bristol had become an important seaport during the Crusades, and Templar ships controlled the industry there. When the slave trade exploded as an economic opportunity, Bristol's business increased, with her merchants responsible for the yearly transport of seventy thousand slaves. Liverpool's history was shorter; it evolved into a seaport as a result of the slave trade. Prior to Liverpool's entry into the trading business, its population numbered five thousand. After entering the cotton, sugar, and slave-trade triangle, businesses such as shipbuilders, textile mills, and supporting industries enlarged the tiny port and its surrounding towns to nearly one million people.

Prominent English families who controlled the trade included the Leylands, Ingrams, Cunliffes, Tarletons, Claytons, Bolds, Kennions, and Banastres. These families started the city's banks and industries, many of which survive today.[2] Not much was done to conceal the ugly business; even the Liverpool city exchange building depicted African heads and elephants.

New England's first slave-trading ship came from the seaport city of Marblehead, but it was built in Salem and was registered there. The *Desire* did not pioneer the trade to Africa but simply sailed to the West Indies and returned with slaves for sale in Connecticut.[3] Marblehead and Salem were capitals of a sea-trading empire that spanned the seven seas. Those who took part in the trade were firmly connected by the Masonic lodge system. In fact, a Marblehead lodge carried American Masonry to China, where in the heyday of opium trading Massachusetts had a beachhead.

The lodges of the Massachusetts seamen were often fraternal and would admit shipowners and common laborers, but as the owners became wealthy, they often gravitated to more prestigious lodges. Within a generation or two they frequently moved to Boston. Colonial Masonry rose above the divisive factors such as religion and color, but it reinforced the barrier between the rich and the poor.[4]

Boston's first families soon entered the trade. Peter Faneuil, a Mason and a Huguenot, was an active trader. He was joined by the Belchers, the Cabots, and the Waldos. While the customers of the slave trade were the southern plantations, the shippers were New Englanders. Modern Boston tries to downplay its role in the slave trade, with Massachusetts historians pointing the finger at its neighbor Rhode Island. Historian Samuel Morison claims, "The 'Guinea trade' had never been an important line of commerce in Massachusetts,"[5] yet at the same time he admits that Salem had a regular trade with Africa, selling rum and fish for gold dust, palm oil, and ivory. "It would be surprising if the occasional shipmaster did not yield to the temptation," notes the author.[6] Morison, who was from a prominent Brahmin family, equally warned readers against exaggerating the opium trafficking.[7] But there is no denying that the bedrock of New England's wealth, including that of many of today's most successful corporations, was funded with the proceeds of both the slave trade and the opium trade.

Despite Massachusetts's claims to the contrary, it was involved in the trade almost as far back as Virginia was. Samuel Vassall, one of the colony's first promoters, is on record complaining about the monopoly of the Guinea Company, an English institution, in the lucrative trade in 1649.[8] A 1724 letter from Irish merchant Thomas Amory suggests that the shippers of the slave trade were predominantly from New England. Other historians also conclude that the slave trade's contribution to the industry of New England is much greater than most will concede. The authors of *New England and the Sea* claim that 30 percent of the traffic in blacks was done on New England ships. Furthermore, the tobacco and rice plantations, fueled by slave labor, were the biggest customers for New England's exports: timber, rum, and fish. As the authors put it, "The coffers of some of New England's proudest families were filled with profits from this trade."[9]

Massachusetts might have been the first New England state to get involved in the trade, but as it devoted its attention to China, the state's slavery business was soon eclipsed by that of its neighbor Rhode Island.

RHODE ISLAND AND THE TRADE

New Englanders like to claim the slave trade was centered in Rhode Island, and they are not completely incorrect in assigning the blame.[10] Rhode Islanders, in turn, like to point the finger at the Jews, which is also in part correct. In 1654 a handful of Portuguese Sephardic families fearing a new Inquisition left their country for the Netherlands. After a brief time they came to America. Rhode Island, founded by Roger

Williams, offered religious freedom. It also offered something even more revolutionary to a small group of families: economic freedom.

This handful of closely related families learned quickly, and soon came to represent most of the slave-trading business of the tiny colony. Sephardic families including those of Aaron Lopez, Abraham Redwood, Abraham Pereira Mendes, Jacob Riveras, Jacob Polock, and the De Wolfs joined English colonists like William Ellery, Henry Collins, Samuel Vernon, John Canning, and Joseph Wanton, who also made money from the trade. The slave trade was not the province of Jews, Episcopalians, or Huguenots. It did, however, pay to band together and operate in secrecy. Christian or Jewish, the slave traders had to be connected, at least to each other. Religious affiliation was often the tie that bound. But not every slave trader was from a persecuted sect.

For this reason it was very important to be accepted into a lodge. The lodge system, which was composed of the elite shipowners, made navigating the treacherous waters of both the Atlantic Ocean and New England political life easier. The Newport Lodge was founded by a merchant from Boston, and once it was established it was populated mostly by Jews from Portugal and the Caribbean. Moses Seixas served as grand master for Rhode Island from 1791 to 1800[11]; he went on to become one of the founders of the Bank of Rhode Island.

Intermarriage among Newport's first families tightened the bonds, as it did among the Boston merchant elite. But intermarriage did not mean marrying within one's race or religion; it meant marrying within one's caste. A Protestant could marry a Jew as long as they were both from the same station in life. Shipowner, sea captain, and merchant were three titles within the higher caste of Rhode Island life.

In America, Jews in general did not suffer the degree of hostility that they encountered in Europe. While in many countries Masonry rejected Jews, and at least one still does, in America Masonry welcomed them. Moses Michael Hay, a Portuguese Sephardic Jew, was instrumental in bringing Scottish Rite Masonry to America, and Paul Revere, a Huguenot, was his deputy grand master. Hay was also instrumental in founding the Bank of Boston.

Not all of the men who were instrumental in fomenting rebellion were Masons. Sam Adams, for example, used the taverns where lodges met as a means of getting mob support. He was very much against the slave trade and refused the gift of a slave. John Adams, too, declared that any slave who entered his house was a free man. He was against the trade and was an outspoken critic of Masonry; the cronyism it bred allowed many to be above the law.

Among Rhode Island's Jewish merchants, Aaron Lopez was possibly the most famous, with thirty ships to his credit. After fleeing a new wave of inquisitorial zeal in Portugal, Lopez arrived in Newport in the 1750s with a second group of Sephardic Jews. He made contacts rapidly in Boston, Charleston, New York, and Jamaica, and began trading rum, furniture, candles, and slaves. In 1775 he was the single biggest taxpayer in the state and had an estate in British Antigua as well. This was Newport's golden age of trade, and Lopez was Newport's most successful merchant. His family takes credit for building Newport's famed Touro Synagogue and for introducing the sperm-oil industry to America. Before his ships went to Africa in search of black slaves, his fleet plied the oceans hunting for whales. A collection of his papers, including ship's manifests, receipt books, and various records, fills 147 volumes and is preserved today.

Rhode Island has been called an American Venice, a tiny area unsuitable for farming but by nature a trading mecca. The state's industry would benefit from the slave trade in other ways. It may have been the center of the rum business, with thirty rum distilleries depending on the triangular trade that depended on African slaves. The rum, sugar, and slave businesses all evolved around each other, which kept Rhode Island prominent in the slave trade. Author Jay Coughtry in his book *The Notorious Triangle* estimates that a hundred thousand Africans were taken aboard more than nine hundred ships registered to Rhode Island owners.

Many families descended from slave traders would later destroy family documents and alter others to absolve the family from guilt. Their wealth and power were never diluted, and many prominent names built their fame on the triangle trade. Traders included the Wanton family, whose Joseph Wanton would be remembered as the fourth governor of Rhode Island; Abraham Redwood, benefactor of the Redwood Library; John Bannister, owner of Bannister's Wharf; Samuel and William Vernon; Philip Wilkinson; and Stephen d'Ayrault.

One family that was extremely wealthy and prominent because of the trade and thus could not erase the past was the De Wolfs. They came to Rhode Island through the Caribbean. Marc Antoine De Wolf, whose migration started in Portugal and proceeded to Holland, Guadeloupe, and finally Bristol, Rhode Island, married the English immigrant Abigail Potter. Bristol was the namesake of England's largest slave port, and there De Wolf was introduced to the trade as a captain on the ship of his brother-in-law, Simeon Potter. Potter traded slaves and rum in the Caribbean, and De Wolf learned quickly.

With his eight sons following De Wolf into the slave business, his extended family may have been responsible for a quarter of Rhode Island's slaving expeditions. Not everyone in his family was happy with the business, however; his youngest son, Levi, was so disgusted after one slaving voyage that he resigned from the family firm. But others showed no signs of dissension. One of Levi's brothers was famous for throwing a slave who had smallpox into the ocean.

Rhode Island had attempted to stop the trade and took several actions against the De Wolf and Brown clans. When a slave ship was confiscated, the slavers united to help the owner to buy it at a rigged auction. When the government sent agents to correct the abuses, they were hauled away or beaten. When the federal government sent a special prosecutor, John Leonard, to try a slave trade case against James De Wolf, a Rhode Island jury failed to convict the trader. Winning the case was not enough, though, and De Wolf sent his own agents to Washington, D.C., to deliver a message. They beat Leonard on the courthouse steps.

The Bristol and Newport trade went on long after it was illegal. James De Wolf quit in 1808, but his brother George continued until

1820, twelve years after the national ban. James married the daughter of William Bradford, who owned a rum distillery and served in the U.S. Senate. He put his slave trade profits into textile mills and became owner of the Arkwright Manufacturing Company, which survived into modern times and is currently part of a Dutch company.

The De Wolf family would also be remembered for founding one of the first New England insurance firms. The firm insured both the slave ships and the "cargo." Today the De Wolfs' imposing mansion, Linden Place in Bristol, is a tourist attraction. It was built in 1810 by General George De Wolf, who moved his headquarters to Cuba and continued growing his fortune in plantations, the slave trade, and West Indian piracy. In 1825, when the sugar crop failed in Cuba, George abandoned his mansion and skipped out of Rhode Island ahead of his creditors.

The family home changed hands several times, but each time to a different De Wolf. Theodora De Wolf married Christopher Colt, the brother of the famous handgun manufacturer, and had six children with him. After Theodora's death, Samuel Colt bought out his brother's interest and remained in the house. Samuel Colt is also credited with founding the Industrial Trust Company, which merged with Fleet National Bank, now called Fleet Boston Financial, one of the largest banks in New England. Samuel P. Colt, Samuel Colt's nephew and Theodora's son, became a prosperous lawyer in New England and handled the Vanderbilt estate. He is also remembered for merging small rubber companies to create U.S. Rubber, which later became Uniroyal.

Rhode Island remained a closed society long after the slave trade was history. Membership in a Masonic lodge appears to have been a requirement for political office in the state. Governors David Russell Brown, Norman Case, Robert Livingston Beeckman, William Gregory, Charles Kimball, Herbert Warren Ladd, and Frank Licht were all Masons, as were and are numerous Rhode Island senators, congressmen, and other officeholders.

PATRIOTS AND PROFITS

It is often said that New England was the core of the Revolution. Those hurt by the restrictive trade covenants of the mother country were the merchants and traders. The early stages of rebellion are traced to the Stamp Act and other mercantile edicts. In 1764, when Britain tried to raise the price of sugar and molasses, the merchants and shipowners of Massachusetts banded together to oppose the action. Such commodities were essential to the slave trade, which was vital to New England commerce. Colonial shipping employed four thousand seamen in New England and was responsible for thousands of peripheral occupations. The Cabot and Russell families of Boston were two of the largest shippers. George Cabot was an Anglophile and a staunch Federalist whose family wealth was built on merchant shipping. He served as a senator from Massachusetts and was appointed the first secretary of the navy but declined the post. Although many of those who sought independence for the colonies were made wealthy through the slave trade, others were opposed to it.

The success of the Revolution may have depended on the money and connections of the merchants, but its ideals were not dependent on the merchants whose politics would carefully straddle the proverbial fence until a decision was forced.

NEW YORK IN THE TRADE

The numbers of slave ships sailing from New York were small compared to those of the New England states. But the wealth of the New Yorkers who prospered through the trade is at least as great. The trade was restricted to the elite families that had often been among the feudal overlords from the colony's earliest days. The intermarried elite core that brought the Scottish Livingston family together with their Dutch neighbors the Schuylers was joined by the Philipses, Thomas Francis Lewis, the Beeckmans, the Marstons, the Van Hornes, the van Cortlandts, and the Walters. Until the American Revolution, the wealth of the

Philipse family might have put them among the top ten in the colonies.

Frederick Philipse had arrived with Peter Stuyvesant as a master builder for the West India Company. Philipse exploited the valuations of native wampum, bought land, and invested in trade from the beginning. His backing of pirate voyages may have been among his greatest ventures, and he would even marry the widow of another transatlantic trader. Philipse's slave trade was just one part of his vast operation. By 1693 the Philipse lands stretched twenty-one miles along the Hudson, for a total of ninety-two thousand acres.

Philip Philipse, an heir to Frederick's fortune, married Margaret Marston, thus linking another powerful family to his own. The Marstons owned land on Wall Street as well as the huge Prospect Farm, a country estate near what is now Eighty-fifth Street. The Marstons too were a mercantile family, and as slave traders they would keep slaves on their Manhattan estate. Margaret's father, Nathaniel, was active in the Anglican Church and is buried in the family vault in Trinity Church, a Manhattan landmark. His portrait in the Museum of the City of New York depicts him with his ledger book, a reference to his participation in the China trade.

Although the volume of ships owned by New Yorkers was less than that of New Englanders, their role might have been just as great. Even after slavery was made illegal, ships owned by New Yorkers were found conducting an Africa-to-Cuba business. In 1859 eighty-five ships from New York City were supposedly working in the Cuban slave trade. The proceeds were used to add "to the treasuries of political organizations" and "carry elections" in nearby states.[12]

Only a few of those in the trade owned slaves themselves. Robert Livingston was one of these people. As the elected speaker of the New York provincial assembly in 1718, business kept Livingston in Albany while his wife, Alida, managed their plantation. One letter Robert received from Alida requested that he find old shoes for the Palatines and slaves, who were barefoot. Robert Livingston is one of the few New Yorkers who actually tried farming with black slaves, and when the experiment did not work the Livingstons kept the slaves as servants.

Another letter shows Robert buying a Negro girl for his son Philip.[13]

As early as 1690 Robert Livingston had an interest in a Dutch ship that sailed to Madagascar, then Barbados, and finally Virginia. In the seventeenth and eighteenth centuries, there was still prejudice against the Scots, even in the melting pot of New York. In order to rise above one's station, the ticket was to marry into a Dutch family, comprising the aristocracy of New York. At the peak of the slave-trading business owned by Philip Livingston, Robert's son, the merchant endowed Yale's first professor's chair.

Alexander Hamilton, the illegitimate son of a Scottish plantation owner in the Caribbean, followed Livingston's road to fame and fortune by marrying a Dutch woman, Elizabeth Schuyler. He became a Freemason for the connections it offered. After the war the fact of his low birth was completely forgotten, as he became a member of the elite Society of Cincinnati.

Hamilton became the antithesis of what Thomas Jefferson held as a role model for the country-in-formation. Like Jefferson, Hamilton owned slaves and called for their freedom; unlike Jefferson, who targeted New York as a city of money-grubbers, Hamilton's lifetime ambition was to found a bank. Hamilton understood that he who controls the money has the most power. George Washington appointed Hamilton the first secretary of the treasury. His first act was to announce that the debts of the new country were to be paid. It was ostensibly a noble idea, but one that was built on an early version of insider trading. Hamilton and his cohorts bought up as much of the war debt as possible at a rate of pennies on the dollar. They were made wealthy when these were paid. Many cried foul at this action, yet Hamilton was a proponent of power without limitation and despised the checks-and-balances system.

Hamilton then founded New York's first bank, the Bank of New York, in 1784 and brought in three other Scots to fill the board. Another early New York bank, the Manhattan Company, was founded by Aaron Burr, who promptly loaned himself a fortune. The Manhattan Company was seized in a hostile takeover by Hamilton's allies—the

Livingstons—who ousted Burr. A war between Hamilton and Burr ended in the infamous duel that left Hamilton dead, Burr a fugitive, and the Stock Exchange (the Tontine Coffee House, at that time) closed for a day. The bank survived the scandal and is still alive and well today under the new name Chase Manhattan.

America's Scottish immigrants were tightly knit through Masonry and other connections and were particularly adept at using these connections to organize syndicates, companies, and institutions. Another Scotsman and merchant, Archibald Gracie, started the first savings bank in New York. He had emigrated from Dumfries in 1784, and within two decades the sea trade made him one of New York's wealthiest citizens. Gracie is described as fabulously wealthy, and there were probably fewer than five men in New York whose fortunes could rival his. Today the Gracie mansion serves as the home of New York City's mayors. Neighbor of the Astors, Rhinelanders, Crugers, and Schermerhorns, Gracie's parties were legend, and the New York glitterati, including Alexander Hamilton, James Fenimore Cooper, and Washington Irving, were frequent guests. In addition, Gracie is often given credit for developing New York as a seaport.

Scotsmen played a key role in establishing banks in Europe as well. The Bank of England was founded in 1694 by William Paterson, a farm-born Scotsman who had a vision of a world banking system controlled by central banks. That system is in place today. Paterson is also remembered as the promoter of the ill-fated Darien scheme, in which many Scotsmen died (see chapter 4), which Livingston would find himself connected to by marriage. Another son of Scotland, John Law, was born around the same time as Paterson and left his homeland for France, where he started the Banque Générale. The bank brought prosperity to France as it made trade more viable. Law, however, lost his proverbial shirt in his own American adventure. He combined the bank with the Mississippi Company, which he established to develop the Louisiana territories in America. The venture ended in bankruptcy and with Law fleeing for his life.

Scots even brought the word *dollar* into the English language. King

James VI introduced a thirty-shilling coin that became known as the sword dollar because of the design. The Scots used the term *dollar* to distinguish their currency from that of their overbearing neighbor to the south. The word took on an anti-English, independent connotation, which the Scots brought with them to the Americas.

PENNSYLVANIA

The first Continental Congress was held in Philadelphia, one of the colonies' most important port cities. The meeting was attended by many in the slave trade. While Pennsylvania was not a plantation state and Philadelphia was not as active in the trade as some colonies, its merchants did participate. Thomas Willing, of the Willing and Morris firm, was one of the merchants in attendance. His partner, Morris, represented one of Europe's largest slave merchants, Foster Cunliffe. Philip Livingston, whose slave ship the *Wolf* plied the Atlantic, also attended. Present from the South were plantation owners including future president Madison, George Mason of Virginia, and Henry Laurens of South Carolina.

Philadelphia's Society of Friends, also called the Quakers, did not approve of the trafficking of human lives. However, some individual Quakers did make profits from the trade. Friends involved in slave trading included William Frampton, who carried the first slaves to Philadelphia, as well as James Claypole, Jonathan Dickinson, and Isaac Norris. Even the always-industrious Benjamin Franklin, who was a friend to the Montaudoin family, considered entering the slave trade. He also entertained the idea to breed slaves, rather than import them, in Florida.

The City of Brotherly Love was founded by William Penn, whose Quaker beliefs earned him the enmity of his own father. In England Penn fought for religious toleration and was imprisoned in the Tower of London. There he penned his text *No Cross, No Crown* and advised his jailers they had better issue his death sentence, as he would not change his philosophy. After his release, Penn continued his fight and was jailed several times. He finally petitioned the king for a charter to start a colony in the New World. The king, no doubt relieved to be getting rid of the trouble-stirring Penn, granted the man's wish.

Penn was a paragon of religious toleration and envisioned a land where all were free to practice their faith. Voltaire, Ben Franklin's brother in the Masonic Nine Sisters Lodge, called Penn the one who could boast of bringing a new Golden Age to earth. From his Pennsylvania paradise Penn wrote that men were "born with a title to perfect freedom." Sadly, followers of this paragon of toleration and freedom were silent on the issue of slavery, although the Quakers would later be counted among the first abolitionists.

VIRGINIA

Virginia was a planter state, and as such the state's aristocracy was made up of people who had great expanses of land and slaves to maintain the plantations. Its history starts with the chartering of the Virginia Company in 1606 to London's leading merchants, including Richard Hakluyt and Sir Thomas Smith, the son of one of Raleigh's financial backers.

From the earliest days, life in Virginia was tough and the actions of the powerful handful that constituted the authority might shock those who accept religious freedom as the reason for the colonization of the Americas. Blasphemy and sacrilege were crimes that were subject to the death penalty, as was the crime of killing a chicken.[14] For stealing oatmeal, one man had a needle driven through his tongue and was then chained to a tree and left to die of starvation.[15] But the white colonists' inhuman treatment of each other for the pettiest of crimes did not extend to the elite members of the colony.

The Virginia Company charter included the island of Bermuda, which allowed Virginia's founders, like Lord Robert Rich, to make a fortune in piracy as they sailed from safe harbor in Virginia to safe harbor in Bermuda. Slave labor would simply replace one cruel system, servitude, with another. Men earned transatlantic passage by agreeing to work for the planter families, often for an indefinite period of time. The planters took advantage of the system and extended the length of service. London's poor and troublesome were disposed of by workhouses, prisons, the gallows, the military, and this new option, Virginia.

Black slave labor came to replace the indefinite servitude of the whites. A head of cattle worth five pounds in Virginia was worth twenty-five pounds in Barbados, and that island would be a great source of slaves for the Virginia plantations. Unlike the sugar industry, in which the way to profits was working one's slaves to death, the tobacco business featured easier work, and slave families were imported to maintain the plantations for a longer term.

Despite the nature of tobacco planting, which was easier than that of the sugar industry, life was still dangerous for people who had no legal recourse. In 1669 the Virginia assembly passed a law allowing the murder of a slave as discipline for bad behavior. When Robert Carter applied to the court in order to be allowed to dismember two disobedient slaves, his application was granted.[16]

Virginia's first families, like the Ludwells, the Byrds, the Carters, and the Spencers, shared the spoils of office and a series of well-placed marriages to become a new aristocracy. They built huge mansions on their landed estates: The Harrisons built Berkeley; the Lees built Stratford; the Carters built Sabine Hall, Nomini Hall, and Carter's Grove; the Byrds built Westover; the Randolphs built Tuckahoe; and the Washingtons built Mount Vernon.

Masonry united the Virginia aristocrats, and important members of high society were lodge members as well. Although lodge records often did not survive the centuries, the membership of George Washington, George Whyte, and George Mason is without doubt. There is evidence that future presidents Monroe and Madison were also Masons, and the Masons do not claim only one of Virginia's aristocracy, Benjamin Harrison, as a lodge brother.

James Madison, a scion of the planter aristocracy, played an active role in the Constitutional Convention. Like fellow planter George Washington, Madison had doubts about the concept of slavery and worked toward sending the black slaves back to Africa.

Benjamin Harrison, the ancestor of Presidents William Henry Harrison and Benjamin Harrison, and a cosigner of the Declaration of Independence, was the descendant of still another Benjamin Harrison, who was most likely a Bermuda planter.[17] The Tucker clan started with William Tucker, a sea captain who arrived in Virginia before 1620. He was entrusted with trading on behalf of the colony. In doing so he concluded a treaty with the Pamunkey Indians by killing two hundred of their tribe with poisoned wine.[18] The Tuckers also had one foot in Bermuda, with plantations there and in Virginia dating to the early days of the Virginia Company.

THE DEEP SOUTH

North Carolina had a plantation-driven economy, although only one Constitutional Convention member from that state, William Blount, was a plantation owner. Like several other signers, he was a lawyer and a Freemason. Blount was also a Revolutionary War hero who earned the respect of many in battle.

Blount started anew after the Revolution as a land speculator. His threatened finances, however, induced him to take a subversive role designed to lead the country back into war. He wanted to see the new country defeat the Spanish and open the West. For this reason Blount became part of a conspiracy that attempted to turn over Florida to the British. He was booted from the Senate as a result. Blount had many friends, including fellow Mason Andrew Jackson, whom he had named attorney general of the Tennessee Territory. These friends in high places and important lodges prevented Blount's impeachment from hindering his family's political dynasty, which would prosper into the next century.

In South Carolina the elite caste, which built its fortunes in the slave trade and plantation industry, was all-powerful and ran the colony in much the same way as the Caribbean states were run. The first governor of South Carolina was Sir John Yeamans, a Barbados planter who founded Charleston and introduced slaves to clear his own plantation.

A hundred years later the planter aristocracy was in full control of the state, even though the country was at the doorstep of democracy.

Henry Laurens, who was at the Philadelphia Convention, was a partner in the firm of Austin and Laurens. The company was the largest of twelve firms in Charleston, capturing 25 percent of the slave trade.[19] Laurens held some of the largest plantations in the colony and was one of the biggest merchants, handling rice, indigo, rum, beer, and wine. Slave traders usually earned a commission of 10 percent of the sale price of their trades, and the slave trade was big enough that the greatest mansions of Charleston were owned by the merchants and slave traders.

Henry's father, John Laurens, was a Huguenot from La Rochelle in France. He was part of the Huguenot wave of immigration that fled Catholic France because of religious war and persecution. John would send his son Henry to England in 1744 to be trained as a merchant.

Henry's education was furthered in South Carolina by making the right friends. He became a member of the Solomon's Lodge and was trained in the craft by another wealthy Charleston merchant, James Crokatt.[20] Membership in the lodge was very important in being accepted by other merchants and businessmen. Stephen Girard of Philadelphia had also joined Masonry through this influential lodge.

Henry Laurens started the family trade, importing rum and other tropical goods from the West Indies, bringing manufactured goods from England, exporting rice and indigo, and buying slaves from British traders and then selling them to South Carolina planters. He was soon sending his own ships to Africa to eliminate the British middlemen. The profits from his trade were invested in land, and by the Revolution he owned eight plantations. He also entered politics, first at the local level and later in increasingly important positions. In 1770, with his fortune made, Henry brought his son to England to arrange for his son's education. There Henry became involved with the American contingent protesting grievances to Parliament. Once he returned to South Carolina, he withdrew from the merchant life and from the slave trade. This did not stop him from keeping his own slaves, however, who numbered three hundred.

While on a mission to Europe to arrange a loan from the Netherlands, Henry Laurens was captured by the British and spent fifteen months in the Tower of London. He returned to South Carolina to find his business ravaged by the Revolution, so he resigned from public life. When asked to join the Constitutional Convention as a representative of South Carolina, he declined, instead sending his new son-in-law.

After the battle of Yorktown, when England's willingness to support the protracted war was over, Laurens's English connection, Richard Oswald, was sent to negotiate the peace. Oswald, a Scottish slave trader who had appointed Laurens as his American agent, was sent by Lord Shelburne to Paris to meet with Benjamin Franklin. As the merchant caste was an elite minority, it was in its best interest to keep the group exclusive. From New England to the Carolinas intermarriage was the norm of the times. Charles Pinckney was the son of Colonel Charles Pinckney, a wealthy plantation owner, a lawyer, and a prominent Mason. Young Charles followed in his father's footsteps but did himself one better: He married Mary Eleanor Laurens. Shortly after Pinckney's marriage, his career and his wealth soared. He became the governor of South Carolina, and along with his cousin Charles Cotesworth Pinckney he represented the state at the Constitutional Convention. Cousin Charles was also the son of a plantation owner and was trained as a merchant and a lawyer. He too was in Washington's elite Society of Cincinnati. South Carolina's third and fourth delegates were also planters and lawyers.

Pierce Butler was the son of a member of Parliament. He came to America because of the institution of primogeniture, which did not allow him to inherit the family estates as he wasn't the eldest son. In 1771 he married Mary Middleton, the daughter of a wealthy plantation owner. They moved south, with Butler resigning his military commission in the British army. He was outspoken in making sure the interests of the slave owner in South Carolina were represented and served in both the Continental Congress and the Constitutional Convention.

John Rutledge was born in Charleston and was sent to London to study law at the Middle Temple. He returned to amass a fortune in plantations and slaves. He served as governor of his state, and after the war he was nominated to the U.S. Supreme Court. The Senate rejected his appointment because of what was perceived as declining mental health and an anti-Federalist position.

James Oglethorpe, the man who founded Georgia, started his career with the Royal African Company. He became a director of the company, whose charter gave it the right to import gold into England and black slaves into the Americas—for a thousand years. Oglethorpe's company included some powerful gentlemen, such as James, the Duke of York, who was the largest shareholder, Lord Shaftesbury, Lord Craven, Sir George Carteret, and Sir John Colleton. All were involved in the plantation business in one way or another; Colleton was a landowner in Barbados before he bought land in the Carolinas. Smaller shareholders included John Locke, the philosopher whose call for liberty obviously did not include all.

Oglethorpe was a Mason in England, and he organized the first lodge in Georgia in 1733 without the benefit of a charter for the first two years. The Grand Lodge soon came around and warranted his lodge, even assisting it financially. Most of Oglethorpe's family were Jacobins and supporters of the Stuart cause. Oglethorpe was placed in an awkward position in 1745; as a military commander for the English he was supposed to help put down the rebellion led by Bonnie Prince Charlie. His lack of concern earned him a court-martial, although he was eventually acquitted.[21]

FLORIDA

Florida still belonged to Spain during the American Revolution. When the state was admitted to the Union, it had a unique status among the slave states in that it allowed blacks many of the same rights as whites. The polarization of early-nineteenth-century politics would eliminate those rights.

The first black slaves were brought from Spain, not Africa, where they were employed in mines and in agriculture. Spanish slaves had unique rights; they were able to hold property, buy and sell goods, and initiate legal suits. These rights added up to the ability to gain their freedom. Free blacks sailed with the Spanish to America and were part of slaving expeditions against the Taino Indians. After 150 years of being part of Spanish Florida, black militias and black fortresses made up of free blacks developed. Members gained status by serving in the militia, and this gave them the ability to acquire titles and privileges.

Many blacks, including Prince Witten, used such activities to achieve a high degree of status in Florida. He and his wife, Judy, fielded a large amount of requests to act as godparents to children in the community, and they evolved into a sort of royalty, with Judy having a slave of her own. The slave revolt in Saint Domingue was led by Jorge Biassou, who commanded an army of forty thousand. Biassou's brother-in-law, Jorge Jacobo, married Prince Witten's daughter Polly, linking a leading Florida family with a leading Haitian family.

Juan Bautista Collins was another northern Florida black whose achievements stand out among both the free black community and the white Florida colony. He became a merchant and built a mercantile firm in Saint Augustine that developed trading links in South Carolina, Saint Domingue, Havana, New Orleans, and central and western Florida. Collins's agents were able to trade among the Seminole nation, which became an amalgamation of the Creek Indians and the runaway blacks. Collins raised cattle, bought and sold livestock, owned property, and, like the upper-caste Spanish, kept the Catholic faith and served in the militia.

In 1763 the British took Florida from the Spanish. British colonies, especially the neighboring Carolinas, felt threatened by armed blacks so close to home, and the rights and status enjoyed by free blacks became threatened. King George III gave his favorite prime minister, the Scottish Earl of Bute, the charge of picking Florida's first British governors; both were aristocratic Scots. The first, James Grant, conceived of a colony where massive plantations, owned by absentee Scottish aristocrats like him, would employ black slave labor to raise cash crops such as indigo. Grant's own plantation was created in 1774, three years after his retirement from the governorship, and produced one quarter of the entire state's indigo production.

In 1763 American and British investors united to form a slave-breeding experiment. Richard Oswald, a Caithness-born trader who started his career in Glasgow and later became a member of London's slave-trading community, teamed up with Henry Laurens and Benjamin Franklin to import and breed Africans. Oswald owned an island in the Gambia River, married into the Scottish Ramsay family (who brought estates in Jamaica into his portfolio), started his own holdings in Virginia near the James River, and by 1764 had a huge home built for himself in Ayr, Scotland.

Britain's designs on Florida did not last long, as the 1783 Treaty of Paris returned Florida to Spain. Freed blacks who had emigrated to the Caribbean islands returned to Florida and went into Spanish courts to confirm their status. Such status was attainable until the U.S. flag flew over Florida in 1821. The years between Florida's becoming a state in the Union and the Civil War witnessed racism become a reality. Independent Spanish Florida did not require that economic status be accorded by color; American Florida saw blacks as a threat, and free blacks soon watched their status disappear. All blacks were soon accorded the status of slaves.

◆

The institution of slavery was not inflicted on the world because of white Europeans, black Africans, or Islamic traders. It was not the exclusive province of Freemasons, Huguenots, Jews, or Muslims. The blame for any institution that allows the rights of one class to be taken away by another class can rarely be assigned to any group or religion, but as an organization religion can lead the way to elitism. The handful who believed they had the right to profit from slavery caused many others to feel that handful was an abomination in a land built on individual freedom. Ultimately the blame lies in the ability of the elite class to dominate through the institutions it could manipulate and control.

Although most American dockworkers and shipwrights were not smugglers or slave traders, their livelihood depended on those who were. As a lodge, union, or congregation, the rank and file went along with whatever they needed to in order to ensure their own incomes, to advance the greater good of the group, or simply to remain a part of the status quo. Thus the world begets blacks trading in black slaves, signers of the Bill of Rights owning slaves, and freedom fighters willing to enslave others.

Still, the worst was yet to come. Many who fought for an American nation, an experiment in individual liberties, a refuge from the tyranny of royalty and religious leaders, would commit to criminal conspiracies to tear apart the nation. Assassination, murder, conspiracy, and a backlash of racial hatred were unleashed upon America because of the manipulations of a few people. This led to America's most deadly war and to the murder of American presidents.

Chapter 13

THE MASONIC BETRAYAL

In 1826 the New York Freemason William Morgan decided to go public with the secrets of the order. Morgan's "brothers" had him arrested on bogus charges, imprisoned, and taken by force to a Masonic lodge, where he was murdered. Prosecutors brought charges against a handful of the conspirators. The jury was packed with Masons, however, and the accused were acquitted. After a special prosecutor was brought in, a few of the Mason murderers were actually convicted, but the longest sentence was thirty months. As an anti-Mason backlash swept the country, membership was lost and lodges disbanded.

The conspiracy that the American public had feared had simply gone underground. Prominent Freemasons controlled the slave trade, the plantations, and the cotton industry, and through their wealth they controlled American politics—from the North to the Deep South.

The history books tell us that the issues of slavery and states' rights led the United States down the path to Civil War. But most Americans did not own or trade slaves, or even own the plantations that required the work of slaves. The average citizen also did not own the textile mills that processed the cotton produced on the slave plantations. A handful of elite and wealthy people did, and they stirred the public to racial hatred and the Civil War.

The southern United States was one of the few remaining areas that still practiced slavery, as did Portuguese Brazil and Spanish Cuba. As the causes of the war are studied, it appears that the "free" states of the North were opposed to the "slave" states of the South. The lines were not always geographical. An abolitionist movement did exist in the North, especially in states that enjoyed no commercial benefits from slavery. The abolitionist movement existed in the South and the West as well.

In the North some people did benefit from the slave trade, and as a result they formed some odd alliances that fought against the tide of emancipation in the twenty years prior to the war. One such alliance was that of Northerner Caleb Cushing and two Southerners, John Anthony Quitman (the governor of Mississippi) and Jefferson Davis. Although Cushing was an active and high-ranking Mason, his mentor, Daniel Webster, advised him to move out of his Newburyport, Massachusetts, home because of his unpopularity. But the thirty-third-degree Mason controlled the plantation trade and the opium trade from his mansion and had friends in high places.

Cushing's coconspirator John Anthony Quitman was born in the Roosevelt territory of Rhinebeck, New York, but moved to Mississippi to become grand master of that state's Masonic hierarchy. He was the grand master for seventeen years. His power in the lodge and the capitol building of Mississippi gave him unbridled ambition, and he was very active in determining the fate of Texas. Quitman, who was against the admission of any new states as "free" states, proposed raising an army and marching west to conquer the new territory that had been taken from Mexico. It was an act of treason that caused Quitman to be brought up on charges of violating American neutrality laws. The other coconspirator, Jefferson Davis, would later become president of the Confederate states.

The three conspirators joined forces to get General Franklin Pierce into the White House. The enemy of this alliance was President Zachary Taylor, who had assumed the presidency in March 1849. Taylor, a slaveholder, had wanted the southwestern states to be admitted as free states. In February 1850 the new president called a meeting of Southern leaders and told them he would hang secessionists who took arms against the Union "with less reluctance than he had hanged deserters and spies in Mexico." It wasn't the last time he threatened hanging. Taylor again publicly spoke out against those who committed acts of treason. He specifically referred to Quitman and his cabal, threatening to see them hanged for their deeds.

The very next day, July 4, 1850, the president took ill. The day was to be a celebration of both the independence of the country and the consecration of the almost finished Washington Monument. It was very much a Masonic celebration, as was everything surrounding the erection of the obelisk. When work was started two years before, the architect wore George Washington's Masonic apron. The stone was quarried from a quarry owned by a Mason. Twenty-one lodges were in attendance at the monument's dedication.

President Taylor, who was surrounded by enemies, did not realize his days were numbered. Later some would insist that the general who had blazed through Mexico in much greater heat to win a war could not handle the climate of Washington. His death, it was said, was brought on because Taylor drank too much cold milk and ate a large quantity of cherries during the celebration, which allegedly causes a stomach inflammation.

Many believe that Taylor was the victim of a plot. Numerous people survived the July 4th picnic. Investigative techniques may not have been as developed back then as they are today, but arsenic was a well-known poison in the nineteenth century. The symptoms of arsenic poisoning include nausea, vomiting, abdominal pain, and diarrhea. Taylor exhibited these symptoms, yet somehow the diagnosis was an overdose of cherries and cold milk. Arsenic can be easily discovered in the body, as it is deposited in the fingernails and hair. When the body of the president was exhumed in 1991 to test for arsenic, the poison was detected, although not in a large enough quantity to kill him. The test was done 140 years after Taylor's death, however, rendering the results inconclusive.

John Quitman and his cohorts were not hanged as Zachary Taylor had threatened. Instead Quitman was elected to Congress, and the conspirators succeeded in getting their man into the White House. When Franklin Pierce was sworn in, Caleb Cushing was rewarded with the

231 The Masonic Betrayal

post of attorney general and Jefferson Davis became secretary of war. Governor Quitman was exonerated of criminal charges.

COTTON WHIGS

In those critical years, the Whig party of the North relied on the leadership of the aristocrat Robert C. Winthrop, who was not concerned with the slavery issue. Although the antislavery movement was strong among the common voters, the people in Winthrop's class—the shippers, merchants, insurers, and railroad builders—relied on cheap labor. But instead of relying on blacks for labor, Northerners exploited the immigrants and the average citizens. The Whig ties with the plantations of the Deep South and the English banking establishment, which financed the cotton trade, were strong.

Georgia planter and Mason Howell Cobb led the Southern Democrats. Cobb was an aristocrat who owned more than a thousand slaves. Between Cobb and Winthrop there was an attempt to maintain the status quo. The spoiler was a party called the Free-Soilers, an antislavery group that had a poor showing in the presidential election but was riding a groundswell of abolitionist opinion.

The fateful ten years between Pierce and Lincoln witnessed the destruction of the Whig party, as it became obvious that the group was playing to the Southern elite. As the antislavery movement grew, the Republican party replaced the Whig party, and the antislavery movement finally had a candidate: Abraham Lincoln.

As the movement against slavery grew, the opposition to it became more violent and secretive. The Knights of the Golden Circle, which was founded by Dr. George W. L. Bickley in Ohio, had secret passwords, handshakes, temples, sworn oaths, and supreme councils. It drew its membership from Masonic lodges. The Knights of the Golden Circle attempted to create one huge slave state, and its largest membership came from Texas, where Governor Sam Houston was a member.

With its funding from England and its push toward secession, the group would be, in the eyes of Abraham Lincoln, the greatest threat to the United States. Lincoln had thirteen thousand members arrested for disloyalty, with Bickley himself being charged with spying.[1] The Knights of the Golden Circle were then led by General Albert Pike, a thirty-third-degree Mason. He too recruited among Masonic lodges, often in the border states and Ohio. Pike also recruited among the Native American tribes. In the spring of 1860 Pike raised to thirty-second degree Peter Pitchlyn, the chief of the Choctaw Nation; Holmes Colbert, national secretary of the Chickasaw; and Elias Boudinot of the Cherokees.

Before the war, Pike was a member of the Democratic American party, which is commonly known as the Know-Nothings. He joined the Confederacy and was among the numerous Masons picked by fellow Mason Jefferson Davis to run the Confederate states. After the Civil War, Pike was the driving force of the Knights of the Ku Klux Klan, in which he was the chief justice. This organization also recruited among Masonic lodges, and in some areas the local Klan membership was limited to Masons. Though the Klan was started in 1866, it was officially disbanded after three years as the wave of violence and riots incited by the organization created a backlash.

In 1905 Walter L. Fleming wrote a pro-Klan book featuring the late Pike on the cover. The organization started up once more, again drawing its membership from Masonic lodges. Somehow Pike, who had been charged with treason for his role in the Civil War, has been honored with a statue in Judiciary Square in Washington. While there have been modern protests against the statue's presence, there is an equally strong movement to keep it there.

THE REVENGE OF THE SLAVE TRADERS

The Civil War did not just end with the surrender at Appomattox. The final act of the war took place at Ford's Theater, where the president was killed by an assassin who was part of a very large conspiracy. John Wilkes Booth, the shooter, was a Mason and a member of the Knights of the Golden Circle. The conspiracy, of course, was much larger than Booth.

Four members of the organization were hanged for their roles and several others went to prison, but still a wider circle provided financial support. The conspiracy in the Lincoln assassination had as many mysteries as the Kennedy assassination would a hundred years later.

After Lincoln's death, Congress formed an Assassination Committee to determine if Andrew Johnson had played a role in the murder. Booth had visited Johnson's residence hours before the shooting. The assassin reportedly met with the future president in 1864 and even earlier, when he was the military governor of Tennessee. Johnson was one of three presidents to come from Tennessee; all three were Masons. He was the first president to receive the Scottish Rite degrees. Johnson was also the target of anti-Masons, and because the clergy had spoken out against him, he later requested that no clergy be present at his funeral.

Lincoln had basically ignored Johnson since the president's Inauguration Day, and his wife, Mary Todd Lincoln, wrote a letter to a friend claiming that Johnson had a hand in her husband's murder. Congress, however, was no more able to find evidence of a conspiracy than it was a hundred years later when President Kennedy was removed from office by a bullet.

Years after the Warren Commission determined that a lone assassin managed to kill President Kennedy with an antique rifle, a new theory emerged: Kennedy had attempted to have Fidel Castro eliminated, and Kennedy's assassination was the retaliation. Coincidentally, Lincoln actually did instigate a plot to attack the Confederate capitol at Richmond and kill the Confederate president, Jefferson Davis, and his cabinet.

Colonel Ulrich Dahlgren was handpicked by Lincoln to lead the attack. Dahlgren was killed in the attempt, and papers found on his body pointed to the plot's origin in Washington. In retaliation, the plot to kill Lincoln was hatched by none other than Davis and his secretary of state, Judah Benjamin.

Benjamin was a unique individual who started in the Confederate government as attorney general and later became the secretary of state.

Born in the British West Indies of Sephardic Jewish parents, he was part of a large and active Jewish community that thrived in the Southern pre–Civil War states. Benjamin's mentor in the pre–Civil War period was John Slidell, an influential New Yorker who became a transplanted Southerner. Because it was in the interest of slave traders to expand the slave states, both Democrat Slidell and Whig leader Caleb Cushing pushed first to declare war on and then to attempt to annex Mexico. Slidell's connections were very much tied to Europe, where his daughter married into the prestigious French-Jewish banking house Erlanger et Cie. Slidell's niece married August Belmont, who represented the even more prestigious Rothschild Bank. The friendships of Slidell helped Benjamin develop connections in Europe that benefited the South during the war. One of these benefits was the floating of a war bond by Erlanger in Europe to raise funds for the Confederate states.

Benjamin also became the head of the Confederate intelligence. He established operations in Canada, where the South had hoped to bring in an ally against the Union. This failed, but the Canada connection was useful in getting money and in running operations. More than one million dollars was held in Canada for the attempt to attack the White House and kill or kidnap the president. Two weeks before the Lincoln assassination, Benjamin dispatched John Surratt to Canada. While there is little indication that Benjamin knew Surratt would play a role in the conspiracy, the Confederate secretary of state helped destroy any evidence by burning all his papers and fleeing to England, where he practiced law. Benjamin was the only member of the Confederate government never to return to the United States.

The murder of Lincoln was most likely planned from at least the time of his second inauguration, when five of the coconspirators— Lewis Paine, George Atzerodt, David Herold, John Surratt, and Ned Spangler—were photographed together. Booth was a guest of the inauguration courtesy of Lucy Hale, the daughter of a senator from New Hampshire and Booth's fiancée.

Just what precautions, if any, were taken to protect the president prior to the assassination is unknown. There was no Secret Service detail, although Lincoln had a bodyguard, John Parker, a member of the Washington Metropolitan Police. Apparently not very diligent, Parker showed up late and took his seat outside the president's box at the theater. Since Parker could not see the play, he decided to find a better vantage point and simply left his post. Parker then invited two other Lincoln employees, his footman and coachman, to join the bodyguard for a drink in a nearby tavern. Investigators have never discovered where Parker actually was when the president was killed.

There was no question where John Kennedy's security detail was many years later in the hours leading up to his assassination. Nine of them spent the previous night in a nightclub run by a friend of Jack Ruby, Pat Kirkwood. Ruby sent over strippers from his Carousel Club to entertain the Secret Service men, who were still drinking at 3:30 A.M.[2] A telexed warning that the president would be assassinated in Dallas was ignored, and the parade route was changed at the last minute and not secured. The driver of the president's car hit the brakes after the first shot and moved again only after the third.[3] Like Lincoln's security detail, Kennedy's much larger Secret Service was not held accountable for his death.

Mortally wounded, President Lincoln was brought to the home of William Peterson, where several doctors, including Charles C. Taft, were present. Dr. Taft wasn't able to save the president, but he reportedly saved some of his hair, which ended up in a locket worn by Teddy Roosevelt at his inauguration. What went on at Peterson's house is lost to history, but another mysterious death occurred shortly after: William Peterson later committed suicide.

The mortally wounded John Kennedy was brought to Parkland Hospital and later to Bethesda Naval Hospital in Maryland. The Parkland doctors completely disagreed with the inexperienced Bethesda doctors about the wounds and the directions of the bullets' entries and exits.[4] Yet the Dulles-controlled Warren Commission ignored the discrepancy,[5] instead claiming that the Bethesda doctors were right and the Parkland doctors had agreed with Bethesda's findings.

The killers of both presidents were soon found and killed. There were persistent rumors that Booth actually survived his shooting, while the body of a patsy was used to give the illusion of Booth going to the grave. Other guests of the Lincolns at Ford's Theater also met with gruesome deaths. For example, Henry Rathbone's wife, Clara, was reportedly stabbed to death by her husband before he tried to end his own life. He would be placed in an insane asylum.

Ten years later Mary Todd Lincoln would also find herself committed to an asylum. Her son Robert was in the White House when his father was shot, with President Garfield in 1881 when he was shot, and in Buffalo when President McKinley was shot in in 1901. For a while Robert Lincoln had been business partners with some of the people connected to his father's death. Later Robert was shocked to discover documents implicating others who survived the plot. He is said to have destroyed the papers.

The conspirators of Lincoln's assassination fled the scene, first to find help for Booth, who was wounded. The group, which included the soldier Boston Corbett, was caught. Corbett shot Booth, and was later declared insane and sent to an asylum.

Mary Surratt, another arrested conspirator, was the first American woman condemned to death by hanging. Just before Mary's death her daughter, Anna Surratt, attempted to see President Andrew Johnson to get clemency for her mother. Two men, both onetime senators, stopped Anna Surratt. Senator Preston King would not see the year's end; he committed suicide by tying a bag of bullets around his neck and jumping off a ferry. Senator James Lane shot himself months later. While there was evidence that the Lincoln conspiracy included his secretary of war, Edwin Stanton, Stanton was involved in the investigation, which would proceed only after those who benefited from its conclusions were in control.

The list of suspicious deaths surrounding the Kennedy murder is even lengthier and has been the focus of several books.

Allen Dulles, the former head of the CIA, was chosen to investigate the assassination of the man who fired him. Kennedy had threatened to dismantle the CIA. Dulles's right-hand man, Charles Cabell, the deputy director of the CIA, was the brother of the mayor of Dallas, where the assassination was staged.[6] The commission that investigated Kennedy's death was named after a thirty-third-degree Mason and Supreme Court justice, Earl Warren. Senator Richard Russell, a Mason from Georgia, and Gerald Ford, another thirty-third-degree Mason, joined the commission. The Warren Commission basically rubber-stamped the findings of the FBI, whose investigation concluded faster than one could fill out a job application. The FBI, of course, was headed by another Mason, J. Edgar Hoover. With the detractors quickly becoming victims and a favorable media system in place, the conclusion of the Warren Commission was allowed to stand—despite its glaring inaccuracy and the sentiment of the public.

◈

The role of secret societies such as the Knights of the Golden Circle did not end with the defeat of the secessionist South. The damage to the United States was already staggering: More than six hundred thousand men had been killed in a population of only thirty million. The national debt rose 2,500 percent. And the divisive politics that existed before the war did not cease. The North generated further hatred through the harsh punitive politics of Reconstruction. In the South and in states like Ohio that sympathized with the South, a new group of secret societies thrived. The Ku Klux Klan became a resurrected version of the Knights of the Golden Circle.[7] Members fostered racial hatred even in areas of the country that were not previously divided by race. As a secret society, the Ku Klux Klan claimed kinship to Masonry and recruited among the ancient order's members. This time the policy of the elite was preached loud enough to become the voice of the mob.

Chapter 14
THE OPIUM BROTHERHOOD

The use of the drug opium had already been around for thousands of years when crusading Templars were introduced to it by the Arabs. Opium had been cultivated from 6000 B.C.E. in Europe and was found in neolithic burials in southern Spain dating to 4200 B.C.E. The culture we recognize as the world's first higher civilization, Sumeria, had a name for opium, *hul-gil,* or "joy plant," a name that was in use up to 5,400 years ago. An Egyptian medical text dating to 1550 B.C.E. listed a long list of ailments opium would relieve. The Greeks, whose mystic cults used opium in religious rituals, prescribed it for problems such as headaches, epilepsy, coughs, and kidney stones. At the same time, they understood it was addictive. Homer refers to opium as the drug of forgetfulness. The Romans used it as a painkiller and as a poison, putting large amounts of the drug in the wine of the intended victim.

From the Mediterranean cultures of Galen and Pliny, the drug spread east to Arabic physicians. Muslim peoples not only inherited the medicinal uses of the drug from these ancient societies but also held the drug in high recreational esteem; in a land that prohibited alcohol, opium was a good substitute. Opium traveled east with the Muslim traders who preceded Marco Polo on land and crossed the Indian Ocean by ship.

During the Crusades, the secretive sect known as the Assassins used the drug hashish to experience the pleasures of heaven. Such enlightenment prepared them for their missions, as they were no longer afraid to die for their faith. The Knights Templar were soon aware of the

Assassins and hashish, as well as of opium. The knights returned with tales of the usefulness of these new drugs, to give courage, as opium did, and to motivate men in battle, as did hashish.

Opium use in Europe had declined after the fall of the Roman Empire, only to increase again after Crusaders reintroduced the drug. After the demise of the Templars in 1307, there is little written on the subject, but opium remained in demand and explorers from Vasco da Gama, a member of the Knights of Christ, to Columbus and Cabot were instructed to obtain the magic elixir.[1] The medieval alchemist Paracelsus called it "the stone of immortality."

During his travels on the Indian Ocean, Afonso de Albuquerque was acquainted with the usefulness of opium and advised the Portuguese king about the potential profit that existed in buying and reselling the drug. In a letter to his king, who was the grand master of the Knights of Christ, Albuquerque wrote, "I would order poppies . . . to be sown in all the fields of Portugal."[2] It was a lesson that the Europeans failed to take to heart. It was easier to buy Turkish or Indian opium.

OPIUM COMES TO THE AMERICAS

The Pilgrims understood the benefit of the drug and took it with them on their travels to America in 1620. *Laudanum* was the name given to the Pilgrims' mixture of opium, wine, saffron, cinnamon, and cloves. The Pilgrims brought a second opium-based concoction, paregoric, in which the drug was mixed with licorice, honey, benzoic acid, camphor, and anise oil.

Dr. Benjamin Rush, a signer of the Declaration of Independence and a member of the Continental Congress, was the surgeon general of the Continental army. He did much to advance the use of medicines and his "heroic therapy," which incorporated opium. In fact, this therapy later provided a name for opium's favored derivative, heroin. Rush prescribed opium for cholera, for relief of intestinal spasms, and as part of a mixture for enemas.

Like all drugs, opium had its downside. Physicians who prescribed it for a period of four days or less best understood the power of the poppy. An opium dependence goes beyond a habit; the opium becomes as fundamental as food and water, as the user's body is actually altered chemically and cannot function without the drug.[3] If one maintains a healthy lifestyle and uses opium properly, the drug can be part of daily existence; many prominent and not-so-prominent people have survived decades-long drug habits. But the nature of opium is not conducive to a healthy lifestyle. Addicts experience physical deterioration, such as gastric and circulatory disorders. The mental effects exhibit themselves in a loss of interest in both personal hygiene and anyone except one's source of the drug. The body appears to feed on itself, becoming emaciated from lack of food. From hepatitis and liver damage to skin disease and respiratory disease, the body begins a descent matched only by the mind's descent. Forgetfulness, lethargy, and irritability are the daily range of emotions suffered by the opium addict.

Today's modern "improvement" of the opium-based group, which includes morphine and heroin, renders the deadly effects of addiction within days. In the eighteenth and nineteenth centuries the opium smoker started on a slower road that led to the final impact: death. Although these effects were fully known, as they are today, knowledge of them did not stop the trade; it continues to this day.

THE OPIUM TRADE

The cornerstone of colonial trade was the supercommodity. The commodity for Portugal had been the black slave; the commodity that grew Spain's empire was silver. The Dutch would lead the way into the spice trade, creating huge demand for pepper and other herbs back home in Europe. Britain and France discovered the commodities that were referred to as food-drugs: sugar, tea, coffee, and alcoholic beverages such as rum. Colonizing America was not just about finding places to dump the undesirable populations of Europe; it was also about making a profit.

Getting England addicted to Chinese tea was easy; keeping a trade balance became more difficult. In 1700 the British East India Company imported twenty thousand pounds of tea. Six years later that figure grew 400 percent to a hundred thousand pounds. By 1766 the cost of tea imports was becoming impossible to meet with silver. When the figure hit six million pounds, it became clear that tea would drain England of silver unless something was done.

Up until the eighteenth century, drug use in the world was never described as an epidemic or plague, but the British would change that. The Chinese had discovered the pleasure of smoking opium, first mixed with tobacco, which was brought by the Dutch, then in a pure form. The British East India Company cornered the opium-producing market and sold its drugs to willing Asians. In every southeast Asian country where Britain's empire was active, the government was forced to admit Indian opium. The Chinese had the most money to spend, and their extravagance easily spread opium use. Opium was expensive to bring to market, but China had such a large wealthy ruling class that there were enough customers who could afford to buy and use the drug on a regular basis. The British East India Company had found a way to correct the tea trade imbalance.

Today we often dismiss the crimes of the past as simply being "the way things were." The British and American traders, however, should not be dismissed so lightly. "They were not ignorant of what sort of substance they were selling. They knew it was a poison. They knew it was addictive."[4]

By 1836 China imported enough opium to make the drug the largest revenue-producing commodity in the world. It enriched a handful while destroying the social and political structure of China. By this time the drug merchants included Americans. The great motivator, greed, was as powerful to Boston's blue bloods as it was to the English. This greed is the reason the drug trade continues today, and why the Western world, specifically America and Europe, is experiencing a drug epidemic. Ironically, it is the former victims of American and European colonialism that are now exporting the drugs to their ex-colonial overlords.

The British and American traders who took part in what was called the China trade often had little the Chinese were willing to buy. The Chinese wanted silver and raw Indian cotton, and America and Europe wanted tea. An exception to the rule was ginseng; America's ginseng, produced in New England and the Appalachian region, was regarded as an aphrodisiac in China. But the market for ginseng was too small to balance America's demand for tea. There were two alternatives. The first was opium. The Chinese were already consumers of opium for almost a thousand years, but they had brewed it into tea. Like many other natural drugs, the opium tea did not cause the debilitating effects that opium smoking and opium derivatives caused. Similarly, the effect of chewing coca leaves on the Andean population of South America had some negative side effects, but nothing like the damage caused by addiction to the refined version of the plant, cocaine. In both cases the refinement of a natural plant created a substance that caused addiction.

The Europeans created the opium addiction. Shortly after discovering the pleasures of tobacco in the American colonies, the Dutch brought the new commodity to China; the Dutch most likely introduced both tobacco and opium smoking. The horrors of addiction quickly became known to the Chinese. In 1729 Chinese Emperor Yung Cheng prohibited the sale and use of opium in his country as anything but medicine. When the British East India Company assumed control over Bengal and Bihar, the opium-producing districts of India, it greatly expanded the trade. By 1767 the company was importing two thousand chests, each filled with 170 pounds of pure opium, each year.

As in America, the British established trade monopolies. The Indian growers, by law, had to sell to the British East India Company. But the British love of profit was no match for the Chinese edict, and the company could no longer sell to China. Instead, the British East India Company became the middleman that bought the opium from the Indian producers and sold to English and American merchants who were willing to run the risk of shipping the product.

In 1799 the Chinese emperor Kia King made all opium trade illegal. This very act most likely served to increase the profits that were made in the trade, as both the price of opium and the amount consumed increased. The British Levant Company, another nationally chartered business syndicate, purchased half the Turkish opium crop and brought it to Europe, where it was sold as medicine.

British and American ships participated in the trade by carrying goods that were attractive to Turkey and India, like tin, lead, and wool. They carried the opium to China, where thousands of pounds of the drug filled chests that were exchanged for tea, spices, and exotic goods.

Another product the Chinese wanted was fur. This provided a lever for the Americans to lift the British monopoly on the China trade. John Jacob Astor's ships were among the first to sail to the Pacific Northwest, where they harvested the coats of seals and otters. Although the Native tribes had hunted the wildlife for centuries, it took only a few years for the hunting to drive the populations to the point of near extinction. This, in turn, made the hunt more expensive.

America as a nation did not sanction the buying and selling of opium, but it did not forbid it either. The American participants in this trade did nothing illegal as far as their own country was concerned. They were, however, breaking Chinese law, as it was illegal to distribute opium there. Like the British, the Americans could rely on their country to invoke protective policy when China attempted to enforce its law. Both Britain and the United States maintained a naval presence to protect their commerce. China, which had no navy, was unable to enforce its laws on its coastline. British and American traders took advantage by occupying Asian islands, where they kept warehouses. Without ships or a coast guard, China could not approach the islands. Just in case of the unlikely inspection by a Chinese mandarin assigned to customs duty, the opium was usually kept aboard floating warehouses—ships that would not make voyages but simply float off the coasts of the occupied islands. From these warehouse ships Chinese merchants bought opium and smuggled it into Canton or the interior of China.

Remarkably, the opium trade was officially prohibited by the British government, but the prohibition was ignored as the government-chartered British East India Company profited from the trade. The partners of the company were the elite of a nation that could simply outlaw competition and disregard the country's own laws. Henry Dundas, the Viscount Melville, was a political boss in Scotland, and his number one goal was to enrich the aristocrats. In Scotland he restored the lands of the nobles. In the United Kingdom he started the Scottish control over the British East India Company, which had no Scottish directors prior to the eighteenth century. Dundas served as president of the company's board from 1793 to 1801. Outside the British Isles he interfered with business from America to Asia. He wrote the blueprint for opium trade with China, and in 1809 was the head of the Board of Control of India. He stocked the Indian subcontinent with friends, all Scots who governed Britain's crown jewel. The Chinese laws could not be changed but they could be rendered insignificant by circumventing the restrictions. Dundas's cronies used "country ships" carrying opium bought from British India, which were accompanied and protected by British East India Company ships. The company would buy tea with the proceeds from the opium sales. The company allowed Americans into the marketplace, and English bankers often assisted them in financing the voyages.

The Dundas family was steeped in Masonry, and the tradition carries into later times. Thomas Dundas, the second Earl of Zetland, became grand master in 1844 and remained in that post until 1870. The Dundas clan brought Masonry to Hong Kong, and the first lodge in that city, chartered in 1846, was named for their lodge in England: the Zetland Lodge No. 525.

LORDS AND DRUG LORDS

At the same time that England defended its right to distribute opium in China, it took to restricting the drug business at home. The government began monitoring the pharmaceutical houses that were expanding the use of opium in Europe. England went to war twice to protect the illegal trade conducted by the country's elite; the 1,000 percent profit was enough to entice the country to protect the illegal trade. In the nineteenth century the drug lords of Britain were the Jardines, the Mathesons, and the Sutherlands—all Scots ushered into prosperity thanks to Dundas. These families built dynasties that are still in power today, while millions of Chinese became addicted to opium.[5]

The first families of the opium trade joined together in small partnerships. William Jardine and James Matheson formed the opium-trading firm of Jardine and Matheson while still in their twenties. Opium was their prime business, and they published regular newsletters called the *Opium Circulars,* which gave information about the drug's markets and prices. A Brit posted in East Asia could pick up a newspaper anywhere from Patna to Singapore to get the current opium prices for Bengal and Patna opium. In this way Britain could claim to be adhering to Chinese policy, and Jardine and Matheson replaced the British East India Company as the largest trading firm in the empire. But they were fully aware of the horrors addiction brought to China. David Matheson, a young partner, assured of nearly unlimited wealth at an early age, chose to resign rather than to profit from the drug trade.

Jardine and Matheson's early success was the result of working in close cooperation with the British East India Company. The British East India Company had a monopoly on tea, which was legal until 1833. When Britain officially agreed not to ship opium, Jardine and Matheson—headquartered in Hong Kong—provide the loophole by bringing in the drug. The British East India Company was provided with tea, but its ships did not actually carry the opium. The drug was still packaged with company seals to ensure its quality, however.

Jardine and Matheson was controlled by family and Masonic relationships, and like their American counterparts they wore their family names like a badge. James Matheson, cofounder of Jardine and Matheson, had a nephew, Hugh, who would invest opium profits in mining. Hugh Matheson founded Rio Tinto Zinc Company, which is still in operation today. Alliances with the key banks Schroeder's and Barings provided the ability to move on a global scale.

The Barings, who later were instrumental in founding the Peninsula and Oriental Steamship lines, were already a force in international trade when they began financing the opium trade. James Matheson's mother's family, the MacKays, who held the title of Earl of Inchcape, until recently controlled the board of the steamer lines. Before steam was the power of choice, opium was carried by clipper ships, which were built for speed. Two of the first opium clippers were the *Alexander Baring* and the *Falcon*. The Barings financed many American firms in various businesses, including the Binghams and Stephen Girard. Girard, like Astor, was an early pioneer of the China trade, but he was quickly eclipsed by New England merchants.

The British had the early lead in the importation of opium and were often the target of Chinese legislation and activity. This is why the British allowed American ships to enter the trade and often financed them. In this way the British were not directly breaking China's prohibition, but the British lenders and shippers would make money from their investments in the American ships.

THE PROFITS OF THE CHINA TRADE

The British families had been benefiting from the trade for a century, but the Americans caught up quickly. To the chagrin of the British, the Americans went to Turkey to buy lower-grade opium that competed with the better British-grown Indian grades. Americans proved themselves adept at smuggling and grew wealthy from the trade.

A recent book called *The Wealthy 100* created a unique ranking of Americans by wealth and the proportion of that wealth in relation to the gross national product. John Jacob Astor, born in 1763, ranked third; Stephen Girard, born in 1750, was fourth; Elias Hasket Derby, born in 1739, was number 38; smuggler John Hancock, born in 1737, was number 54; and the not as well known Thomas Handasyd Perkins, born in 1764, was ranked number 78.[6] While opium traders Astor and Girard ranked much higher, Thomas Perkins was even more influential, as he brought scores of American blue bloods into the trade.

THE HOUSE THAT PERKINS BUILT

Thomas Perkins deserves credit for being one of America's first and foremost opium dealers, as well as one of the greatest drug smugglers in history. His amazing fortune places him ahead, in comparable dollars, of even the computer billionaires of the 1990s. Perkins's wealth made him a very influential man in American politics and the power behind the Boston Brahmin class. Old reports state that the first families of Boston were from Salem, which implies they made their fortunes in shipping. What is not often understood is that these first families all made their start in the opium trade. The Appletons, Cabots, Endicotts, Hoopers, Higginsons, Jacksons, Lowells, Lawrences, Phillipses, and Saltonstalls made their money by being related to Thomas Perkins or by riding on the coattails of the mercantile prince.

Not only did these families create wealth, but also they then created industries that survived and prospered for decades to come. One industry was insurance. The Perkinses understood the value of spreading risk; they would often be financed in part by the first families of New England, who wanted their share of the area's most lucrative trade, and in part by insurance.

Marine insurance is regarded as the grandfather of all modern forms of insurance in America, and it got its start in New England insuring cargo from basic commodities to slaves and opium. Connecticut was home to some of America's first insurance companies. Many have survived intact or as parts of larger companies, though few realize their foundation was insuring the drug and slave traders in the early nineteenth century.

Born in 1764, Thomas Perkins decided early that Harvard was not where he would seek his fortune. Instead he apprenticed with shipping merchants and his older brother, James, who was in the Santo Domingo–New England part of the triangle trade. Thomas married Sarah Elliot, whose father was a British tobacco trader, and through his new family connections made his start in business aboard one of Elias Derby's ships.

Derby was Salem's most important merchant, and the shipping

business made him very rich. Today he is regarded as America's first millionaire and a trailblazer of global commerce. Derby's father started their business importing sugar from the West Indies. Because this was made illegal by Britain's restrictive trade acts, it was a fine sort of revenge that led Derby into privateering against British cargo ships during the Revolution. While many succumbed to the risks, Derby prospered. In the postwar period his ships sailed around the world, and his *Grand Turk* was the first New England ship to reach the Chinese port of Canton, in 1785. Thomas Perkins sailed as the supercargo, the person responsible for transacting the ship's business, with the ship commanded by Captain James Magee, who was related to Derby's wife.

Perkins was responsible for obtaining a good price for the cargo on board the ship. He would then take the proceeds, in whatever form, and invest them in a suitable cargo to bring home. The trade was not always direct, which made the job of the supercargo even more important. Often the supercargo would receive instructions to buy and sell in any way deemed necessary to ensure the owner's profit. On slave ships the captain and supercargo often conspired to abandon some of the crew in order to increase the share of the profits for those who remained.

The Perkins family had little problem with the morality—or lack of morality—of the trade, as its previous business was the slave and sugar trade in Santo Domingo. In 1792 a slave insurrection in that country ruined the Perkinses' business, so James and Thomas formed a new partnership as J. and T. H. Perkins. It did not take more than one successful voyage to become wealthy, and the many successful Perkins voyages made Thomas both wealthy and powerful.

For the crew who traveled on a Perkins ship, life was not as comfortable or as lucrative. In 1814 Charles Tyng was a thirteen-year-old who had run away from school. Colonel Thomas Perkins, who received his title by serving in the Massachusetts militia, took the boy aboard a China-bound ship; Thomas's brother had married the boy's aunt. If the four-foot eight-inch teenager had expected any benefits from being related to the wealthy shipowner, he soon found out the opposite was true. His uncle John Higginson was supercargo aboard the ship, and the first words young Charles heard from him were instructions to the carpenter to beat the boy. Tyng was beaten daily for minor infractions, for not knowing his way about the ship, and for the amusement of those in charge. He was thrown in the hog pen as punishment. Tyng was even denied adequate clothing for the passage around Cape Horn, and he was handed over to three unusually obese women, wives of a Hawaiian king, for their sexual amusement. Charles Tyng survived his brief stint working for his uncles, and after being twice cheated by them later, he left their employ. Tyng left his memoirs preserving the tales of the opium trade and of the Perkinses' role.[7]

The other men aboard the Perkinses' ship fared better, but the ship was underprovisioned and ran out of food on the way to Canton. This also happened on the return trip. The ship's owners netted four hundred thousand dollars for their efforts, or lack thereof, as they sat home in New England.

While today the memoirs of New England's first families and the museums dedicated to those clans downplay the role of opium and black slaves in building New England's fortunes, their involvement in those trades is undeniable. Shippers could fare well carrying tobacco and cotton to Rotterdam and London, but fortunes were built on trading opium for tea in China. Salem's wives had grown fond of Chinese lacquer furniture and Eastern silk gowns,[8] and when the East India Marine Hall opened, Asian dress was the order of the evening. Smuggling opium had its rewards, and both T. H. Perkins and opium kingpin Joseph Russell became extremely prominent merchants as a result of their shipping businesses. Their wealth gave them power and access to government. Perkins and Russell traveled to France to carry out their ventures and to act on behalf of their country during the Monroe administration. During the War of 1812, Russell was made chargé d'affaires of the United States at the Court of Saint James's.

Perkins was a principal member of the Federalist party and was elected to the Senate eight times. He was also the president of the Boston branch of the United States Bank (in which post he was succeeded by a Cabot). Perkins made his money from the opium trade before the drug business led to open war in China, and invested the profits into sawmills, gristmills, textiles, and the railroad business— including the Boston and Lowell, the Boston and Providence, and other railroads farther west. With his combined interests, Perkins was soon considered the wealthiest man in New England. Many New England family fortunes began with investments in the Perkins China ventures. As a community leader, Perkins did what many slave traders, drug smugglers, and robber barons would do: He became a philanthropist. His charities included the Perkins Institute for the Blind and Massachusetts General Hospital.[9]

As Thomas Perkins devoted himself to European affairs and his business interests in New England, he turned over the day-to-day responsibilities of opium trafficking to his relatives. His children also made connections through marriage, wedding Cabots, Gardiners, Higginsons, Forbeses, and Cushings.

THE CUSHING INHERITANCE

While relationships to the Perkins business and family were the start of many fortunes, they were also the start of several political careers. One of the most powerful political families that had ties to the Perkinses were the Cushings.

In China the Boston-based Cushing family soon became responsible for operating the Perkins family business. Thomas Cushing was already an active merchant during the eighteenth century. As a businessman, Cushing would sometimes collect intelligence on the Tories, but he was reluctant to share it. He was against the Revolution, as he feared it would interfere with his shipping business. But Cushing overcame his fears when he found that he could make a fortune overcharging both the Americans and the French for supplies. Such excessive profiteering was shared by Otis and Gerry, and even smaller merchants did not consider it wrong to gouge the military.

Chief among a cadre of Thomas Cushing's nephews was John Perkins Cushing, who started out as the head of the American *hong,* or house of foreign trade, in Canton. John Cushing's mother was Ann Perkins, and her connections would allow him access to wealth known to very few. After the early death of his mother, young Cushing was raised by T. H. Perkins.

John Cushing started his career in the countinghouse of the Perkins home office, but was sent to Canton at age seventeen to further his education. A year later he was in charge of the Canton branch, the epicenter of Perkins's profit machine. Cushing developed an early friendship with one of China's most powerful merchants, Houqua, who was head of the Cohong, the community of Chinese merchants. The friendship of Houqua meant everything for a foreign merchant. Soon Cushing was regarded as the most influential American in Canton.

Cushing stayed in Canton for twenty-five years and increased his personal wealth by buying ships and shares in ships. In 1830 he retired from the China trade and sold his own interests. He returned to New England, where he married Louisa Gardiner and built city mansions and country estates for himself. But he never fully retired, as he made investments in the Chinese voyages of others. Cushing's family wealth was earned entirely in drug trafficking with China, and his descendants ensured that the trade did not end.

Caleb Cushing was the heir apparent. A graduate of Harvard at the age of seventeen, Caleb Cushing became a lawyer and represented the family's interests. He also became a thirty-third-degree Mason.

Caleb Cushing's political career started in the House of Representatives, and after the suspicious death of William Henry Harrison in 1843, Cushing was sent by the new president Tyler to China as U.S. Commissioner. In China, Cushing did more to represent the Perkins-Cushing interests in the opium-smuggling business than the interests of his country. China, beaten by the British navy in the war, lacked the ability to stand up to the threats of Cushing. The country granted American ships the use of five ports.

Cushing went on to promote war against Mexico, plot with secessionists, and conspire against Zachary Taylor. The death of Taylor elevated Cushing to attorney general of the United States.

THE STURGIS FAMILY

At the same time that John Perkins Cushing was beginning his career in the opium trade, another Perkins relative was also achieving success. The Sturgises were one of the first families of Massachusetts, claiming descent from Edward Sturgis, who arrived in 1630. The family started in farming, but the marriage of Russell Sturgis to Elizabeth Perkins, Thomas's sister, ensured the Sturgis family's fortune in the shipping business. Thomas Perkins would invest with Russell Sturgis in the *Hope,* and Sturgis set sail for China.

Meanwhile, one of Russell's sons, James Perkins Sturgis, was sent to the island of Lintin, just outside of Hong Kong, to manage the storage facilities for all the opium traders. Because opium importing was illegal, Lintin served as what might be called a drop house—a large terminal for all the ships carrying opium.

As the Sturgis family wealth grew, Nathaniel Russell Sturgis teamed up with George Robert Russell, who started Russell and Company, the most important opium-trafficking firm of the 1830s. A Russell Sturgis headed Barings Bank, which financed the opium trade. The women in the Sturgis clan did their part as well. Elizabeth Perkins Sturgis married Henry Grew, and their daughter, Jane, married J. P. Morgan's only son, John Pierpont Morgan.

RUSSELL AND COMPANY

As the China trade expanded in the 1830s, the most important shipping family was Samuel Russell's. A latecomer to the business, Samuel Russell founded Russell and Company in 1823. He directed the company's ships to Smyrna in Turkey to buy opium; the ships then brought the opium to China. The company grew by hiring the right people and by buying out their competitors.

Russell's chief of operations in Canton was Warren Delano Jr., the grandfather of future president Franklin Roosevelt. Russell partners who contributed funds to mount his overseas ventures included John

Cleve Green, who financed Princeton, and Abiel Abbot Low, who financed construction at Columbia University in New York.[10]

The Russell family had a tremendous influence at Yale, and their relationship continues to the present day. Yale was originally called the Collegiate School. In early colonial times Elihu Yale served with the British East India Company. He made a fortune with the company and became governor of Madras in India in 1687. Later in life Yale gave away much of his wealth, and Cotton Mather renamed the Collegiate School in Yale's honor in 1718.

Joseph Coolidge was another Russell investor, as were members of the Perkins, Sturgis, and Forbes families. The Perkinses and Russells were soon united in a merger. Coolidge's son organized United Fruit, which kept the colonial interests of many of New England's influential families tied together. His grandson, Archibald C. Coolidge, was a founder of the Council on Foreign Relations.[11]

Samuel Russell's cousin William Huntington Russell set up a trust a Yale that created a unique organization of elite families under the name of the Skull and Bones. Russell's cofounder was Alfonso Taft. The Skull and Bones is a very secretive order that admits only fifteen new members each year. Prominent families that have been part of this organization include the Harrimans, Bushes, Kerrys, Tafts, Whitneys, Bundys, Weyerhaeusers, Pinchots, Goodyears, Sloanes, Stimsons, Phelpses, Pillsburys, Kelloggs, Vanderbilts, and Lovetts.

While the Russell shipping empire became one of the greatest and most far-reaching, there is still one more New England family that played a significant role in the trade.

THE FORBES CLAN

When the Cushings left China, the Forbes family took over operations. The Forbeses were not the first in the opium trade with China, but they brought drug smuggling to its highest level of profitability and left a legacy that extends into modern times.

The Forbes family roots reach well back into Scotland, where they can be traced to at least the thirteenth century. Sir Alexander Forbes, the first Lord Forbes, was granted lands in 1423 and was made a lord of Parliament in 1445. Incessant warfare in both Scotland and England made loyalty to the king precarious. Well before the massive Scottish immigration after Culloden in 1745, the Forbeses, who were Protestants (and therefore not Jacobites), were already situated in Massachusetts and connected with the families that would become American "aristocracy." As with the Gardiners and others illicit traders, the fortune accumulated by the Forbeses in opium trading was invested in land and industry. John and Robert Forbes would lead the way to the family fortune.

John Murray Forbes (1813–1898), the son of Ralph Bennet Forbes and Margaret Perkins Forbes, started his business career at age fifteen in the Boston countinghouse of his uncles James and Thomas Perkins. John Forbes was soon allowed to travel to Canton to represent the Perkins syndicate, and he stayed for seven years. In 1837, at the age of twenty-four, Forbes returned from Canton so wealthy that he could finance the construction of several railroads, including the Michigan Central Railroad, which he bought unfinished and extended to Lake Michigan and Chicago.

Forbes became a prime mover, leading a group of capitalists who could raise millions to complete acquisitions of companies. Many had previously invested with Forbes in the China trade, and they remained grateful for and loyal because of the fortunes they had reaped. Forbes continued to extend the Michigan Central's service, to Detroit and into Canada, and he built other railways including the Hannibal and Saint Joseph Railroad in Missouri and the Chicago, Burlington, and Quincy Railroad, of which he served as president.

NAUSHON ISLAND

Following the lesson of Gardiner, John Forbes bought an island where he could conduct business isolated from the prying eyes of neighbors. Like Gardiner's Island, the island of Naushon, just south of the Woods Hole area of Cape Cod, served as a protectorate for smugglers for as long as Massachusetts was a colony. The shifting sandbars and the isolation from the active ports of the New England coast protected many lawbreaking merchants.

The island first belonged to one of Massachusetts's most elite families, the Winthrops. There is little evidence that they were involved in the merchant trade. John Winthrop, the leader of seven hundred Puritans, was the first of the family who came to America. John Winthrop's idea of religion was that it was something to be imposed on others. The Taliban form of Islam is an apt comparison to the religious vision of John Winthrop. Puritans made it a crime to miss church, to dance, to sing, and to celebrate Christmas; likewise, the Taliban made it a crime to miss prayers, to dance, to sing, and to celebrate (as opposed to observe) Islamic festival days. Both fundamentalist groups punished their people with torture and humiliation.

As governor of the Massachusetts Bay Colony, Winthrop opposed democracy as well, believing his colony should be governed by a handful of pious leaders. Fleeing religious persecution apparently did not mean that Winthrop would hesitate to persecute others, and in America's first incidence of religious persecution, he banished Anne Hutchinson from the colony. Such elitism pervaded the thinking of the rulers of Massachusetts up to—and even after—the American Revolution.

The second family to own the island was the Bowditches. They would never enjoy the power of the Winthrops or the wealth of the Forbeses, but the Bowditches were industrious seafarers and the family was very well connected with Massachusetts blue bloods. William Bowditch sailed to America in the seventeenth century, when the family began making its living from the sea. Habakkuk Bowditch, a son who began a career at sea in the mid-eighteenth century, lost two ships and two sons to the sea and had taken up the cooper trade when his fourth son, Nathaniel, achieved long-lasting fame. Born in 1773 in Salem, Nathaniel enjoyed mathematics more than anything else, and this skill would revive the family's status. Even while in his teens, Nathaniel was renowned for his knowledge of mathematics and languages, to the point that others brought him books to further his education. He spoke French, Spanish, and German and understood Latin, and he even studied two dozen other languages. Remarkably, he found an error in Newton's *Principia*.

During the Revolution a privateer from Beverly captured a ship carrying the library of a noted Irish scholar. A group of merchants bought the books and housed them in the Philosophical Library, where Nathaniel Bowditch could continue his mostly self-taught education. Despite his widespread reputation, he still had to go to sea to make his fortune. Bowditch worked as a supercargo and made five voyages and a huge fortune, while at the same time making lunar calculations to navigate without the use of a chronometer. Legendary status came when Bowditch navigated into Salem Harbor during a blinding snowstorm.[12] He combined his book knowledge and practical experience to enhance the ability of American merchants to navigate their own country. Bowditch rewrote the *American Coastal Pilot* and then later produced his own book, *The New American Practical Navigator,* which served as a tool for navigating treacherous American waters until the government took over the responsibility fifty years later.[13] Bowditch's premier work is simply referred to as "Bowditch" by sailors; it remains a classic in the field. Since 1802 it has been reprinted in seventy editions.

Bowditch, who married his cousin Mary Ingersoll, refused mathematics chairs at several universities, including Harvard, the University of Virginia, and West Point, instead preferring his position as president of the Essex Fire and Marine Insurance Company.[14]

At the entrance to Buzzards Bay, Naushon, the Bowditches' private island, was more of an island kingdom than a summer home. When Kidd rushed around planting his treasure, Naushon's Tarpaulin Cove and Gardiner's Island were his last stops. In the years preceding the Revolution, the cove served as a hiding place where smugglers could wait to unload their merchandise.

A lighthouse was built on Naushon just before the Revolutionary War to protect the ships navigating the shoals. During the Revolution it served as a meeting place for privateers. James Bowditch, Nathaniel's brother, fought the government's efforts to improve the lighthouse, as guests were unwanted. When James died in 1817, an improved light-house was erected. At this point the Bowditch family, which had owned Naushon for more than a century, sold the island to the Forbeses. Since then the "kingdom" has been in the hands of various Forbes family members and trusts.

THE FORBES FAMILY AND NAUSHON ISLAND

John Murray Forbes married into another first family of New England when he wed Sarah Hathaway of New Bedford. Their five children included William Hathaway Forbes, who married Edith Emerson (a relative of Ralph Waldo Emerson's) and became president of the newly formed Bell Telephone, John Malcolm Forbes, and Mary Hathaway Forbes, who married a Russell.

The Hathaway, Forbes, and Perkins families were united in a merger with Russell and Company even before John and Sarah Forbes were united in marriage. Money from the opium trade and later investments ensured the prominence of the family for generations to come. The grandson of John Murray Forbes, William Cameron Forbes, was appointed by Teddy Roosevelt as governor general of the Philippines, and was later appointed to a post in Asia by President Harding.

John Forbes's brother was Robert Bennet Forbes (1804–1889), who was known as "Black Ben" Forbes. His historical biography notes his exploits as a sea captain in the China trade but ignores his involvement in the opium business. At age thirteen Robert Forbes sailed for his uncles to China, and at age twenty-four, when Perkins and Russell merged their companies to form the most powerful American house in China, young Robert secured the lucrative post of running the Lintin operation.

Forbes left China in 1834 to marry Rose Green Smith, and he almost lost his fortune in the Panic of 1837. Seeking to rebuild his wealth, Forbes went back to China and played a prominent role in the outbreak of the Opium War, during which Russell and Company prospered. Forbes was made the head of the company, replacing John C. Green. By 1850 Forbes owned interests in more than sixty ships and was the American vice-consul to China and France. In his later life Forbes was noted for his contribution to the U.S. Navy during the Civil War, and he became the first commodore of the Boston Yacht Club.

THE SYNDICATE

The early shipping business was unusually risky and the loss of a single ship was a disaster to some companies. Often the way to spread the risk was to "syndicate" the business so that merchants took shares in one another's companies. In addition to the Perkins and Russell syndicates, a third syndicate drew in some important personages.

Augustine Heard was an Ipswich merchant whose father participated in the often illegal molasses and sugar trade. He too relished the thought of getting revenge on the harsh and restrictive trade laws that favored the home country at the expense of the colonies, so he became a privateer. Heard started his career in the countinghouse and then became a supercargo. In 1807 he sailed to Smyrna aboard the *Betsy*.[15] The Heard Company started by selling ginseng and otter skins but soon joined the opium trade. Heard's partners included John Forbes, John Green, and Joseph Coolidge.

◈

The American base of the opium trade moved south from the ports of New England to New York. Families who were prominent in Connecticut became equally important in New York. Ultimately, the drug-smuggling families would attain the White House.

Chapter 15

OPIUM: FROM THE LODGE
TO THE DEN

During the glory years of the China trade, New York succeeded Boston as the center of American shipping. Ships and warehouses lined South Street's three-mile-long stretch of piers a few short blocks from Wall Street's Tontine Coffee House, which served as the center of the growing financial industry. The waterfront was so busy that spectators came to watch the hustle of dockworkers, shipbuilders, and auctioneers. Hammers clanged, barrels rolled, auctioneers shouted, and thousands worked hard building and loading ships. Skilled labor was so in demand that a sail maker was paid a previously unheard of four dollars a day.

Ships sailed from New York to all ports. Similar to New England's Brahmin families, many New York families achieved great wealth in the drug trade. American shippers had as many excuses for involvement in the trade as their British counterparts. And like the British, the Americans had less to offer as exports, and the new country became the dumping ground for British wares. The American families brought to China ginseng, furs, and opium, their only valued goods.

It should be noted that the trade was not illegal in the United States. What has become labeled the "China trade," which included tea and opium, furs, and furniture, reduces the stigma that might be perceived in modern times. Not all of the China traders carried opium, and their activity was not considered criminal. The laws that were broken were only those of another nation's, a common enough attitude in colonial expansionist times. Although the morality of the opium trade was questioned by a handful, both the British and American governments had no quarrel with any aspects of the China trade.

NEW YORK'S WEALTHIEST CITIZEN

America's richest opium smuggler was possibly John Jacob Astor. In 1800 Astor was worth $250,000 when the average American family had an income of $750. When he died in 1848 his wealth was equal to almost 1 percent of the entire country's gross national product.[1]

Astor's wealth was made in numerous ways, but his opium fortune was a direct result of the British East India Company's granting him a license to sell furs to China and to engage in the opium trade. The fur business was soon abandoned in all but name. In 1816 Astor's American Fur Company actually sailed directly to Turkey to buy ten tons of opium, which was then sold illegally in Canton.

◈

Astor's rapid rise to great wealth is an unlikely story. The son of a German butcher, Astor came to America in 1784 at age twenty-one. He reportedly spoke very little English, although he had lived for a short time in London. He is described as having no grace, charm, or wit; he is even said to have once wiped his hands on the table linens at a dinner party. Yet Astor's gruff manners and poor English did not stop him from rapidly entering society. He quickly married into wealth and breeding in the form of Sarah Todd of New York's Breevort family.[2] This connection most likely prompted his invitation to join New York's most prestigious Masonic lodge, the Holland No. 8. Here he mingled with Archibald Russell, the Livingstons, De Witt Clinton and George Clinton, and members of New York's other first families.

The Holland No. 8 Lodge was founded in 1787 after negotiating with the Masons to be allowed to hold meetings in the Low Dutch language. At first the new lodge admitted only eight members. The number 8 is significant to elite Masonry: There were eight original Templar knights, there are eight points on the Masonic cross, and there were eight prominent and wealthy New Yorkers in the new lodge.

From his new connections Astor discovered the lucrative fur pelt business. Pelts that could be bought for a dollar from a New York Indian could fetch six times the price in London.[3] Astor typically cheated the Indians by getting them drunk and then overcharging for the liquor.[4] He cheated his own workers with low-paying contracts, although his own records show he was more generous in bribes: He once made a thirty-five-thousand-dollar payment to Michigan Governor Lewis Cass.[5] In short, Astor prospered in the fur business.

Astor's proceeds from the fur trade were invested into New York City real estate during the year Washington was elected president and New York was in recession. And Astor instinctively knew how to take advantage of people. For example, when Aaron Burr shot Alexander Hamilton in a duel, Burr had to flee the country and so Astor bought Burr's Greenwich Village home for cash. In 1825 Astor bought land from the U.S. government and immediately evicted seven hundred farmers.

Astor's China connections were made through his fur business, as the Chinese bought beaver pelts that Astor's trappers and traders took from New York and the Oregon territory. He was the first New York merchant to join the China trade, and soon he replaced the furs with opium.

In 1807 New York City entered another recession as the Embargo Act stopped shipping. A letter from Punqua Wingchong, a visiting Chinese merchant and a mandarin connected to the ruling family in China, claimed the embargo had stranded him in New York City and requested permission from President Jefferson to be allowed to sail home. Jefferson made an exception and asked on what ship he intended to sail. Punqua Wingchong requested the *Beaver,* an Astor ship. The ship left New York with Punqua Wingchong and a hull full of furs. When it returned Jefferson discovered that Punqua Wingchong was not a merchant but a dockhand, and the voyage was a ruse created by Astor. The

Beaver made a two-hundred-thousand-dollar profit from the trip.

The profit was put into still another farm, which extended from Broadway to the Hudson in midtown New York.[6] But the American government got even when it went to war with Britain. Astor lost his fur capital in Astoria, Oregon, which was worth eight hundred thousand dollars.

Nevertheless, Astor's drug business grew unhindered. In writing he requested that a Constantinople merchant "please send returns in opium" for a consignment of 1,500 red fox furs.[7] With three separate fleets sailing the world, Astor made enough drug and pelt money to dip into an immense amount of real estate. By 1826 the German immigrant who made his fortune in America was buying the mortgages of Irish immigrants and foreclosing on them to add to his holdings at lower prices.[8]

In 1847 Moses Yale Beach compiled a list of the wealthiest New Yorkers. Some had a million or two; Astor towered above them.[9] Astor stopped at nothing to increase his fortune. In 1848 he was eighty-four years old and extremely wealthy, yet he still demanded rent even from widows. He died in March of that year, and his second son, William Backhouse Astor, inherited most of his father's twenty-million-dollar fortune.

John Jacob Astor's son learned well. In the 1860s, when working-class New Yorkers were going through a severe economic depression, officers of a Russian fleet docked in New York raised $4,760 to buy fuel for the poor. William Astor, however, raised rents 30 percent.[10] When he died in 1875, he owned seven hundred buildings and houses—most of them crammed with poor tenants. His legacy is the multitude of slums where the poor starved. Yet the Astor name still graces communities from Queens in New York to Oregon.

NEW YORK'S OTHER CHINA TRADERS

Astor receives the credit for launching New York City into the opium trade, but others soon followed. Many were New Englanders who moved operations to New York. Prominent families included the Griswolds from Old Lyme, Connecticut; the Lows from Salem; and the Grinnells from New Bedford.[11]

The Griswold Family

Nathaniel Griswold and George Griswold III built the family fortune through their ownership of a large fleet of trading ships that called on ports all over the world. Originally based in East Lyme, a small port on the Long Island Sound coast of Connecticut, the Griswold brothers ran an empire. Their black-and-white-checkered flag was seen in China, the West Indies, and South America. Although the Griswolds have not become a household name in subsequent centuries, many family members achieved prominence as a result of trading in the eighteenth century. The Griswolds' agent in Canton was Russell and Company, in which a Griswold relative was a partner.

Nathaniel Griswold was content to be a merchant, but his brother George had greater ambitions. George was a director of Columbia Insurance, was involved in the Bank of America, and dabbled in other ventures including gold mining. Other family members also made the merchant connection. For example, Nathaniel's daughter Catherine married Peter Lorillard, New York's first tobacco merchant.

The Griswolds played a role in early American politics, as Matthew Griswold was brought to the position of Federalist governor of Connecticut through family money. Future Griswolds served in the U.S. House of Representatives and the Senate as politicians for Connecticut and Pennsylvania. John D. Lodge, the great-great-grandson of sea trader George Griswold III, was Connecticut's governor from 1951 to 1955. Still other Griswolds became captains of industry, bishops, and college professors.

John Cleve Green

One Griswold employee who later achieved prominence on his own was John Cleve Green, who is usually remembered as one of the major benefactors of Princeton University. Born in Lawrenceville, New Jersey, in 1800 to an elder of the Presbyterian Church, Green began his career in the counting room of N. L. Griswold of New York City. He was soon promoted to a supercargo and traveled to South America, Spain, and finally China at the height of the opium trade. Green married the boss's daughter, Sarah Griswold. Green's connections and his knack for being in the right place at the right time landed him a position with Russell and Company. After six years in Canton working for the pre-eminent opium house, Green returned to New York. He continued in the China trade and also advanced his career as director of the Bank of Commerce and other banks, railroads, and New York Hospital.

The Low Family

The Low family was a group of Massachusetts merchants that moved to New York. Seth Low was born on Cape Ann in 1782. He moved at an early age to Salem, where he earned his living as a trader and a merchant. In *Tall Ships to Cathay* Helen Augur mentions that Seth Low married Mary Porter, which connected the Lows with the prominent Lord family. Seth had twelve children, and as the Salem area was losing its importance, he moved his family to New York. There Seth and his brother William Henry Low, a senior partner in Russell and Company, helped expand the American role in the trade that Russell inherited from the Perkins syndicate.

Several of Seth Low's children were involved in the China trade, but his son Abiel Abbot Low achieved the greatest fame. Abiel Low joined Russell and Company as a clerk just a short time before the Opium Wars started. He took over the Forbeses' position of personal secretary and agent for Houqua, which helped to expand his wealth and power. After acquiring work experience and connections, Abiel decided to go out on his own. He returned to New York and commissioned the fastest clipper ships money could buy; only the Forbes ships could compete with his. His A. A. Low and Brothers remained in the forefront and continued trading with China and Japan even when most other companies had left the trade.

Profits from his Abiel Low's Asia business were invested in the first

Atlantic cable and the building of the Chesapeake and Ohio Railroad. His son Seth graduated from Columbia University in 1870 and went on to become mayor of Brooklyn and then the first mayor of New York City after it consolidated in 1898. Seth Low the younger is famous for donating a million dollars, supposedly one third of his fortune, to build the Low Library at Columbia.

Abiel Low, who married Ellen Almira Dow, had a daughter also named Ellen, who in 1869 married into the Pierrepont family—which would later be known as the Pierpont family. The Pierpont and Morgan families were eventually united and played a significant role in the development of American finance.

The House of Morgan was actually started by China trader George Peabody. Described as a solitary miser, Peabody nevertheless joined forces with Barings Bank to get American states to pay on their bond debts, much of which was in British hands. Barings went as far as to bribe famed statesman Daniel Webster to make speeches on the issue. Peabody bought the bonds for pennies on the dollar and reaped a fortune when they were finally repaid. Like other Salem merchants, he amassed great wealth in the China trade and invested in railroads. Because he was heirless, Peabody gave his money to philanthropic causes, including a library in Salem, and he turned over his company to young Junius Spencer Morgan. Junius Morgan's heir was son J. Pierpont Morgan, whose stamp on Barings Bank would last for more than a century.[12]

The Grinnell Family

The Grinnells are another China-trading family whose origins are sketchy, but they most likely possess a Huguenot background. Cornelius Grinnell was an American sea captain who became a privateer during the American Revolution. He married Sylvia Howland, which established the Grinnells among New England's first families. Other Grinnells married into Rhode Island's Brown dynasty and into the Russell family.

Joseph Grinnell, son of Cornelius, cultivated the family wealth in the shipping and whaling businesses. Grinnell collaborated with a man by the name of Preserved Fish and Joseph's brother Henry to establish the firm of Fish, Grinnell, and Company. Over time *Fish* was dropped from the name and the business became Grinnell, Minturn, and Company. The company would become one of New York City's largest shipping firms.

The Grinnell family roots were in New Bedford, where the first of the Greek Revival mansions was built for Joseph. His profits, like those of many other merchants, were put into the textile trade, and he founded the still-in-operation Wamsutta Mills. Various Grinnells later financed polar explorations and rescue missions, pioneered real-estate development in Key West, and even found a town—Grinnell, Iowa— and its local college (Grinnell College).

Howland and Aspinwall

Another company that moved from New England to New York during the golden years of the opium trade was Howland and Aspinwall. This merger of two founding families spawned great wealth for generations to come.

John Howland was the first of the clan to travel to America, where he married a fellow *Mayflower* passenger. John's son, Joseph Howland, started in the whaling business in Connecticut. Joseph's sons also considered the sea to be a road to wealth and went into shipping. Howland shipping would take part in the sugar and slave trade in the Caribbean and in ventures in Cuba, Mexico, and the Mediterranean before discovering the China trade. The Howland children made good matches, with one daughter marrying James Roosevelt and another marrying James Brown of Brown Brothers Harriman.

The most significant Howland marriage was a business merger with the Aspinwall family. Like the Howlands, the Aspinwalls were in the shipping business prior to the American Revolution. Around the turn of the nineteenth century, John Aspinwall married Susan Howland. The new Howland and Aspinwall firm generated great profits in the China trade, and in 1837 William Henry Aspinwall's fortune was estimated to be greater than Cornelius Vanderbilt's. Post–China trade ventures included building America's oldest steamship line and several railroads, and, like most other China traders, participating in philanthropy.

Aspinwall was considered both an honest and a pious man, and has been referred to as a visionary. He was a cofounder of the Metropolitan Museum of Art in New York and led America in new adventures around the world while he lived quietly in New York.

Aspinwall claimed that his Panama Railroad, which was erected before the famous canal, could be built in six months. Not having traveled there himself, he didn't realize that the first thirteen miles went through dense jungles and impenetrable swamps filled with poisonous insects and snakes. From mosquitoes and sand flies to alligators and other hazards, the area was know as a pesthole from the days of Spanish exploration. General Grant, who visited the construction site, described the conditions of the rainy season as "beyond belief."[13]

The conditions took their toll on the workers, who often toiled in mud up to their necks, fighting off the swarming insects from sunrise to sunset. Sickness and disease—including cholera, yellow fever, smallpox, and dysentery—claimed many lives, as did harsh treatment similar to what was enacted on slaves. A commonly told story holds that there was a dead Irishman for every railroad tie. Howland and Aspinwall declared the death toll at one thousand, but estimates actually run up to six thousand. Chinese workers, called coolies, who did hard labor for low wages, were imported. Eight hundred arrived; two hundred survived. Many committed suicide by hanging themselves, paying companions to stab or shoot them, or simply drowning themselves in the ocean. Aspinwall was in New York at the time, where, ironically to modern sensibilities, he helped created the Society for the Prevention of Cruelty to Animals.

Like their Boston counterparts, New York's first families used marriage to ensure that their wealth and prominence would remain intact. Harriet Howland married James Roosevelt, President Franklin Roosevelt's great-grandfather, and Mary Aspinwall married Isaac Roosevelt, the same president's grandfather. The son of Mary Aspinwall and Isaac Roosevelt, James Roosevelt, married Rebecca Howland.

THE ROOSEVELTS AND THE DELANOS

The Roosevelts and the Delanos were among America's first Dutch families. Claes Martenszen van Roosevelt arrived in America before 1649 and died in 1660. Like John Jacob Astor, Roosevelt's only son, Nicholas, got his start in the fur business. He in turn had two sons who split the family into two lines: the Oyster Bay, New York line, from which President Teddy Roosevelt was born, and the Hyde Park New York line of Franklin Delano Roosevelt. The Oyster Bay branch got most of its wealth from the merchant business; the Hyde Park branch invested primarily in real estate.

Membership in the elite societies of their day, including Masonry, and intermarriage increased the Roosevelt family fortune. Isaac Roosevelt married into a sugar-trading family, which often implied the triangular trade of sugar, molasses, and slaves. After the Molasses Act of 1733, anyone who wouldn't smuggle couldn't survive. The Roosevelts survived and prospered,[14] and Isaac's brother James joined the business. Isaac became close with William Walton, and both were involved in founding the Bank of New York. James would also make a connection to the Waltons when he married Maria Walton.

Other Roosevelts married Howlands and Aspinwalls, which is how they were introduced to the China trade. The Howland and Aspinwall families were also active in building clipper ships and later in the steamship and railroad businesses.

By the 1820s the Roosevelt clan were more than just wealthy; they were also very well connected. James Roosevelt, son of Rebecca Aspinwall Roosevelt, sat on boards with the Vanderbilts and J. Pierpont Morgan. James Roosevelt's son James "Rosy" Roosevelt became engaged to Helen Schermerhorn Astor. At their engagement party, one of the guests in attendance was Sara Delano.

The Delanos were another of America's first families. Descendants of a Huguenot family by the name of de la Noye, who fled Holland for America, they arrived on the *Fortune* in 1621. Philip de la Noye came to America at age nineteen and became a Massachusetts landowner. He modified the spelling of his surname to Delano and married into the family of John and Priscilla Alden. Philip's son, Thomas Delano, married the Alden's daughter, also named Priscilla, although the couple was fined ten pounds for engaging in intercourse before the wedding.

Farther down the family tree, Warren Delano, Franklin's grandfather, made his fortune in the opium business, starting through the Grinnell firm. Warren's daughter Sara Delano became the mother of President Franklin Delano Roosevelt. Sara's sister Dora married a Forbes, and their sister Annie married Fred Hitch, a Russell and Company associate in Shanghai.

The Delano family seemed to gravitate toward the sea and the trading business. Warren Delano was an associate of James Roosevelt's father and was a partner in Russell, Sturgis, and Company (also known as Russell and Company at various stages). Warren was the China representative and owned a mansion in Macao. For a while he retired from opium trading and sank his fortune into New York real estate and coal and copper mines in Pennsylvania and Tennessee.

In August 1857 the failure of the Ohio Life Insurance and Trust started a domino effect that wiped out many banks. All but one bank in New York suspended specie payment. By the end of the year, five thousand businesses had failed, tens of thousands of workers had lost their homes and jobs, and people starved and froze to death both in the cities and in the coal towns. While his workers died, Warren lived in Algonac, his estate, complete with high-ceilinged rooms with rosewood furniture, teakwood screens, potted plants, and Buddhist bells.

Although Warren Delano suffered no loss of creature comforts, his net worth suffered dearly. He was desperate to keep his status and decided to go back to China and the drug-smuggling business; it was the simplest way to rebuild his fortune. "It would be denied in these later years that the opium he bought and shipped was intended for the tremendously profitable market provided by addicts," writes Kenneth Davis, who mentions specifically that it was opium, and not tea, that brought wealth along with a touch of notoriety.[15] By this time the New England drug smugglers were bringing the drug to American addicts.

The family later claimed that the opium Warren brought to America was for the relief of the Civil War wounded, but he returned to China in 1859, which predated the Civil War by two years.

The future President Franklin Roosevelt announced his engagement to Eleanor in grandfather Warren's room, surrounded by China-trade regalia. More prominent than his cousin Teddy was, Franklin took his role in Masonry seriously, becoming active in the Holland No. 8 Lodge in New York City and a Scottish Rite Temple in Albany.

Theodore Roosevelt is famous, of course, as a U.S. president and for leading the charge on San Juan Hill. Roosevelt's public persona depicts him as a "trustbuster," fighting the giant Standard Oil and mediating mining strikes. Despite his Masonic membership, however, he was far from egalitarian. He was also closely tied to big business, and was able to raise the necessary corporate donations for his candidacy; his trust-busting activities, though, would leave him at odds with the Rockefeller and Carnegie interests.

The twenty-sixth president of the United States is on record as being a racial elitist with an attitude that bordered on favoring ethnic cleansing. He has been quoted as saying, "Some day we will realize that the prime duty, the inescapable duty of the good citizen of the right type is to leave his or her blood behind him in the world; and that we have no business to permit the perpetuation of citizens of the wrong type." He also said, "I wish very much that the wrong people could be prevented entirely from breeding. . . . Criminals should be sterilized and feebleminded persons forbidden to leave offspring."[16]

While Teddy was crying out against the unwashed masses, the country was gripped by a fear of anyone who was foreign—Chinese, African, Italian, or Eastern European. The Eugenics Records Office (ERO) was created and funded by the wealthiest people of the day to reduce the population of the poor. The ERO, which was funded by John D. Rockefeller, the Carnegie Institution, George Eastman, and the widow of E. H. Harriman, singled out specific undesirable traits, from alcoholism to an inordinate love of the sea, and then sought to sterilize those who exhibited such traits. The movement grew in America and was adopted by Nazi Germany, which then showed the world the ultimate expression of these beliefs.

President Grant and Julia Dent

The Delano family's influence continued, as Susannah Delano married Captain Noah Grant in June 1746. They had a son Noah, also a sea captain, who married Rachel Kelly. They also had a son Jesse, who married Hannah Simpson. Jesse and Hannah Grant's son was Ulysses Simpson Grant, the renowned Civil War general and U.S. president, who married Julia Dent.

The Dent family of England ranked alongside the Jardines and Mathesons in the opium trade,[17] but the prosperity of the trade may not have extended to the American Dents. *The Memoirs of Julia Dent Grant* mentions her father as a prosperous landowner descended from a Maryland plantation owner and her mother's father as a China trader in the firm of Wrenshall, Peacock, and Pillon. The American Dents were a New England family who took part in the early China trade first by exporting ginseng to that country. Julia Dent's mother and father came to the Midwest to trade along the Mississippi River with Edward Tracy.

Ulysses Grant was a late bloomer who had drifted down to failure and disgrace during his early army career. He drank to the point that he was broke and finally resigned from the army. He failed at farming, failed at selling real estate, and made only a modest income as a clerk until someone convinced him to return to the military. The Civil War saved his reputation and gained him the presidency of the United States.

AMERICA'S MERCHANT FAMILIES GO TO WAR

The elite merchant families of Boston and New York grew wealthy in the opium trade, which was inherited from England; China, however, suffered.

The Chinese rapidly became addicted in increasing numbers. The importation of opium chests numbered five thousand in 1821 and grew to thirty-nine thousand by 1837. This figure represents 6,630,000 pounds of opium. Soon the addiction reached the royal palace. Emperor Tao Kwong lost three sons to drug addiction, and it was estimated that China had four to twelve million addicts.[18] The emperor conducted a study of the effects of opium on his country. He was told that for the first time his treasury was being drained of silver rather than being resupplied by the tea trade. Brigandage plagued the highways. Soldiers refused to fight, and when coerced to fight against other warlords the soldiers were defeated. It was obvious that corruption was spreading in the army and the civil service. Mandarins were regularly bribed to allow the importation of illegal products. And at Canton the marketplace was stocked with the apparatus of the opium trade.

The emperor ordered a crackdown and numerous drug users were arrested. To drive home the emperor's point, an opium merchant was publicly crucified in Canton. A Chinese boat was caught unloading opium believed to have been bought from Thomas Perkins. At first nothing was done, but then all trade came to a halt. On the day Bennett Forbes became a partner at Russell and Company, he complained that they could not unload a chest of opium.[19] Russell and Company made an announcement that it would cease trading opium. Its agent, John Green, sent instructions to India to stop all opium trading. But it was too late for them and for others. The agent of the emperor, Lin Tse-hsu, surrounded all the British and American ships and subjected them to house arrest. He then confiscated twenty thousand chests of opium and staged the Chinese version of the Boston Tea Party, mixing the opium with lime and throwing it into the water. Russell and Company lost 1,400 chests, Jardine and Matheson lost 7,000 chests, and the British Dent and Company lost 1,700 chests.

Even after the destruction of millions of dollars' worth of drugs, the house arrest continued. Wealthy Americans in China, including Warren Delano, A. A. Low, and John Green, were forced to do without servants and had to cook for themselves for the first time. The punishment was considerably less harsh than that inflicted on their Chinese partners in the trade, who were jailed and quickly executed.

Finally the opium debate reached Parliament. Statesmen like William Gladstone decried the trade in opium and its effect on the Chinese, but in the end the money was the key. The only way to compensate the British businessmen for their loss was to declare war on China. The brief war compelled China to sign a treaty giving the British Hong Kong and access to its markets.

THE LEGACY OF THE CHINA TRADE

The area that would become Hong Kong replaced the tiny islands and floating warehouses that served as the storage facilities for opium. From Hong Kong, ships could sail up along the coast and spread opium to even greater numbers of the Chinese population. But along with legality came a decrease in profits. The shipping firm called the Peninsula and Oriental Steamship line allowed Chinese buyers to place orders for opium directly with India, eliminating the British middleman.

But some companies thrived in the new situation. For the firm of Jardine and Matheson, the Opium War represented a new beginning. Made famous by the James Clavell novel *Noble House,* Jardine and Matheson, the house that opium built, grew and prospered as a result of having the power of England behind it. Today Simon and Henry Keswick, direct descendants of William Jardine, run the company, which is not known to have broken English or Chinese rules since the Opium War days. It has its many tentacles in shipping, the Cunard Line, trading, auto sales, brokerage, engineering, restaurants and hotels, property investment and management, insurance, and banking.

The power Jardine and Matheson once wielded in London is no longer as strong, as the company was unable to persuade Margaret Thatcher to hang on to Hong Kong. In 1984 Hong Kong was thirteen years away from reverting back to Chinese rule. Jardine and Matheson moved its exchange listing to Singapore, which infuriated China. The hard feelings between the company and modern China still persist. Jardine and Matheson is thought by many, including China, to have played a role in getting Chris Patten appointed Hong Kong's last gov-ernor under British rule. Patten's democratic reforms, and Henry Keswick's criticism of China after Tiananmen Square in 1989, have kept the relationship tenuous.[20] In 1995 more than half of Jardine's profits were still earned in China and Hong Kong.

A competing company from the Persian-English family of Sassoon also had a major part in the China trade. Like their Scottish counter-parts the Sassoons brought opium to China, but theirs was homegrown. Saleh Sassoon was the treasurer to the Ahmet Pasha, or governor of Baghdad. When the pasha was overthrown, the family moved to Bombay. Sassoon's son David became a merchant and was granted a license to trade in Indian opium and cotton. The Opium Wars were a brief setback, but David's son Edward Albert brought opium profits home to England, where he increased the family fortune in the textile trade. Being knighted by the queen was Edward's reward for his con-tribution to the economy. And marrying a Rothschild was a means of ensuring his power.

THE OPIUM LEGACY IN AMERICA

For their part in the drug business the Americans took home a lot of money. In 1844 Caleb Cushing created the American treaty with China, which officially allowed American ships in the China trade.

After the wars in China the drug-smuggling business became more dangerous, as there was Asian competition and there were much faster steamships. British and American firms started bringing drugs to safer shores—their own. In Britain, the cities of Liverpool, Dover, Bristol, and even London were the import drug centers. This was around the time that the attempts to regulate opium use became serious.[21] Between pre– and post–Opium Wars the opium imports in England tripled to 280,000 pounds.[22] The drug was even prescribed to children in such concoctions as Mrs. Winslow's Soothing Syrup, and unwed mothers dis-covered it was an easy way to terminate an unwanted pregnancy. Opium would be regulated as a poison in 1868, but without substantial penalty. Opium's derivative morphine was soon the cause of massive addiction of returning Crimean War veterans, who learned to inject the drug.

The drug trade in Europe became widespread, and it was the product of an alliance between criminal families from various nations and Swiss and German pharmaceutical companies. A large number of these firms were happy to deal with the smugglers, simply shipping drugs under deliberately misleading labels.[23] For instance, German firms shipped heroin, the latest derivative of opium, as aspirin. Turkey was the one nation that resisted the demands of the League of Nations and profited from its own production of opium. Turkey held out until 1931, when it officially closed its factories. Bulgaria took up the slack.

The drug trade, of course, never stopped. More and more customers bought the products, and as regulation grew, so did the profits from the trade. The only part that has changed is the level of violence. When corporations controlled the industry, they had no need to compete differently from how they had in selling other products. When the corporations were replaced by criminals, those who felt the need to get rid of the competition often killed it.

In 1840 New Englanders imported twenty-four thousand pounds of opium into the United States. This garnered much attention, but the U.S. reaction was to slap a duty on the product. Drug importers, once dependent on a small group of addicts in their homeland, soon had thousands as the Civil War saw an increase in prescribed opium and opium abuse. Horace Day wrote *The Opium Habit,* blaming the Civil War for the massive spread of addiction.

Chapter 16

WEALTH: THE LEGACY OF THE OPIUM TRADE

New England always had an elite class. Some of the early families were wealthy or at least titled in England, while others were prominent in their respective churches. For nearly four hundred years status was accorded by just how far back the family name could be traced. There were two classes of people who came to early Massachusetts: the original blue bloods, the religious dissenters from the East Anglia district north of London, and a more geographically varied group of "others."

The blue bloods became Massachusetts's first and original upper class. They were Puritans led by John Winthrop of the East Anglia town of Groton. Winthrop was likened to the biblical Nehemiah, who led his people out of Babylonian captivity. In England the Puritans might have made up 20 percent of the population; in East Anglia it was closer to 40 percent. The map of New England provides the evidence of the Puritan infiltration: Boston, Ipswich, Lynn, Norfolk, Suffolk, and Essex are among the many town names brought to seventeenth-century New England from the mother country. Puritans were in and out of favor and risked persecution as the kings of England came and went, married, or converted. The New World, they hoped, would provide relief and the Puritan version of religious freedom.

The second group was from a much wider geographic range. This included Huguenots who fled Catholic persecution in France and were not always welcome in other countries. In 1585 the Edict of Nantes gave them religious freedom, but it was later rescinded. Troops in Catholic France supervised the reconversion. This prompted many families, including the Faneuils, Bowdoins, Reveres, and Olivers, to relocate to New England. It brought the Jays and Bayards to New York.[1] The Huguenots were merchants first, and because of the precarious nature of their existence and survival in Europe, they were possibly a much more adaptable people.

Prestige was brought from Europe, achieved with the money accumulated in the New World, or acquired by marriage. By the late seventeenth century distinctions among European brands of Protestantism were blurred and the struggles pitted the English Protestants against the Scottish and Irish Catholics. The English favored Parliamentary rule while the Catholic Irish and Scots often favored the king, especially if it was a Stuart king.

Boston was a microcosm of this old society, where the top tier of a class system was built on status in Europe and in the church and was later joined by those who made their fortunes in the New World. Members of this class were bent on self-preservation and accomplished this in many ways: intermarriage, dominance in business and politics, and endowment of public institutions. Cabots married Lowells, Roosevelts married Astors, and Paines married Whitneys. Such names were like tribal tattoos; they indicated royal lineage and thus prestige. Names also served to exclude certain groups, and pressure was put on individual family members to marry within their station.

Fortunes amassed in real estate, privateering, merchanting, or smuggling were reinvested in railroads, textile mills, insurance companies, and banks, allowing the elite class to control the economy. Money bought politicians and elected those who chose to brave the political waters. Money—often from opium trading, smuggling, and slave trading—was used as an endowment to build educational institutions and buy professorial chairs that would then control just who would be approved to enter the elite and how history would be viewed.

The universities and museums determined how the history books would be written. They could color the past to suit themselves or others. The opium clippers were referred to as "tea clippers." The slave trade became the "sugar and molasses trade." Wartime profiteering and price gouging were simply not discussed. Slave traders who were now bank presidents were "prominent businessmen." And many people whose fortunes were built on opium and slave trading became those prominent businessmen.

THE APPLETONS

The Appletons' fortune began to accumulate almost upon their landing in the New World in the seventeenth century, but it was later enhanced by association with the China trade and with cronyism. The family lived at the pinnacle of Boston society, which was referred to as the Boston Associates,[2] a tight-knit group that included two Appletons, a Cabot-Lowell, two Jacksons, and a handful of others who would lay the foundation of New England industry.

The Appleton family can be traced to the sixteenth century in England. Samuel Appleton (1766–1853) fought in King Philip's War and was a member of the first provincial council and a Connecticut judge. He also owned a sawmill and invested in an early ironworks in Massachusetts. An Appleton married a Perkins in 1701, and descendants of the earliest settlers include Jane Means Appleton Pierce, who became the first lady to the fourteenth president, Franklin Pierce; and Calvin Coolidge, the thirtieth president.

Samuel Appleton started the family in the textile business and made significant investments in real estate and railroads. He married Mary Gore. Appleton was actively involved in the Massachusetts Historical Society, was a trustee of Massachusetts Hospital, and was a contributor to Dartmouth, Harvard, and the Boston Female Asylum.

Nathan Appleton (1779–1861) was a founder of the Boston Manufacturing Company, the Waltham Cotton Factory, the Hamilton Company, and numerous other mills. The Appletons, along with the Lowells, Jacksons, and Thorndikes, brought to Massachusetts the first looms that operated in the United States. As a group they are responsible for putting both Waltham and Lawrence, Massachusetts, and Manchester, New Hampshire, on the map as textile cities. Nathan Appleton was one of the founders of the textile city dubbed Lowell after John Lowell, scion of another New England first family. Appleton served several terms in the Massachusetts state legislature and the U.S. House of Representatives, and he also became an organizer of the Boston Athenaeum.

Nathan owned ships, founded banks and insurance companies, and invested in railroads and in infrastructure projects. His brother William became president of the Boston branch of the United States Bank. Appletons, Jacksons, and Lowells controlled the board of the Suffolk Bank, which acted as the central bank for New England.

Henry Wadsworth Longfellow was lucky enough to be born into one of New Hampshire's first families, the Wadsworths, which afforded him the ability to travel throughout Europe and write poetry. He married Frances Appleton, the daughter of Nathan Appleton, which substantially increased Longfellow's wealth. The Longfellow House in Cambridge was a gift from his father-in-law. Longfellow owned shares in at least five textile companies that his father-in-law invested in, and when his friend and contemporary Charles Dickens visited the mills of Lowell, it is no small wonder he compared them favorably to England's.

Jesse Appleton was a man of principle. He served as the president of Bowdoin College, where Longfellow had been a student and a professor. Jesse's daughters benefited from both his station and his lessons and developed a knack for marrying well. Daughter Frances married a Bowdoin professor. Daughter Mary married John Aiken, a prominent attorney and significant investor in the textile industry.

Despite the family's involvement in the China trade, Jane Appleton had a sense of morality that seems at odds with her fortune. When she met Franklin Pierce, who attended Bowdoin, he was studying to become an attorney. The Appleton family discouraged the match, as Pierce was not as prominent as the Appletons, despite the fact that his father was the governor of New Hampshire.

Pierce entered politics early, a career that went hand in hand with being an attorney. He was a Jacksonian, which pitted him against the Whig class of Massachusetts's monied elite, but at the same time he was pro-slavery. Pierce soon retired from politics to enlist as a private in the war against Mexico. He emerged a general and a war hero. When his war hero status raised his value as a candidate, Pierce was swept into national politics by the same faction that had removed Taylor. Jane Appleton Pierce did all she could to keep her husband from becoming a presidential candidate. His getting the party nomination caused her to faint, and for a while she fought his going to Washington, as it had a reputation for hard drinking that to her was immoral.

Incredible tragedy struck Jane and Franklin Pierce, as their third and only surviving son was killed on the way to the inauguration in Washington. Jane avoided public life, and a childhood friend took her place at White House functions.

Pierce was a one-term president who had a flair for creating divisiveness. He was the first president to appoint a non-Protestant cabinet member. The postmaster general was James Campbell, a Pennsylvania Catholic whose appointment and reception of a papal delegate helped create the backlash that would become the Know-Nothing (American nativist) party. Pierce endorsed the Kansas-Nebraska Bill, which was the eye of the slavery hurricane and led to the splitting of the Democratic party and the ending of the Whig party—and the creation of the Republican party. He brought England and America to the verge of war for a third time over policy and further strained relations with Europe when plans to annex Cuba were leaked to the European press.

Pierce's attorney general, Caleb Cushing, was the real power behind the "throne." The thirty-third-degree Mason and opium trader was the grand master to the divisive politics that threatened the nation. Pierce's secretary of war, Jefferson Davis, completed the conspiracy, leading the Southern states into war against the Union.

Jane Appleton's marriage to Pierce was not the only connection the Appleton family had to the presidency. Nathan Appleton became father-in-law to Thomas Coolidge, whose descendant would also reach the White House. Coolidge money too had been increased in the China trade, and Thomas Coolidge had no qualms about admitting his devotion to the acquisition of wealth, as "money was becoming the only real avenue to power and success both socially and in the regard of your fellow-men."[3] Coolidge money was spread at Harvard and at the Museum of Fine Arts in Boston, among other institutions. Coolidge money would also start the United Fruit Company, which linked other prominent New England families for a hundred years.

THE CABOTS

Samuel Eliot Morison, one of America's highest authorities on the history of the sea trade, writes, "Seaboard Massachusetts has never known such a thing as social democracy. . . . Inequalities of wealth have made political democracy a sham."[4] Writing on the mansions of pre-Revolutionary New England, which include George Cabot's at Beverly, Jonathan Jackson's at Newburyport, and John Heard's at Ipswich, Morison points to the sea as the source of wealth. Bluntly referring to the Revolution as an effect of George III's harsh maritime policy, Morison calls Boston the headquarters of the Revolution. What England called smuggling, he emphasizes, Americans called free trade.[5]

The Cabot family began the family fortune upon arrival in America, when John Cabot emigrated from the Channel Islands to Salem in 1700. His son Joseph became a successful merchant and married into the Higginson family, one of the most prominent in the colony.

George Cabot was the seventh of Joseph's eleven children, and despite his Harvard education he was shipped off as a cabin boy under the command of two older brothers. Their father's ships were active with the Spanish colonies in the trade of rum and fish, two staples of the slave plantations. At age eighteen George was made captain. After four years at sea, George married and took over a share in the distillery business from his wife's side of the family, as well as control of his brothers' shipping interests. George made his last voyage at age twenty-seven, at which time he was already a captain of industry.

The Revolutionary War was great business for George as he fitted out forty ships as privateers and shared richly in many prizes. What Cabot and his fellow merchants had fought for, in addition to prizes, was to make a union of the colonies in the belief that it would expand their mercantile business. And for a while it did. In 1784 George Cabot was already trading through the Baltic Sea, pioneering the Russian trade with his ships *Bucanier* and *Commerce*.[6] In 1787, with the war at an end, the Cabot family established the Beverly Cotton Manufactory. Cabots also owned fishing fleets in Beverly, which led Senator George Cabot to draft and push through an act giving fishermen a bounty to expand the codfishing business.

From 1789 to 1799 Alexander Hamilton had dictated the financial and foreign policy for the nation's first two administrations. His privy council was called the Essex Junto.[7] Made up of George Cabot, Stephen Higginson, Jonathan Jackson, John Lowell, and Thomas Pickering, the Junto almost created a second revolution when the policies of Jefferson were not in accord with the council's own financial interests.

The fortunes of the Essex Junto were made mostly from the sea and from unrestricted trade. Its credit needs were met not by the infant government in Washington but by the same facilities members had relied on before the Revolution: the London banking houses. The Essex Junto was actually a traitorous conspiracy, as it broke away from the United States because of Jefferson's embargo. When home among his fellow aristocrats, George Cabot was a pillar of the compact society; outside New England he was an anarchist, a charge he had made against Jefferson. The conspiracy blew over as the embargo was lifted.

Senator George Cabot, whose mother was Elizabeth Higginson, married his first cousin, also named Elizabeth Higginson. The union was one of many dynastic marriages among the opium families who became the Brahmin class of Boston. George further cemented his role in the establishment by serving as president of the Boston branch of the United States Bank, as director of Suffolk Insurance, and as president of Boston Marine Insurance.

The next famous Cabot was Edward (1818–1901), the third of

eleven children of Samuel Cabot and Eliza Perkins (daughter of Thomas Handasyd Perkins). The offspring of two of the most powerful China trading families, Edward Cabot decided to be a sheep farmer. After losing a fortune in that business in Illinois, he returned home and became an architect. Edward would get commissions to design Johns Hopkins University and the Boston Athenaeum, both of which were financed by family.

The best-known Cabot might be Henry Cabot Lodge, a Harvard Ph.D. historian-turned-politician. A true elitist, he fought against women's suffrage and even against the direct election of U.S. senators. To foster these elitist politics the Cabot family endowed organizations such as the Brookings Institute, where world leaders like James Wolfensohn of the World Bank; Henry Schacht of Warburg, Pincus; David Rockefeller; and Barton Biggs of Morgan Stanley bridge the corporate-political divide and influence government policy.

THE LOWELLS

A Boston elitist saying holds that the Lowells speak only to the Cabots, and the Cabots speak only to God.

The Lowell family achieved its status in Brahmin society by its early arrival in the colonies and its development of Newburyport as an early center of shipbuilding and a merchant community. The early families did everything they could to preserve their status and wealth, including marrying into other wealthy and prestigious families.

John Lowell was part of the class of 1721 at Harvard and shared classrooms with Hancocks, Winslows, Hutchinsons, and Woolcotts. A great example of what the dynastic marriage can produce is the relationship of John Lowell and Jonathan Jackson. John "Old Judge" Lowell, a Harvard graduate in 1761, married the daughter of Stephen Higginson, a leading merchant, and Elizabeth Cabot Higginson. As Lowell was a lawyer, this connection maintained his status in the merchant community, which had already been established by his family.

John's close friend Jonathan Jackson had inherited twenty thousand pounds and married the daughter of Patrick Tracy, one of Boston's richest merchants. The marriage increased Jackson's wealth and his status as a merchant, and extended his connections into England—a necessary connection for financing. For Jackson, John Lowell represented connections; for John Lowell, Jackson meant more clients. Their partnership was cemented by marriage between the families. John Lowell's son, Francis Cabot Lowell, was born to his second wife, Susan Cabot. Francis Cabot Lowell married Hannah, the daughter of Jackson and his first wife.

John and Elizabeth Lowell were New England's finest couple, and their Boston home on High Street was next door to that of their best friends, the Jacksons. From this power base the two men were able to increase their fortunes, thanks to the Revolution. John represented the business affairs of British families, handled the wills of leading patricians in Boston, collected seven hundred separate fees related to privateer actions, and was in charge of liquidating many Tory-owned properties after the war. His legal machine benefited from his action in the early politics of the new country.

John Lowell served as a member of the State Constitutional Convention, which advocated that "all men are born free and equal," but it is doubtful that he personally advocated such sentiments. Both Lowell and best friend, Jackson, were slave owners. John Lowell has the distinction of being the last man in Boston to own a black slave.

After the war the classes were further divided in America as economic depression and higher taxation struck home. A huge chasm existed between the haves and the have-nots, and the Lowells were among those who had it all. In order to have a place to keep it all, Lowell, along with members of the Russell and Higginson families, started the Massachusetts Bank, which became the First National Bank of Boston.

While the Lowell family wealth was already one of the greatest and they were one of the most powerful clans in the new country, Francis Cabot Lowell further increased the family wealth and made an imprint on the American textile industry.

In England, Richard Arkwright launched the industrial revolution by bringing machinery to the textile industry, which was formerly dependent on people in their homes. Spinning, carding, and weaving yarn on hand looms was the original cottage industry. A woman often went to a storekeeper, bought the yarn on consignment, and returned woven cloth to earn a profit. Women could weave at home while earning a wage at the same time. The industrial revolution would change the home-based industry to a factory-based one, starting with the spinning frame, the first fully powered machine for spinning yarn.

An assistant to Richard Arkwright, Samuel Slater, memorized the design of the spinning frame and brought it to America, where slave trader Moses Brown financed the first cotton-spinning wheel in Pawtucket, Rhode Island. For Brown it was a natural progression from one type of cruel labor to another; instead of exploiting captive labor, there was an entire new class of labor ready to be used—children. The company Brown built was named in honor of the machine's inventor, Arkwright.

Francis Cabot Lowell followed Brown's example and went to England in 1810 to get plans for his own factory. His first factory would be a partnership with brother-in-law Tracy Jackson, as well as with Paul Moody and Nathan Appleton. Lowell's mill combined all the operations of making raw cotton into finished clothes. As soon as he realized it could be done, he used his political influence to push for high duties on imported cloth, in order to lessen his competition.

Lowell's inner circle of Boston Associates then scouted for a location to build even larger mills. They found that the confluence of the Concord and Merrimack Rivers was perfect for providing the waterpower needed to power their looms. Thus the sleepy farming village of East Chelmsford was turned into a factory village called Lowell.

Lowell was much more than a single factory; it was the first corporate town. Several corporations were formed and scouts were sent throughout the state to find the necessary machine operators. Children were the best source of labor. Times were tough and children as young as ten were in great supply. The youngest of the factory girls were "doffers," doffing, or taking off, the full bobbins from the spinning frames and replacing them. These girls worked fourteen-hour days, starting at five in the morning, for the munificent sum of two dollars a week.[8]

As in mining towns, unscrupulous textile operators would often allow workers to run up charges at factory stores. The combination of inflated prices and accumulated debt ensured that workers would stay. The women and children brought to the factory town often could not afford to leave, their condition reduced to something not much different from slavery.

The elite factory owners were able to color things differently. John Greenleaf Whittier, poet and newspaper editor, lived near Lowell and wrote of the mill town, describing it as a "city springing up like the enchanted palaces of Arabian Tales." These brick "palaces" ran six days a week, fourteen hours a day, and when it was dark whale-oil lamps extended the day. The living conditions were worse. Accommodations were in blocks of sixteen "houses," with five hundred people forced to use one privy. In another tenement in Lowell the tenants had to carry their waste, human and otherwise, to Austin Avenue. In another Lowell block the commissioners counted 396 people living in conditions Whittier described as filthy, unsanitary, foul, and wretched. But the women had to live there as a condition of their employment. What Mr. Whittier and other writers who were tainted by those who paid their salaries seemed to miss, a Massachusetts labor commissioner pointed out: The state's laws protected horses better than people.[9]

Despite the conditions, the wage was higher than a teenage girl could make outside the factory system, and children could send home money to their families. Despite the abuses, the millworkers did not fight for raises. Eventually they were forced to fight to keep the same wage, as factory owners started cutting wages after competition from other mills grew. The plight of the mill women achieved national attention many decades later when seventy-three-year-old Mary Jones marched with several hundred textile workers, half of them under the age of sixteen, from Philadelphia to New York to visit President Teddy Roosevelt. By this time American mills and mines employed two million children. Marching in rags, many of the women missing fingers from machine accidents, the group attempted to call on a New York senator first and then on Teddy Roosevelt at his mansion. Both men avoided the demonstration, but the public outcry created by the march finally led to child protection laws.

Although many of New England's elite kept their family money and power intact, it was the Cabot name that remained a political force. Henry Cabot Lodge served in Congress and the Senate from 1893 to 1924 and was even nominated for president by Teddy Roosevelt at the 1916 Republican Convention. Lodge's grandson Henry Cabot Lodge was John F. Kennedy's ambassador to South Vietnam, and was involved heavily in the secret negotiations that led to the assassination of South Vietnam's president, Ngo Dinh Diem.

CHASING THE DRAGON

After the first Opium War, the California gold rush diverted attention from the opium trade in China. The great rush to reach the West meant there was more money to be made shipping goods to California than to China. The eastern magnates, made wealthy by the opium trade, were the driving force behind the rush to build a transcontinental railroad. With slavery banned, the next best labor was imported and cheap. The railroad owners turned to China, where coolies, or unskilled laborers, could be carried over on ships along with opium.

Many Chinese desired to leave their country as famine and taxes hurt farming. Many of the immigrants came from the same coastal provinces where the opium business had thrived. The means of getting out of China was as harsh as the immigration on the death ships from Ireland—sometimes worse. Dubbed the pig trade, the immigrants were treated like slaves as they got on the transport ships, which were often managed by Americans. The Chinese were marked with the letter *C* for their destination, California. They commited themselves to an indenture period that many did not understand. Thousands would be "relieved" of their obligation, as the death rate was a startling 40 percent, higher than that of the African slave trade.

Most of the immigrants whose passage was paid—at the price of indenture—were men who were destined to work on the railroads. To service the men, Chinese overseers bring them drugs and occasionally prostitutes. Many of the women brought to serve as prostitutes were sold by their families or kidnapped; some were as young as eight years old.[10]

Emigration from China spread the use of opium to Australia and Peru, two other common destinations, as well as to California. In America the nation was discovering the negatives of drug addiction, but there was no public outcry until opium became associated with the immigrants.

While in the grips of a new hysteria against immigration and the poor, the attitudes of Americans changed. One could buy heroin in the Sears catalog or at the grocery store and cannabis at the drugstore, but now the American government and the Hearst media sought to convince Americans that such evils were being foisted upon the country by foreigners. The Chinese brought the opium, the Mexicans brought the marijuana, and the blacks brought the cocaine. The head of the Federal Bureau of Narcotics, Harry J. Anslinger, and the Hearst newspapers spoke out against anything that was associated with people of these heritages, including their music. Even the labor unions, threatened by the large numbers of hardworking Asians, called the Chinese drug smugglers.[11]

The editorial opinion of the Hearst organization mirrored the position of the Ku Klux Klan in seeking 100 percent "Americanism." Thomas Edison's first films were on the Chinese and their alleged proclivity for opium. Americans soon got the message. It was one thing when old women drifted off to sleep after sniffing an opium pipe; it was another when strangers were using the drug.

At the turn of the century, Roosevelt relied on the word to suppress Asian opium. Although it was ironic that the nineteenth-century Roosevelts and Delanos had built a family fortune on addicting Chinese to opium, the tide had turned. America was smoking more opium each year than the six largest nations of Europe put together.

The man who might be dubbed America's first drug czar, Hamilton Wright, claimed that the Chinese brought the problem to American shores and that opium's use had grown beyond the Chinese workers. He pointed out that five hundred thousand pounds of opium were used each year, and less than 10 percent was for legitimate medicinal purposes. Wright placed the blame on "ignorant physicians" and "law-defying retail druggists," and called on the country to establish laws that would curb opium use. But cocaine was also becoming popular, and Wright claimed, "It is current knowledge . . . where large numbers of Negroes congregate, cocaine is peddled pretty openly."[12]

The result of the racist hysteria was the Harrison Act, which started the ban on drugs such as heroin. The ban had two immediate results: It drove the price of heroin up 1,500 percent[13] and it induced the use of the syringe to help addicts get more bang for their bucks. Another long-term effect was violence. As it was no longer a drug that was used primarily by middle-aged women, opium and heroin found the young and the poor to be receptive and repetitive clients. The illegal trade was the source of wealth for those who braved the risks. A new generation of smugglers became America's legacy. And the poor learned that you no longer had to have a name like Cabot or Lowell to get rich in the drug trade.

Chapter 17

THE POWER
OF THE NEW SKULL
AND BONES

One of the stranger buildings on the Yale Campus resembles a mausoleum. Inside, a young man, one of fifteen juniors chosen each year, lies naked in a coffin. He is not dead; he is reciting a sexual autobiography of his life before being "tapped" for the Skull and Bones. The ceremony is called Connubial Bliss, and it no doubt helps the bonding process that will last a lifetime.[1] Standing around are the fourteen other initiates and the current membership, who are all seniors at Yale. The goings-on get stranger, and it is said that if one would climb to the top of nearby Weir Hall, one "could hear strange cries and moans coming from the bowels of the tomb."[2] Unlike a normal fraternity, no one actually resides in the building; it only conducts rituals there. Also unlike a fraternity, the Skull and Bones initiates emerge wealthier and with connections that can ensure a lifetime of success.

Former president George Bush is one of those who has lain in the coffin. He is not the only famous member; his son George W. Bush is another. A third president, William Howard Taft, was a "Bonesman," and his father, Alphonso Taft, was one of the founders. The odds of three presidents coming out of the same fifteen-member-a-year fraternity are infinitesimal. Then again, the support from fellow Bonesmen means they have clout—enough clout to get to the White House. The membership list of Skull and Bones is one of the greatest concentrations of power in the United State. Names like Pillsbury, Kellogg, Weyerhaeuser, Phelps, and Whitney abound. They rule in the business world and they rule in the political arena.

Besides the three presidents, numerous congressmen, justices, and military leaders have been members of the Skull and Bones. Rhode Island Senator John Chafee is a member. Senator Robert Taft was a member. Conservative William F. Buckley is a member, and so is his CIA-proponent brother, James. The CIA as an employer is a virtual class reunion of Yale; both organizations have the same statue of Nathan Hale,[3] and both are regarded as a "campus," which is not a usual designation for the headquarters of a government intelligence unit. And among the active Yale class reunion at Langley, membership in Skull and Bones is regarded as a most prominent background. The director of personnel in the early years was F. Trubee Davison, who was made a Bonesman in 1918. When the CIA made Chile safe for the interests of American businessmen, the deputy chief of station was Bonesman Dino Pionzio. Bonesman Archibald MacLeish started his career in intelligence and then moved to fellow Bonesman Henry Luce's *Time* magazine. MacLeish's appointment to an intelligence position was granted by another member of Yale's secret societies, Wilmarth Sheldon Lewis of the Scroll and Key.[4]

McGeorge Bundy, the man who gave us a war in Vietnam, is a member of the Skull and Bones. William Sloane Coffin, who went from the CIA to protesting the war, is also a member. Russell Davenport, founder of *Fortune,* is a Bonesman. Senator John Forbes Kerry, an heir to the China trading Forbes family, is also a member.

For many, note the authors of *Wise Men, Six Friends and the World They Made,* "Membership in a senior society at Yale was the capstone of a successful career at Yale. The oldest and greatest, indeed the most legendary . . . was Skull and Bones." Two of those six friends alluded to in the book's title were Skull and Bones members William Averill Harriman and Robert Abercrombie Lovett. When Harriman carried secret dispatches in the First World War, he coded them 322, a code understood only by Bonesmen. When third wife Pamela Churchill asked Harriman about it in 1971, he told her he couldn't tell even her.[5]

For those who wonder what goes on inside the iron gates of this quasi-Masonic sanctuary, there are few answers. If a Bonesman is in a room and the subject of the organization comes up, he not only will not reply but also he will leave the room. The oaths taken among the bones and skulls of celebrity skeletons have never been broken. Nor has the power.

In recent years Ron Rosenbaum and Antony Sutton, authors of *America's Secret Establishment,* have shed light on the secret organization. The Skull and Bones is the beneficiary of a trust set up by the Russell and Company heirs. How much money from the vast China trading fortune went into the Russell Trust Association is unknown, but each tapped member starts with fifteen thousand dollars and countless valuable connections. Old-money names include Adams, Bundy, Cheney, Lord, Stimson, and Wadsworth. New-money names include Harriman, Rockefeller, Payne, and Bush.[6] Averill Harriman, of the Wall Street firm Brown Brothers Harriman, is another member and the patron of the Bush fortune. And Brown Brothers Harriman is the repository of the Skull and Bones's funds.

From this remarkable base of power the heirs to the Russell Trust maintain control as the inner circle of power. The outer circle, which consists of organizations that exist in at least semi-daylight, include the Trilateral Commission, the Brookings Institute, the Council on Foreign Relations, and the Round Tables of Commerce in numerous cities. These in turn ensure that the elite stay in control of American business, government, universities, and the media. In fact, a revolving door of Trilaterals and Council on Foreign Relations members serve in key positions in both government and business. They make the rules. They allow themselves to use tax-free foundations to ensure the ideas of the ruling class will always prevail by funding the "right" people and projects. The elite system perpetuates itself.

Though a blanket of secrecy protects the inner workings of such organizations, the secrecy has been under attack. In April 2001 the *New York Observer* and Ron Rosenbaum actually filmed the secret rites of the Skull and Bones' initiation. Using high-tech night-vision video equipment, the organization—whose members gave birth to the OSS and the CIA, filled numerous secretary of state posts, and served as national security advisers—were spied on themselves. While the vulgar scene need not be retold in these pages, it would have been a much greater embarrassment if other media had carried the story further.

Is there a Skull and Bones agenda? Bonesmen "believe in the notion of 'constructive chaos,' which justifies covert action," writes Joel Bainerman in *Inside the Covert Operations of the CIA and Israel's Mossad.* The foreign policy of the Bonesmen is almost always carried out through a secret agenda.[7] Alphonso Taft was secretary of war when he pressured McKinley to declare war on Spain. After McKinley was assassinated, Teddy Roosevelt took over and brought in Bonesman William Howard Taft. Others of the order who have held warrior posts include Henry Stimson, secretary of state under Hoover; Robert Lovett, secretary of defense at the height of the Cold War; General George Marshall, who became Truman's secretary of state; McGeorge Bundy, Kennedy's national security adviser; and Averell Harriman, ambassador-at-large for southeast Asia during Vietnam. Following the Stimson doctrine that there should be regular periodic wars to divert discontent and rally the nation to a single purpose, Bonesmen George Bush and George W. Bush would uphold the tradition with brief military excursions in Asia and Latin America.

Just how much clout has the order of the Skull and Bones exerted on twentieth-century history? In Asia, American policy started with the policy of the New England opium families. After reaping their fortunes in Asia, the families turned their attention homeward to railroads, mills, and mines. An American presence remained in China as missionaries then tried to "reform" the Chinese to further accept Western ways. Henry Luce was the son of a missionary to China. He was sent to Yale for an education and was tapped for the Skull and Bones. In *Whiteout: The CIA, Drugs and the Press,* Alexander Cockburn and Jeffrey St. Clair write, "Tap Day was a critical turning point for Luce. He yearned to be tapped for Skull and Bones, the supreme society at Yale, the ultimate honor."[8] With eighty-six thousand dollars borrowed mostly from other Yalies and family friends, Luce, with the help of Yale students serving as assistants, started *Time* magazine, which would later be *Life* magazine.

Luce married Clare Boothe Brokaw, who took as much of an interest in China as he did. Together they acted on behalf of the China Institute of America to bring Chinese students to the United States. Luce and his wife were very close to the ruling Chinese Soong family, whose corrupt activities helped the rise of Communism. When Chiang Kai-shek's army was defeated, Luce's China Lobby united John Foster and Allen Dulles, the Rockefeller family, Thomas Lamont, and Cardinal Spellman to push for American assistance. Chiang lost credibility as his army was defeated in one battle after another and he and his family looted three hundred million dollars of American funds. But Chiang would not lose the support of Luce, who was still rabid that Mao Tse-tung had beaten Chiang. *Time* magazine would constantly play up the Nationalist cause.

Mao Tse-tung was a Yale student, perhaps as a result of Luce's China efforts. The Yale Divinity School had established a number of "branch" schools in China, and Mao was their most famous student. Although he was not tapped for the Skull and Bones, just about every recent ambassador to China was a Bonesman: George Bush, Winston Lord, and James Lilley, all alumni of the Skull and Bones, all served as ambassador to China.

With the outspoken Luce leading the way, America was rallied to take up the French battle in Vietnam as a means of curtailing further Communist expansion. The result was a long, drawn-out, and expensive war that took tens of thousands of lives and wreaked havoc on America by bringing heroin addiction to eighty thousand returning war veterans.[9]

The China Lobby and the Skull and Bones were firmly behind the Vietnam War, and they were unfortunately in position to ensure that the war continued. The so-called best and the brightest, like Bonesmen McGeorge Bundy, Henry Cabot Lodge, and Dean Acheson (whose son is a Bonesman), gave bad advice to one president after another, while Americans wondered how many lives the country would be forced to sacrifice twelve thousand miles away. The issue, however, was greater than the war itself. The Yale-driven CIA had never stopped fighting and then supporting the KMT army of Chiang Kai-shek, and soon the war became a turf battle for blue-chip corporations and drug traffickers alike.[10] The conflict in Vietnam was a source of profits for the corporations that received the greatest amount of business from the war: Textron's Bell Helicopter Company, chemical firms including Dow Chemical and Monsanto, which produced Agent Orange and other defoliants, and construction company Brown and Root, a key backer of President Johnson.

THE UNITED FRUIT CONNECTION

Just as the debate on Vietnam was decided by a handful, so too would relations with Latin America be decided by a few. When the opium business lost its luster, the Russell partners found opportunity elsewhere. Joseph Coolidge, a Russell partner, turned over the marine trade heritage to his son Thomas Coolidge, who organized United Fruit. The company started as a banana importer but soon became master of the so-called banana republics it controlled, owning their railroads and communications systems.

The Yale blue bloods and their CIA were firmly in control of the company, which was also doing business with New Orleans mobsters. Joe Macheca, the reputed boss of organized crime in New Orleans, merged his shipping line into United Fruit in 1900. His underworld successor, Charles Matranga, stayed close to United Fruit throughout his life, and at his funeral United Fruit executives paid their respects.[11] The New Orleans mob was then controlled by Carlos Marcello, during which time it imported morphine and cocaine from Honduras. In the same year that Marcello took control, the board of directors bought out its greatest rival, Samuel Zemurray, with stock in its company. A few years later, when Zemurray became a nuisance as a board of directors member, Thomas Cabot sacked him.

Later a new challenge emerged. Jacob Arbenz, the democratically elected president of Guatemala, decided the land should be given back to the people, and so he had the audacity to buy United Fruit's land at the value the company had stated it was worth.[12] United Fruit shareholder John Foster Dulles said the country was under "a Communist-type reign of terror" and that America must act.[13] Massachusetts Congressman John McCormack assailed the Guatemalan government for its attack on his constituents' investment, declaring that 90 percent of New England's foreign investments were in Latin America.[14] Senator Henry Cabot Lodge, whose family owned stock, led the attack[15] and was joined by Thomas Cabot and his brother John Moors Cabot, assistant secretary of state.

The United Fruit story was fed to the media and trumped in Congress, and finally a top executive made the case to the Council on Foreign Relations. The council hired a lobbyist, Thomas Corcoran, to act as liaison to the CIA. Tommy the Cork, as he was called, was friends with Walter Bedell "Beetle" Smith, the CIA director. Corcoran had served as the legal representative to the CIA's "airline" in Laos and Vietnam.[16] The American intelligence agency actually had a proprietary airline first called CAT, Civil Air Transport and later dubbed Air America, that would be the subject of a 1990 movie by the same title.

In 1954 the CIA used Honduras to topple the government of Guatemala. A series of graft and drug scandals in Honduras brought down the leadership in the 1970s, but the CIA ensured that Honduras would be a main staging point for actions in nearby Guatemala and Nicaragua. When the showdown came with the DEA, which was making the CIA uncomfortable, it was the DEA office that closed.[17] Despite the so-called War on Drugs, the drug-free plan was much less important than the agenda of United Fruit, its shareholders, and the CIA.

THE BUSH CONNECTION

George Bush's best-known lie about taxes eclipses his other great lie: "Take my word, this scourge will stop," which was part of his inauguration speech. The amount of American heroin addicts, which dropped from five hundred thousand to two hundred thousand in the years after Vietnam, rose sharply again after America—through the CIA—lent assistance to Afghanistan. The CIA backing of the opium growers fooled few. The president's Strategic Council on Drug Abuse was frustrated enough by the CIA's silence on the issue that it pointed out in a *New York Times* editorial that drug use would rise just as it did with the CIA adventures in Laos. The prediction was correct, as the addict census grew to 450,000 and heroin deaths in New York rose 77 percent.[18]

A creative form of the Skull and Bones constructive chaos had the government spending billions to fight a war on drugs and billions more to jail users, while making the world safe for drug lords from the Afghan hills to the Golden Triangle of southeast Asia and the Honduran coast.

GEORGE BUSH, GEORGE W. BUSH, AND DICK CHENEY

The Bush tradition in the Skull and Bones began with George's father, Prescott, who was a Bonesman and served in Army intelligence. At the wedding of Prescott Bush and Dorothy Walker, five Bonesmen served as ushers. Bush family members were close to the Rockefellers and Harrimans and served on numerous corporation boards. George Herbert Walker Bush was born and raised in Greenwich, Connecticut, and schooled at Andover and Yale. With money from the owner of the *Washington Post* and connections from family and his Bones cabal, George headed to Texas to make his fortune.

Bonesman Henry Neil Mallon, one of four Mallons in the group, gave George the chance to learn the oil business through his company, Dresser Industries, which had been bought from its founding family by Mallon with Harriman money. After George's apprenticeship at Dresser he started his own company, Zapata Oil, with two partners. Zapata Oil drilled in the eastern Gulf of Mexico. The company's island base in the Cay Sal Bank would be used for CIA operations against Castro. The Bay of Pigs invasion in 1961 was actually known as Operation Zapata. Two vessels used in the operation were *Barbara* and *Houston,* the names of George's new wife and newly adopted home base.[19] While it is generally denied, George's CIA career began at this time, and he was still active in the organization in 1963. He later became director of the CIA.

George W. Bush's career went according to the same game plan as his father's with the exception of CIA involvement. George W. went to Yale, was a member of the Skull and Bones, worked in the oil business, and then moved into politics. In the 2000 presidential race he picked Richard Bruce Cheney as his running mate. Although the soon-to-be vice president was not a Bonesman, there are nine Cheneys in the membership list of the Skull and Bones. The Cheney ancestor who came to America in 1667 landed in Massachusetts, entitling the family to be counted among the blue bloods. Like George H. W. Bush, Cheney was connected to military intelligence, and he was a strong supporter of Lieutenant Colonel Oliver North. Cheney was even George's secretary of defense during Operation Desert Storm. Cheney too went to Texas, where he became the head of Halliburton, an oil-drilling company that bought Dresser Industries in 1998 under his tenure as boss. The company's Brown and Root subsidiary remains an important campaign donor, now to Republican candidates rather than to Democrats, and a beneficiary of large government contracts.

THE BONES AND THE OCTOBER SURPRISE

In November 1980 President Jimmy Carter, who had so far survived two assassination attempts and the intrigues of a powerful machine he could not fully comprehend, lost the presidential election. The powers that were had thrown their weight behind the charismatic Ronald Reagan and Bonesman George Bush. But what the Republicans feared the most was that the hostage situation in Iran would end just before the election. Despite the constant mismanagement by the Carter White House, a last-minute release of the American hostages, the "October Surprise," could spike Carter's popularity enough to carry the election.

The conspiracy theory covered in numerous books tells the story of George Bush, fellow Bonesman Senator John Heinz III, and a handful of intelligence operatives flying to Spain to meet with members of Iran's government. The deal was that Iran would hold the hostages until after the election in exchange for arms. This deal would also start the strange Oliver North–Iran-Contra Affair that was unearthed years later.

After the election, a series of murders and strange deaths began that included Reagan's campaign manager and spymaster William Casey; Amaram Nir, an Israeli officer; arms dealer Cyrus Hashemi[20]; and broadcast journalist Jessica Savitch. In a remarkable coincidence, Senators John Heinz and John Tower were killed in separate plane crashes within hours of each other, in April 1991. Both were allegedly connected to the October Surprise. And both were powerful men in the Senate.

The father of Senator Heinz was John Heinz II, who was a Skull and Bones member in 1931. John III, prince of the Heinz ketchup company fortune, married Teresa Simoes Ferreira, who was born of a Portuguese family in Mozambique, which at the time was still a colony. Ferreira, a board member of the Carnegie Institute, a member of the Brookings Institute, and a member of the Council on Foreign Relations, suddenly inherited a fortune worth $860 million. She then would marry another senator, Bonesman John Forbes Kerry. John Kerry, whose ancestors were among the opium pioneers in China, investigated the Iran-Contra Affair, unearthed Oliver North's private aid network to the Contras, and exposed the Bank of Commerce and Credit International (BCCI). He was given credit for his courage in attacking the mainstream corruption in Washington and intelligence drug dealing, but others say his investigation stopped short. The coincidences don't.

COINCIDENCE AND THE JFK ASSASSINATION

The murder of President John Kennedy is a half century old, but many believe it will never be solved. The first suspicions of foreign involvement, given credence by J. Edgar Hoover and Clare Boothe Luce, were quickly discredited. Luce had said an anti-Castro agent had called her the day JFK was killed and said Oswald was a Communist.[21] The next victim of suspicion was the American right wing, as allegedly someone named George Bush tipped off the authorities of the assassination plot. The next suspects were organized criminals, such as the Mafia, and even Texas oil producers. Finally, the American CIA took over as the most likely culprit. Surveys of skeptics of the Warren Commission Report, which Allen Dulles predicted no one would ever read, indicate that the CIA was the power behind the conspiracy. One skeptic was Robert Kennedy, who asked CIA Director John McCone point-blank, "Did the CIA kill my brother?"[22] McCone said no.

A motive for the murder of President Kennedy could be that he had failed to take back Cuba, and this threatened other Caribbean islands where United Fruit and a handful of sugar companies reaped the rewards of exploitative capitalism. Another motive might be that Kennedy had threatened to end the Vietnam profit center, which brought fortunes to the numerous blue-blood investments in aviation, particularly Textron, which owned Bell Helicopter, and the Brown and Root construction company, which had provided Lyndon B. Johnson with his campaign war chest. This chapter will not attempt to solve the mystery of the Kennedy assassination, but it will try to shed light on some of the awkward coincidences that authors of the Warren Commission Report, such as Kennedy haters Earl Warren and Allen Dulles, believed no one would ever read.

The conspiracy as traced by the Warren Commission may have started when a young marine named Lee Harvey Oswald, who had contact with the Office of Naval Intelligence, started studying Russian while stationed in a high-security base in Japan, and then left the marines and defected to Russia.[23] In Russia the soldier was treated well, was given an apartment and a job, and was able to get married. He also had his picture taken with an American "tourist," Marie Hyde, who said she became lost while on her tour, a near impossibility in the 1960s Cold War Russia.

The defector, who had been suspected of passing information on the U-2 flights to his Russian hosts, returned home without even a slap on the wrist from his government. Instead he was given a loan by the government to buy a home with his Russian bride. He then got a series of jobs, with at least one requiring a security clearance. He also met George DeMohrenschildt, who was connected in the oil business and knew both George Bush and Jacqueline Bouvier Kennedy. DeMohrenschildt introduced Oswald to Michael Ralph Paine and Ruth Hyde Paine, both of whom belonged to the United World Federalists, which was started by Cord Meyer of the CIA.

Another member of Meyer's United World Federalists was Priscilla Johnson. Supposedly turned down for a CIA job because of her membership in United World Federalists, Johnson nevertheless turned up in Russia and met Oswald.[24] Michael Paine's mother was Ruth Forbes Paine, of the same family whose ships carried opium to China in the nineteenth century. Ruth Paine's brother, William Forbes, was on the board of United Fruit. On his father's side, Michael's ancestors include Cabots, one of whom is a cousin who sat on the board of directors of United Fruit. Michael's wife, also named Ruth, was the daughter of William Avery Hyde. She was close to her husband's family, and in July 1963 went to Naushon Island, the Forbes kingdom off Woods Hole, to visit her mother-in-law, Ruth.

Mother Ruth's best friend, Mary Bancroft, was not only in the CIA but was also involved in a long-term relationship with Allen Dulles. Bancroft wrote all about her twenty-year affair in her autobiography, *My Life as a Spy*. Bancroft's father was elected mayor of Cambridge four times and was president of the Boston Elevated Railway. Her stepmother's stepfather was Clarence Walker Barron, who published *Barron's* and the *Wall Street Journal*. Bancroft's first husband worked as chief of United Fruit in Cuba, and her daughter married the son of Bonesman and Senator Robert Taft.[25]

When Ruth Paine, wife of Michael, returned from Naushon, the Paines took in young Lee Harvey Oswald and his Russian wife, Marina. Ruth found her adopted defector a job in the Texas School Book Depository. Ruth and Michael also provided a key piece of evidence that would help convict their new friend, should the police department protect Oswald long enough to get him to trial. In a declassified document, an informant describes a phone call Michael made to Ruth right after the shooting, with Michael saying he didn't believe Oswald was involved and that "we both know who is responsible."[26]

◈

Why would Robert Kennedy ask if the CIA killed his brother? The CIA had caused the biggest blunder of John Kennedy's short presidency, the Bay of Pigs invasion. It caused Kennedy to dump Allen Dulles, who advised for the operation, and threaten to smash the CIA into a million pieces. And it was also surprising when the committee set up to investigate the murder of the president was made up of Earl Warren, who was beholden to the Teamsters, whom Robert Kennedy had investigated; Gerald Ford, who was also beholden to the Teamsters; and Allen Dulles. The CIA was a natural suspect in the assassination.

The greatest piece of evidence in the Warren Commission investigation was what became known as the Zapruder film, which was quickly bought by Luce's Time/Life Corporation. The film showed President Kennedy's head snap in a way that could be caused only by a bullet from the right front. It was made to appear that the President's head was falling forward indicating a shot from the rear, which meant that the frames in the film were reversed.[27] Later this reversal of frames was said to be an accident.

After the Warren Commission fell out of favor with the thinking public, other commissions were set up to investigate the CIA and the growing amount of political assassinations in America. The newer evidence pointed to the involvement of intelligence in the Kennedy assassination, and forensic evidence showed the improbability of there being a single shooter. It is more likely that a two- or three-man hit team had been in place. Marita Lorenz testified that she was part of the operation and named two of the CIA operatives and a number of Cubans who were also involved. In her short and remarkable life, Lorenz had been a lover of Fidel Castro and then part of the CIA Operation 40 plot to kill him. At that time she was "dating" Venezuelan dictator Marcos Perez

Jimenez, whose government was so corrupt that even the Roman Catholic Church took issue with it.[28] How did Lorenz survive to testify? Her mother was Alice June Lofland, a cousin of Henry Cabot Lodge,[29] and she worked for the NSC.[30] Lorenz testified to the Select Committee on Assassinations about the Operation 40 plot against the president: "From the time I rejoined Operation 40 . . . all I heard was 'We're going to get Kennedy.' "[31] She said no one would murder her because of her mother's "power in the National Security Agency."[32]

Among the series of strange deaths that took place shortly after JFK was murdered was that of Mary Pinchot Meyer, the ex-wife of Cord Meyer. Pinchot Meyer was murdered while walking along the Chesapeake and Ohio towpath. Georgetown murders are rare, but this one included some very strange circumstances and was never solved.

Cord Meyer was the Yale-educated CIA agent who was linked to Ruth and Michael Paine through the United World Federalists, which he had founded before Dulles brought him into the CIA. Pinchot Meyer had been having an affair with JFK. Meyer was one of the most influential people in the CIA. Just after Pinchot Meyer's death, the CIA counterintelligence chief James Jesus Angleton entered her house "with a key he kept to the place" and took her diary.[33, 34] Angleton was joined by Ben Bradlee of the *Washington Post,* who was Pinchot Meyer's brother-in-law.

Although a series of unlikely coincidences, no matter how suspicious, cannot be conclusive evidence of a conspiracy, it does suggest something that exists far from the eyes of the public. The coincidences point to an elite handful of interlocking relationships that have a hold over national affairs—a grip that most citizens could not imagine possible. The coincidences further suggest that the media, in the hands of such an elite, may stop far short of serious investigative reporting.

That there is a conspiracy is not in doubt; there are numerous conspiracies. An elite class has always been in power and always will be. When the chauffeur of a Rockefeller pays more in taxes than the man he drives, the will of the elite is in evidence. When the House Select Committee on Assassinations concludes that the assassinations of Kennedy and Martin Luther King were conspiracies but nothing further is done, this is more evidence. When officers of the DEA complain of being told to back off because they are causing a problem for the CIA, this gives evidence that a higher power that goes unchecked is in control.

The fact that a nation allows itself to be ruled by an elite class has become old news to those being ruled, and has become a given to those who do not need to aspire to power because it is already theirs.

The story of the night that George W. Bush was tapped for entry in the Skull and Bones is told in Bill Minutaglio's *First Son*. George was not sure he wanted the rigor of meeting with fellow Bonesmen two nights a week. He was already born into wealth and, thanks to his father, into power. George told a fellow classmate that he would rather join "Gin and Tonic." His father, probably anticipating his son's doubt, knocked on his door at 8 P.M. and told young George that it was time to do the right thing, to become a "good man." George accepted.[35]

NOTES

Chapter 1

1. Malcolm Barber, *The New Knighthood: A History of the Order of the Temple* (Cambridge, England: Cambridge University Press, 1994), pp. 267–71.

2. Charles G. Addison, *The History of the Knights Templar* (Kempton, Ill.: Adventures Unlimited Press, 1997), p. 83.

3. Ibid., p. 88.

4. Ibid., p. 89.

5. John Westfall Thompson and Edgar Nathaniel Johnson, *An Introduction to Medieval Europe* (New York: W. W. Norton Co., 1937), p. 564.

6. Barber, p. 237.

7. Ibid., p. 241.

8. John J. Robinson, *Born in Blood: The Lost Secrets of Freemasonry* (New York: M. Evans & Co., 1989), p. 228.

9. Desmond Seward, *The Monks of War: The Military Religious Orders* (London: Penguin, 1972), p. 78.

10. Piers Paul Read, *The Templars* (New York: St. Martin's Press, 2000), p. 250.

11. Seward, p. 207.

12. Read, p. 259.

13. Peter Partner, *The Murdered Magicians: The Templars and Their Myth* (New York: Barnes & Noble, 1987), p. 60.

14. Universe Lodge No. 705 Web site, http://www.yesic.com/~mason/lodge/universe.htm.

15. Christopher Knight and Robert Lomas, *The Hiram Key: Pharaohs, Freemasons and the Discovery of the Secret Scrolls of Jesus* (Boston: Element Books, 1997), p. 313.

Chapter 2

1. From Dom Pedro Alcazar, *Seakeeping*, edited by Mark S. Harris, as posted on the Web site www.florilegium.org/ files/TRAVEL/Seakeeping.

2. Ibid.

3. Knight and Lomas, p. 297.

4. Thompson and Johnson, p. 596.

5. Frederick Pohl, *Prince Henry Sinclair* (New York: Clarkson Potter, 1967), pp. 62–3.

6. Ibid., p. 90.

7. Joseph R. Strayer, *The Albigensian Crusades* (Ann Arbor: University of Michigan Press, 1992), pp. 61–70.

8. Will Durant, *The Reformation: A History of European Civilization from Wycliff to Calvin 1300–1564* (New York: Simon & Schuster, 1957), p. 112.

9. Robinson, p. 21.

10. Seward, p. 43.

11. Ibid., pp. 230–1.

12. Seward, pp. 234–6.

13. Ibid., p. 330.

14. Ibid., p. 313.

15. Guy Patton and Robin Mackness, *Web of Gold: The Secret Power of a Sacred Treasure* (London: Sidgewick & Jackson, 2000), p. 242.

Chapter 3

1. Patrick Pringle, *Jolly Roger: The Story of the Great Age of Piracy* (New York: W. W. Norton, 1953), p. 22.

2. Robert C. Ritchie, *Captain Kidd and the War Against the Pirates* (Cambridge, Mass.: Harvard University Press, 1986), pp. 203–227.

3. Clare Brandt, *An American Aristocracy: The Livingstons* (Garden City, New York: Doubleday, 1986), p. 38.

4. Jan Rogozinski, *Honor among Thieves: Captain Kidd, Henry Every, and the Pirate Democracy in the Indian Ocean* (Mechanicsburg, Penn.: Stackpole Books, 2000), pp. 69–76.

5. Ritchie, p. 36.

6. Ibid.

7. Brandt, p. 21.

8. Stephen Birmingham, *America's Secret Aristocracy* (New York: Berkley Books, 1987), pp. 33–4.

9. Brandt, pp. 30–6.

10. Edward Robb Ellis, *The Epic of New York City* (New York: Kondansha, 1997), p. 107.

11. Ritchie, p. 26.

12. George Francis Dow and John Henry Edmonds, *The Pirates of the New England Coast 1630–1730* (New York: Dover Publications, 1996), p. 77.

Chapter 4

1. Steve Wick, *The Settler and the Sachem*, from the Web site www.Lihistory.com. Also see Bernie Bookbinder, *Long Island: People and Places, Past and Present* (New York: Henry N. Abrams, Inc., 1998).
2. Robert Ellis Cahill, *Pirates and Lost Treasures* (Peabody, Mass.: Chandler Smith Publishing, 1987), p. 84.
3. David M. Fletcher, *The Diplomacy of Annexation* (Columbia: University of Missouri Press, 1973), p. 71.
4. Edwin P. Hoyt, *John Tyler* (New York: Abelard Schuman, 1969), p. 72.
5. Fletcher, p. 135.
6. Hoyt, p. 132.
7. John Prebble, *Darien: The Scottish Dream of Empire* (Edinburgh: Berlinn Limited, 2000), p. 185.
8. Brandt, p. 55.
9. Ibid., p. 105.
10. Ibid., 103–8.
11. Axel Madsen, *John Jacob Astor: America's First Millionaire* (New York: John Wiley, 2001), p. 32.
12. David Leon Chandler, *The Jefferson Conspiracies* (New York: William Morrow and Company, 1994), p. 151.
13. Ibid., p. 100.
14. Louis B. Davidson and Eddie Doherty, *Strange Crimes at Sea* (Binghamton, N.Y.: Vail-Ballou Press, 1954), p. 105.
15. Birmingham, pp. 100–2.
16. Dow and Edmonds, p. 89.
17. Ibid., p. 42.
18. Ritchie, pp. 113–6.
19. Birmingham, p. 203.
20. Stephen Hess, *America's Political Dynasties* (New York: Doubleday, 1966), p. 191.

Part Two: Introduction

1. Michael Baigent and Richard Leigh, *The Temple and the Lodge* (New York: Arcade Publishing, 1989), p. 174.
2. Ibid., p. 143.
3. William Bramley, *The Gods of Eden* (New York: Avon Books, 1989), p. 228.

4. Ibid., p. 276.
5. Steven C. Bullock, *Revolutionary Brotherhood: Freemasonry and the Transformation of the American Social Order 1730–1840* (Chapel Hill: University of North Carolina Press, 1996), p. 46.

Chapter 5

1. A. J. Langguth, *Patriots: The Men Who Started the American Revolution* (New York: Simon & Schuster, 1988), pp. 95–7.
2. Samuel Eliot Morison, *The Maritime History of Massachusetts 1783–1860* (Boston: Northeastern University Press, 1921), pp. 27–8.
3. Herbert Allen, *John Hancock: Patriot in Purple* (New York: Macmillan, 1948), pp. 61–9.
4. Robert Leckie, *George Washington's War: The Saga of the American Revolution* (New York: HarperCollins, 1992), p. 53.
5. Michael Klepper and Robert Gunther, *The Wealthy 100: From Benjamin Franklin to Bill Gates: A Ranking of the Richest Americans, Past and Present* (Secaucus, N.J.: Citadel Press, 1996), pp. 191–3.
6. Langguth, p. 179.
7. Paul Lewis, *The Great Incendiary: A Biography of Samuel Adams* (New York: Dial Press, 1973), chapter 9.
8. Ellis, p. 155.
9. Baigent and Leigh, p. 209.
10. Ibid., p. 116.
11. Langguth, p. 294.
12. Christopher Hibbert, *Redcoats and Rebels* (New York: W. W. Norton, 1990), pp. 64–75.
13. Bullock, p. 79.
14. Baigent and Leigh, pp. 260–2.
15. Robert Hieronimus, *America's Secret Destiny: Spiritual Vision and the Founding of a Nation* (Rochester, Vt.: Destiny Books, 1989), p. 26.

Chapter 6

1. Richard B. Morris, *Seven Who Shaped Our Destiny* (New York: Harper and Row, 1973), p. 11.
2. Bullock, p. 60.
3. Ibid., p. 118.
4. Catherine Drinker Bowen, *The Most Dangerous Man in America: Scenes from the Life of Benjamin Franklin* (Boston: Little, Brown, 1974), p. 130.

5. Morris, p. 23.

6. Michael Howard, *The Occult Conspiracy: Secret Societies, Their Influence and Power in World History* (Rochester, Vt.: Destiny Books, 1989), p. 80.

7. Leckie, p. 29.

8. Ibid., p. 39.

9. David Schoenbrum, *Triumph in Paris: The Exploits of Benjamin Franklin* (New York: Harper and Row, 1976), p. 10.

10. Howard, p. 58.

11. Hieronimus, p. 32.

12. Helen Augur, *The Secret War of Independence* (Boston: Little, Brown, and Co.,1955), p. 17.

13. Kevin Phillips, *The Cousins' War* (New York: Basic Books, 1999), p. 147.

14. Anton Chaitkin, *Treason in America* (Washington, D.C.: Executive Intelligence Review, 1984), p. 247.

15. John Dos Passos, *The Shackles of Power* (New York: Doubleday, 1966), pp. 87–9.

16. Hess, pp. 369–85.

Chapter 7

1. Augur, pp. 70–1.

2. Ibid., p. 37.

3. Ibid., 66–9.

4. André Maurois, *Adrienne: The Life of the Marquis de la Fayette* (New York: McGraw Hill, 1961), p. 23.

5. Burke Davis, *The Campaign That Won America: The Siege at Yorktown* (New York: Dial Press, 1970), p. 113.

6. Morison, p. 7.

7. Baigent and Leigh, p. 40.

8. Augur, pp. 200–1.

9. Hess, p. 227.

10. Langguth, p. 279.

11. Ibid., p. 342.

12. Ibid., p. 32.

13. Augur, pp. 70–1.

14. Klepper and Gunther, p. 27.

15. George Wilson, *Stephen Girard: The Life and Times of America's First Tycoon* (Philadelphia: Combined Books, 1995), p. 188.

Chapter 8

1. David Cordingly, *Women Sailors and Sailors' Women* (New York: Random House, 2001), pp. 5–9.
2. Langguth, p. 467.
3. Ibid., pp. 473–4.
4. Barbara W. Tuchman, *The First Salute* (New York: Ballantine Books, 1988), p. 250.
5. Baigent and Leigh, p. 218.
6. Tuchman, p. 191.
7. From Robert A. Selig, *Deux-Ponts Germans*, from the Web site www.americanrevolution.org.
8. Seward, p. 330.
9. Tuchman, p. 229.
10. Tuchman, p. 141.

Chapter 9

1. David Ovason, *The Secret Architecture of Our Nation's Capital* (New York: Harper Collins, 1999), pp. 142–9.
2. A. Ralph Epperson, *Masonry: Conspiracy against Christianity* (Tucson: Publius Press, 1997), p. 281.
3. Hieronimus, p. 39.
4. Ibid., p. 28.
5. Baigent and Leigh, p. 261.
6. Thomas Fleming, *The Duel* (New York: Basic Books, 1999), p. 109.
7. Bullock, p. 150.
8. Ovason, p. 85.
9. Ibid., p. 269.
10. Ibid., p. 237.
11. Howard, p. 88.
12. Fleming, p. 4.
13. Bramley, p. 226.

Chapter 10

1. Brent Staples, "How Slavery Fueled Business in the North," from the Web site www.fresnobee.com (July 25, 2000), pp. 1–4.
2. Pringle, pp. 17–18.
3. Hugh Thomas, *The Slave Trade: The Story of the Atlantic Slave Trade 1440–1870* (New York: Simon & Schuster, 1997), p. 296.

4. Thomas Brosnahan, Kim Grant, and Steve Jermanok, *New England* (Hawthorn, Victoria, Australia: Lonely Planet Publications, 1999), p. 346.
5. Wade Davis, *The Serpent and the Rainbow* (New York: Warner Books, 1985), p. 66.
6. Eric Williams, *From Columbus to Castro: The History of the Caribbean 1492–1969* (New York: Harper and Row, 1970), p. 245.
7. Davis, p. 231.
8. Thomas Handasyd Perkins, *The Memoir of Thomas Handasyd Perkins* (1856; reprint, New York: Burt Franklin, 1971), p. 10.

Chapter 11

1. Jack Weatherford, *The History of Money* (New York: Three Rivers Press, 1997), p. 22.
2. Seward, p. 161.
3. Elaine Sanceau, *Henry the Navigator: The Story of a Great Prince and His Times* (New York: W. W. Norton, 1947), p. 255.
4. Ibid., p. 224.
5. Ibid., p. 255.
6. Sale Kirkpatrick, *The Conquest of Paradise* (New York: Penguin, 1991), pp. 50–1.
7. Benjamin Keen, trans., *The Life of Admiral Christopher Columbus by His Son Ferdinand* (New Brunswick, N.J.: Rutgers University Press, 1959), p. 5.
8. Gianni Granzotto, *Christopher Columbus: The Dream and the Obsession,* Stephen Sartarelli, trans. (Garden City: Doubleday, 1985), pp. 39–41.
9. Keen, pp. 16–17.
10. Samuel Eliot Morison, *Admiral of the Sea: A Life of Christopher Columbus* (Boston: Little, Brown and Co., 1942), p. 57.
11. Ibid., p. 93.
12. Granzotto, p. 44.
13. Ibid., pp. 594–5.
14. Samuel Eliot Morison, *Christopher Columbus, Mariner* (Boston: Little, Brown and Co., 1942), pp. 127–9.
15. Thomas, p. 90.
16. Ibid., p. 96.
17. Williams, p. 34.
18. James Pope-Hennessy, *Sins of the Father: A Study of the Atlantic Slave Traders* (New York: Alfred A. Knopf, 1968), p. 45.
19. Will Durant, *The Reformation: The Story of Civilization VI* (New York: Simon & Schuster, 1957), p. 194.

20. Thomas, p. 191.

21. Seward, p. 294.

22. Davis, pp. 36–38.

23. Rod Davis, *American Voudou* (Denton: University of North Texas Press, 1999), pp. 8–9.

24. James A. Rawley, *The Trans-Atlantic Slave Trade* (New York: W. W. Norton, 1981), pp. 105–6.

25. Ibid., pp. 136–8.

26. Will Durant and Ariel Durant, *Rousseau and Revolution: The Story of Civilization X* (New York: Simon & Schuster, 1967), p. 939.

27. Augur, pp. 3–27.

28. Charles Nicholl, *The Creature in the Map: A Journey to El Dorado* (New York: William Morrow and Company, 1995), pp. 127, 309–11.

29. Thomas, p. 155.

Chapter 12

1. Thomas, p. 204.

2. Ibid., p. 248.

3. Ibid., p. 177.

4. Bullock, p. 59.

5. Morison, *The Maritime History of Massachusetts,* p. 32.

6. Ibid., p. 33.

7. Ibid., p. 278.

8. Thomas, p. 176.

9. Robert G. Albion, William A. Baker, and Benjamin W. Labaree, *New England and the Sea* (Mystic, Conn.: Mystic Seaport Museum, 1972), p. 37.

10. Pope-Hennessy, p. 226.

11. Bullock, p. 59.

12. Thomas, pp. 771–2

13. Brandt, pp. 68–9.

14. Edmund S. Morgan, *American Slavery, American Freedom* (New York: W. W. Norton, 1975), p. 77.

15. Ibid., p. 80.

16. Ibid., p. 315.

17. Ruth Harrison Jones, ed., Harrison Heritage vol. VI, no. 4 (Dec, 1986) "Unknown Possible Ancestors of the Presidents Harrison," from the Web site http://moon.ouhsc.edu/rbonner /HHDOCS/86decHH.html.

18. Morgan, p. 121.

19. Pope-Hennessy, pp. 223–4.
20. Bullock, p. 80.
21. Baigent and Leigh, p. 180.

Chapter 13

1. Jim Marrs, *Rule by Secrecy* (New York: HarperCollins, 2000), pp. 209–12.
2. John Davis, *The Kennedy Contract* (New York: HarperCollins, 1993), p. 81.
3. Jim Garrison, *On the Trail of the Assassins* (New York: Warner Books, 1988), p. 328.
4. David S. Lifton, *Best Evidence* (New York: Penguin, 1992) pp. 64–7.
5. Robert J. Groden and Harrison Edward Livingstone, *High Treason* (New York: Berkley Books, 1989), p. 104.
6. Groden and Livingstone, p. 154.
7. Marrs, p. 216.

Chapter 14

1. Martin Booth, *Opium: A History* (New York: St. Martin's Press, 1996), pp. 16–24.
2. Alfred W. McCoy, *The Politics of Heroin: CIA Complicity in the Global Drug Trade* (New York: HarperCollins, 1991), p. 79.
3. Booth, pp. 82–3.
4. Carl A. Trocki, *Opium, Empire and the Global Political Economy* (New York: Routledge, 1999), p. 32.
5. Edward A. Gargan, "The Humbling of a Heavyweight," *New York Times,* 30 November 1995.
6. Klepper and Gunther, p. 11.
7. Charles Tyng, *Before the Wind: The Memoir of an American Sea Captain* (New York: Viking, 1999), pp. xiii–xviii.
8. Charles Corn, *The Scents of Eden: A History of the Spice Trade* (New York: Kodansha, 1999), p. 303.
9. Thomas G. Cary, *Memoir of Thomas Handasyd Perkins* (Boston: Little, Brown and Co., 1856; reprint, New York: Burt Franklin, 1971), p. 209.
10. Fay, Peter Ward, *The Opium War 1840–1842,* (Chapel Hill: University of North Carolina Press, 1995), p. 140.
11. Chaitkin, p. 135.
12. Morison, *The Maritime History of Massachusetts,* p. 115.
13. Albion, Baker, and Labaree, p. 92.
14. Nathaniel Bowditch, *Bowditch's Coastal Navigation* (New York: Arco Publishing, 1979), Notes.

15. Thomas N. Layton, *The Voyage of the* Frolic: *New England Merchants and the Opium Trade* (Stanford: Stanford University Press, 1997), p. 25.

Chapter 15

1. Klepper and Gunther, p. 28.
2. Ibid., page 29.
3. Ellis, p. 177.
4. Lucy Kavaler, *The Astors: An American Legend* (New York: Dodd, Mead, 1968), p. 30.
5. Ibid., p. 30.
6. Ellis, p. 210.
7. Ibid., p. 211.
8. Ibid., p. 244.
9. Klepper and Gunther, p. 19.
10. Ellis, p. 318.
11. Albion, Baker, and Labaree, pp. 97–100.
12. Ron Chernow, *The House of Morgan: An American Banking Dynasty and the Rise of Modern Finance* (New York: Touchstone Books, 1991), pp. 8–16.
13. From the Web site www.trainweb.org/panama/history1.html.
14. Kenneth Sydney Davis, *FDR: The Beckoning of Destiny 1882–1928* (New York: Random House, 1996) pp. 15–20.
15. Ibid., p. 42.
16. Jeremy Rifkin and Jeremy P. Tarcher, *The Biotech Century* (New York: Putnam, 1999), p. 117.
17. Jeffrey Steinberg, (editor) et al. *Dope, Inc.* (Washington, D.C.: Executive Intelligence Review, 1992) p. 127.
18. Booth, p. 128.
19. Fay, p. 132
20. Gargan, "The Humbling of a Heavyweight."
21. Booth, pp. 51–66.
22. Ibid., pp. 51–74.
23. Kathryn Meyer and Terry Parssinen, *Web of Smoke: Smugglers, Warlords, Spies and the History of the International Drug Trade* (Lanham, Md.: Rowman and Littlefield, 1998), p. 125.

Chapter 16

1. Phillips, p. 13.
2. Nelson W. Aldrich, *Old Money: The Mythology of Wealth in America* (New York: Allworth Press, 1996), p. 61.

3. Ibid., p. 13.

4. Morison, *The Maritime History of Massachusetts,* p. 23.

5. Ibid., p. 27.

6. Ibid., p. 154.

7. Ibid., p. 167.

8. Harriet H. Robinson, "Early Factory Labor in New England" (Boston: Wright & Potter, 1883), pp. 380–92, from the Web site of the Massachusetts Bureau of Statistics of Labor, http://www.fordham.edu/halsall/mod/robinson-lowell.html.

9. Page Smith, *The Rise of Industrial America: A People's History of the Post-Reconstruction Era* (New York: Penguin, 1990), p. 221.

10. Booth, chapter 9.

11. Thom Metzger, *The Birth of Heroin and the Demonization of the Dope Fiend* (Port Townsend, Wash.: Loompanics Unlimited, 1998), p. 132.

12. Edward, Marshall, *New York Times,* "The Story of the Opium Fight," March 12, 1911, from Schaffer Library of Drug Policy Web site, http://www.druglibrary.org/schaffer/.

13. Metzger, p. 176.

Chapter 17

1. Jonathan Vankin, *Conspiracies, Cover-ups and Crimes* (New York: Dell, 1992), p. 234.

2. Ron Rosenbaum, *The Secret Parts of Fortune* (New York: HarperCollins, 2000), p. 1.

3. Robin W. Winks, *Cloak and Gown, Scholars in the Secret War 1939–1961* (New Haven: Yale University Press, 1996), p. 15.

4. Ibid., p. 96.

5. Walter Isaacson and Evan Thomas, *Wise Men, Six Friends and the World They Made* (New York: Simon & Schuster, 1986), pp. 80–2.

6. Antony Sutton, *America's Secret Establishment: An Introduction to the Order of Skull and Bones* (Billings, Mont.: Liberty House Press, 1983), p. 8.

7. Joel Bainerman, *Inside the Covert Operations of the CIA and Israel's Mossad* (New York: SPI Books, 1994), p. 164.

8. Ralph G. Martin, *Henry & Clare: An Intimate Portrait of the Luces* (New York: Putnam, 1991), p. 61.

9. Alexander Cockburn and Jeffrey St. Clair, *Whiteout: The CIA, Drugs and the Press* (New York: Verso, 1998), p. 238.

10. McCoy, pp. 162–73.

11. Peter Dale Scott and Jonathan Marshall, *Cocaine, Politics, Drugs, Armies and the CIA in Central America* (Berkeley: University of California Press, 1992), p. 52.

12. Stephen Schlesinger and Stephen Kinzer, *Bitter Fruit: The Untold Story of the American Coup in Guatemala* (New York: Doubleday, 1982), p. 76.

13. Ibid., p. 11.

14. Ibid., p. 72.

15. Ibid., pp. 82–4.

16. Ibid., pp. 90–2.

17. Scott and Marshall, p. 57.

18. Cockburn and St. Clair, pp. 259–61.

19. L. Fletcher Prouty, *JFK, the CIA, Vietnam and the Plot to Assassinate John F. Kennedy* (New York: Carol Publishing Group, 1992), pp. 131-2.

20. Vankin, pp. 182–4.

21. Gaeton Fonzi, *The Last Investigation* (New York: Thunder's Mouth Press, 1994). pp. 52–3.

22. Arthur M. Schlesinger, Jr., *Robert Kennedy and His Time,* (New York: Ballatine, 1978), p. 665.

23. Groden and Livingstone, pp. 160–1

24. John Newman, *Oswald and the CIA* (New York: Carroll and Graf, 1995), pp. 61–7.

25. Martin, pp. 264–5.

26. Fonzi, p. 10.

27. Fonzi, p. 217.

28. Gerard Colby with Charlotte Dennett, *Thy Will Be Done: The Conquest of the Amazon—Nelson Rockefeller and Evangelism in the Age of Oil* (New York: Harper Collins, 1995) p. 312.

29. Marita Lorenz, *Marita* (New York: Thunder's Mouth Press, 1993), p. 33.

30. Ibid., p. 58.

31. Ibid., p. 127.

32. Ibid., p. 168.

33. Timothy Leary, "The Murder of Mary Pinchot Meyer," *The Rebel* (November 22, 1983).

34. Burton Hersh, *The Old Boys: The American Elite and the Origins of the CIA* (New York: Charles Scribner's Sons, 1992), p. 358.

35. Bill Minutaglio, *First Son: George W. Bush and the Bush Family Dynasty* (New York: Random House, 1999), pp. 103–5.

INDEX

BOOKS OF RELATED INTEREST

The Lost Treasure of the Knights Templar
Solving the Oak Island Mystery
by Steven Sora

The Secrets of Masonic Washington
A Guidebook to Signs, Symbols, and Ceremonies at
the Origin of America's Capital
by James Wasserman

The Templars and the Assassins
The Militia of Heaven
by James Wasserman

An Illustrated History of the Knights Templar
by James Wasserman

Secret Societies
Their Influence and Power from Antiquity to the Present Day
by Michael Howard

The Secret History of Freemasonry
Its Origins and Connection to the Knights Templar
by Paul Naudon

Founding Fathers, Secret Societies
Freemasons, Illuminati, Rosicrucians,
and the Decoding of the Great Seal
by Robert Hieronimus, Ph.D. with Laura Cortner

The Templars
Knights of God
by Edward Burman

Inner Traditions • Bear & Company
P.O. Box 388
Rochester, VT 05767
1-800-246-8648
www.InnerTraditions.com

Or contact your local bookseller